YOUR SICK DOG

This book is dedicated to my parents, Nicholas
and Elero, who taught me the joy of learning and
the value of knowledge

YOUR SICK DOG

The Dog Owner's Guide to Understanding and Managing Breeding, Illness and Injury

N G Maritz BVSc MRCVS

SWAN·HILL
PRESS

DISCLAIMER

Whilst every effort is made by the Publishers to see that no inaccurate or misleading data, opinion or statement appear in this book, they wish to make it clear that the data and opinions appearing in this book are the sole responsibility of the author. Accordingly the Publishers and their employees, officers and agents accept no responsibility or liability whatsoever for the consequences of any such inaccurate or misleading data, opinion or statement.

The Author has made every effort to ensure the accuracy of the information herein. However, appropriate information sources should be consulted, especially for new or unfamiliar drugs, procedures or current clinical opinions. It is the responsibility of every pet owner to evaluate the appropriateness of a particular opinion in the context of actual clinical situations, and with due consideration to new developments.

Cover photograph: Ross Bland
Cover design: Nick Raybould
Text illustrations: Phil Capsey

Copyright © 2004 Nico Maritz
Illustrations copyright © 2004 Phil Capsey

First published in the UK in 2004
by Swan Hill Press, an imprint of Quiller Publishing Ltd

British Library Cataloguing-in-Publication Data
A catalogue record for this book
is available from the British Library

ISBN 1 904057 36 5

Typeset by Phoenix Typesetting, Auldgirth, Dumfriesshire
Printed in Singapore by Stamford Press Pte. Ltd

Swan Hill Press
an imprint of Quiller Publishing Ltd
Wykey House, Wykey, Shrewsbury, SY4 1JA, England
E-mail: info@quillerbooks.com
Website: www.swanhillbooks.com

Contents

FOREWORD

Each chapter of this book is written as if it were a consultation with your vet. The title of each chapter is one of the common symptoms that people consult their vets on. The chapter will explain how the vet's thoughts will guide them to the final diagnosis and why they ask various questions and suggest various tests. The chapter will explain how you can do much of the detective work yourself and often reach the diagnosis on your own. Each chapter will also offer a useful reference work after you have had a consultation with the vet to help you understand what happened during the consultation and to offer more information on the final diagnosis. Each chapter starts with a flow diagram which is intended to serve as a map to guide the reader through the chapter. The book has been written in this way because traditional veterinary home reference books usually only give a long list of alphabetical medical conditions and are only useful to the dog owner after the vet has made the diagnosis.

When you notice that there is something wrong with your dog you will usually take them to your vet and describe the symptoms you have seen. The vet will then use these symptoms as a starting point in their search for the specific diagnosis. They will usually need to gather more information to help them make a specific diagnosis. They will ask you a number of questions, they will examine the dog and they may suggest various types of test. The most common reasons for taking your dog to the vet include simple symptoms like itching or limping or diarrhoea. There are however a vast number of possible causes for each simple symptom noticed and this is why people need vets to identify the individual cause of the common symptom they have noticed. This book is written from the perspective of you, the dog owner, who has noticed a problem with your dog. The book explains how the vet will use the information you give them to arrive at an exact diagnosis.

I have found that most people want to know how the vet reaches a specific diagnosis and they want to know what all the various treatment options are for each diagnosis. People have expressed the need to understand how the vet's diagnosis explains the symptoms that they have noticed at home and they want to know about the pros and cons of each treatment option. This book has been written from this perspective i.e. how is the vague symptom that one notices at home translated into an accurate diagnosis with a very specific treatment?

One possible cristicism of this type of book is that there is inevitably some information that is repeated in two or more chapters. This is because each chapter is intended to be read individually as if it were a personal consultation with your vet. Each chapter is intended to offer a stand-alone reference source without the reader needing to flip forwards and backwards into other chapters to get all the information they need.

This book is intended to empower the dog owner by helping them to understand every aspect of the veterinary care of their pet and to demystify the visit to the vet. The intention is that the vet and the dog owner should meet on more equal terms and be able to discuss the care of the dog more fully. The intention is not to try to replace the vet or to prescribe how individual medical conditions should be treated. My rationale is simply that we should all have as much information on a subject as possible to allow us to be in control of the situation and make informed decisions.

There are many grey areas in the world of medicine and surgery where different vets would have very different opinions on the same subject. There are often situations where one would get ten different answers from ten vets all asked the same question. This happens because different techniques and treatments seem to yield different results when used by different individuals. This means that two vets may have very different ways of treating the same problem but both will achieve the same results.

This is why every person should select their vet not only on the results that they achieve but also on how they achieve them. There should be a good sense of trust in your vet because this will help you through difficult times when you may have to rely completely on their judgement and advice. This book deals with many contentious issues and thus reflects my personal opinions on these issues. Different vets often have different opinions on the same subject and this demonstrates that there is often more than one solution for every problem.

This book is not intended to be an exhaustive and definitive work on the subject of medical conditions affecting dogs. It is intended to be an easy to use reference work to help people understand the most common medical conditions affecting dogs and the most commonly noticed symptoms. It would be beyond the scope of this book to try to include every known condition and every known treatment option. I have simplified matters by describing what tests and treatments I would suggest for my patients.

I hope this book will be of benefit to all dogs and their owners.

1

BREEDING AND PREGNANCY
IN DOGS

T he reproductive cycle of dogs has some very important differences to the reproductive cycle in human beings and the basic pattern of the reproductive cycle must be understood if you decide to breed from your dogs. The terminology various people use when discussing breeding in dogs varies and may be confusing. To simplify this discussion I will first clarify what various terms mean.

- I will refer to male dogs as 'dogs' and female dogs are called 'bitches'.
- A bitch is described as being 'in season' or 'in heat' when she is in the pro-oestrus or oestrus stage of her cycle (see the next paragraph for a full explanation of these terms). When the bitch is in season the vagina is swollen and initially will release small amounts of blood. During her season the bitch will attract the attention of male dogs who will attempt to mate with her.
- The term 'mounting' or 'to mount' means that the male dog is standing or attempting to stand on his back legs with his chest and front legs resting on the bitch's back.
- The term 'mating' means full penetrative sex.
- The concept of the male and female dog 'tying' during mating (also referred to as 'the tie') means the five to thirty minutes time for which the penis is held in the vagina and the male dog cannot withdraw from the bitch. During this phase the male dog will often move off the bitch's back and they will stand stuck together but facing in opposite directions. The tie has a very important function in that it stops the sperm from leaking out of the vagina and thus the only route for the sperm to travel is through the cervix and into the uterus. This ensures that the maximum number of sperm cells will move into the uterus and fallopian tubes and this improves the chances of the eggs being fertilized. An interesting point to make about the tie is that it is in fact the bitch that is holding onto the dog and not the other way around. The bitch does this by clamping the vagina around two swellings in the penis and thus prevents the penis from being withdrawn from the vagina. The male dog or the bitch may cry out or yelp in apparent pain during the tie and most people assume that it is the male dog that is hurting the bitch. They will then sometimes try to pull the male dog away from the bitch or in extreme cases even start hitting the male dog. This is the wrong thing to do because this may damage the penis and vagina. The male dog is usually the one who wants to separate and it is the bitch that is holding onto him preventing him from doing so. The tie is a normal part of mating and one should leave the two dogs alone to release when the bitch is ready.

The reproductive cycle of a bitch is divided into four stages that together represent one cycle:

The first stage is called pro-oestrus

This is the time at which we will see blood coming out of the vagina. The appearance of blood from the vagina signals that she is preparing to ovulate i.e. she is preparing to release eggs from her ovaries which will then be available for fertilization by sperm from a male dog. Many people will refer to this stage as being 'in season' or 'in heat'. During this stage a variable amount of blood will be released from the vagina and most bitches will produce spots of blood on the carpets and bedding at home. This process is thus also sometimes called 'spotting' or 'showing colour'. When the bitch is in pro-oestrus she will become very attractive to male dogs and most bitches will also show an increased interest in the male dogs pursuing her. This bleeding period is not the stage at which the bitch will ovulate and thus she will usually not allow male dogs to mount her to attempt to mate with her. She will however usually flirt outrageously with any male dog who shows an interest in her. Pro-oestrus usually lasts for about nine days but may be as short as two days or as long as twenty-seven days.

The most common misconception that I encounter is that many people think that the bleeding seen during pro-oestrus in the dog is the same process as menstruation or 'having a period' that women experience. These two processes are entirely different. The first difference is that the bleeding occurs immediately before ovulation in dogs and in women it occurs about two weeks after ovulation. The second difference is that in the case of human menstruation the blood comes from the uterus (womb) as the lining of the womb is discarded. In the case of dogs, the blood comes from the lining of the vagina and is due to the fact that the lining of the vagina is swelling and thickening to prepare for the act of mating.

The second stage is called oestrus

This stage starts on the first day that the bleeding stops and this is the stage in the reproductive cycle when the bitch is fertile and may become pregnant if mating occurs. This stage lasts for about seven days and it is during this stage that the bitch will ovulate and release eggs from her ovaries. The eggs are usually released on the second or third day of oestrus (thus the eggs are usually released about ten days after bleeding is first noticed from the vagina i.e. ovulation usually occurs about ten days after the start of the bitch's season). The most common mistake people make when they do not want their bitch to become pregnant is that they avoid all contact with male dogs for as long as they see blood from the vagina. When the vaginal bleeding stops they think that the season is over and will then allow the bitch to mix with male dogs again. This is a mistake because it is precisely this time after the bleeding has stopped that the bitch will allow male dogs to mate with her and it is the time that she is fertile i.e. the time that she is most likely to become pregnant. My advice to people who do not want their bitch to become pregnant is to avoid all contact with male dogs for at least two weeks after the vaginal bleeding (pro-oestrus) has stopped.

The third stage (if the bitch has not become pregnant) is called met-oestrus

During this phase the ovaries, the uterus (womb) and vagina slowly shrink back to their normal size as the reproductive system settles back to its resting inactive state. This usually takes about three weeks.

The fourth stage is called an-oestrus

This is the long interval between seasons in which the reproductive system is inactive.

Most bitches will come into season every six to eight months and thus one complete cycle takes six to eight months. Bitches reach puberty at about six months of age when they have their first season. This age is a generalization because the very small breeds of dog may reach puberty at a younger age for example at five months old, and the very large breeds may only reach puberty when they are as old as one year of age. The first season marks the bitch's step from being a puppy to being sexually mature. Once she has had a season she is sexually mature but is not yet an adult dog, as she is not yet fully grown. This is similar to the process in human beings in that sexually mature adolescent children are not necessarily adults. A young girl who has started menstruating at ten to twelve years of age is able to become pregnant but we would certainly not regard her as being an adult in physical or emotional terms. The same principle applies to bitches at the time of their first season in the sense that although they can become pregnant, they are in fact still adolescents and we should wait for them to grow into adults before breeding from them. The reason for this is because the bitch herself is still growing at the time of her first season and we should not place the burden of pregnancy on her body until it is fully-grown. The second reason is that there is a higher risk of complications in the pregnancy if bitches are bred at their first season. These complications may include puppies with birth defects and difficulties in giving birth to these puppies. If one decides to breed from a bitch I would generally only breed from her at her third season.

Pregnancy

The length of pregnancy is called the gestation period. The gestation period in the bitch is approximately sixty-three days from the day of ovulation. The exact day of ovulation is only known if the bitch has been tested at the time of mating. This testing may take the form of blood tests or the tests may be done on smears taken from the vagina. The most common reasons for performing these tests to determine the day of ovulation are that the bitch needs to be transported to the male stud dog and thus we would need to know which day they need to be brought together, or that the bitch has failed to become pregnant when mated during previous seasons. The length of pregnancy from the day of mating may appear to be as long as seventy-two days or as short as fifty-six days. This is because sperm can remain alive in the uterus for as long as a week after mating and thus if the female was mated a week before ovulation, the gestation period from the day of mating would appear longer that the average of sixty-three days. The eggs released from the ovaries can also remain alive for a few days and thus if the bitch is only mated a few days after she ovulated the length of the pregnancy may appear to be less than sixty-three days. Thus, although the true length of pregnancy is always sixty-three days after ovulation, the length of pregnancy after mating may appear to be longer (up to seventy-two days) or shorter (as little as fifty-six days).

Once a bitch has been mated many people would want to know if she has become pregnant. She is only likely to become pregnant if she and the male dog 'tied' during mating. If we know that they tied then we can arrange to test the bitch for pregnancy. The pregnancy test in the dog may be done by blood tests from as early as twenty days after ovulation or by ultrasound scanning from as early as eighteen days after ovulation or by the vet carefully feeling the bitch's belly about twenty-one to twenty-five days after ovulation. Because the exact day of ovulation is often not known most vets would suggest performing the blood test or scan one month after mating occurred. Vets all have their own preference for which test to use to confirm pregnancy and the various options should be discussed with your own vet after the bitch has been mated.

Pregnancy in the bitch can be regarded as having three stages or trimesters just as human pregnancy does. The third trimester of pregnancy is the one of interest to dog owners as this is the stage that one will notice obvious changes in the bitch. The bitch's belly and her mammary glands (breast tissue) will start to enlarge and swell from as early as three weeks before the puppies are due. Milk can be expressed from the nipples from about one week before the pups are due. The bitch will become restless and possibly have a reduced appetite and increased interest in making a bed for herself and the impending pups from two to three days before the pups are due. A good final measure of when the pups are due is that the body temperature of the bitch will briefly drop by one degree Celsius about twenty-four hours before the pups are due. Many people are interested in documenting this drop in body temperature so that they know when to make the final preparations for the process of giving birth. People who want to take this measurement should start to take the bitch's temperature with a thermometer from the time that milk can be expressed from the bitch's nipples. This temperature should be taken several times a day until they have recorded the one degree drop in temperature. The reason one needs to take the temperature several times a day is that the temperature only drops briefly for a few hours then returns to normal. If this temperature drop is recorded the pups will be due in twenty-four hours.

An important point to make at this stage is that one should not keep milking milk out of the nipples after it has first appeared and been identified. The reason for this is that the milk produced in the first few days is a special kind of milk called colostrum and this special milk is very important for the puppies. If we repeatedly remove this milk by checking the bitch's nipples then a lot of the colostrum may be lost. Thus one can repeatedly check the nipples for milk but once the milk has appeared (up to one week before the pups are due) then it should not be checked again.

Giving birth (parturition)

The process of giving birth is technically called parturition and is divided into three stages.

Stage one

The first stage of parturition is characterised by restless behaviour. The bitch will appear restless, agitated and uncomfortable. She will often pace around the house trying to select a place to give birth. The best idea would be to arrange a place for her to give birth in a quiet familiar room in the house. She should be provided with a comfortable and spacious bed with soft bedding material. This process of selecting a place to give birth is called nesting behaviour and the bitch will often scratch at the bedding and blankets to rearrange it to her liking. Once she has selected the place to give birth she will tend to stay there and will appear to become more agitated and uncomfortable.

She will often stand up frequently, sit down and keep turning around as she tries to make herself more comfortable. This stage of parturition may last for as long as twenty-four hours.

Stage two

The start of stage two of parturition is when one sees the bitch's abdomen contracting in the same way that one would expect if she were constipated and trying to pass faeces. These contractions may however be very subtle initially and sometimes the first sign that stage two has started is that we may see clear liquid pass out of the vagina. This liquid is colourless with little or no smell and this is what people mean when they say 'her waters have broken'. The liquid is called amniotic or foetal fluid and comes from the bag of fluid that the puppy is in. When this fluid appears it means that the bag has broken and the puppy is ready to be born. At this stage the contractions should become more obvious and more frequent. Once the bitch has been straining and has had continuous contractions for about thirty minutes a puppy should be born. If no puppy has been born within thirty minutes of continuous contractions then it would be a good idea to telephone your vet for advice.

The first puppy to be born is often the largest one of the litter and generally if the bitch can give birth to the first pup she should be able to give birth naturally to all the pups. The pups may be born either head first or bottom first; both types of birth are quite normal in dogs. Statistically half of all pups are normally born bottom first so there is no real concept of a 'breach birth' such as may complicate birth in human beings. When each pup is born it may still be inside the 'sack' of foetal membranes. If the pup is born still inside this sack then give the bitch a few moments to open the sack and get the puppy out. If she does not do this herself then you should tear the sack open for her. If you need to do this then it is important that you tear the sack open, do not cut it open with a knife or a pair of scissors as you may injure the pup. Pups may be born in this sack or without it, both types of birth are quite normal. If the pup is born out of the sack, the sack will normally be squeezed out of the vagina within a few minutes of the pup being born. Once the pup is born and out of its sack the bitch should start to vigorously lick and clean the puppy. The objective of this often quite rough licking is to stimulate the pup to start breathing which it will normally start doing within a few moments of being cleaned. Once the pup has started breathing it will often start shouting and complaining in the same way that newly born human babies do. This loud screaming is nature's way of clearing all fluid from the lungs, throat and nose.

Once the first pup has been born and is breathing normally it will start to crawl around looking for a nipple to feed from. I would generally give the bitch and her pup about ten minutes to get the pup to a nipple by themselves. If after ten minutes the pup has not found a nipple then I would help it onto a nipple and help it until it started sucking. The process of the pup feeding from the nipple will help to stimulate the birth of the other puppies still inside the womb. The puppies are generally born within thirty minutes of each other but this time frame may be longer or shorter. The same general rule with the subsequent puppies applies i.e. if no puppy is produced after thirty minute of continuous contractions then telephone the vet for advice. I have however seen cases where, after producing a few pups, the bitch may stop contracting and rest for two to four hours before giving birth to the rest of the puppies. The signal that the bitch has finished giving birth and all the puppies have been born is that she will settle down with them and they will be feeding or sleeping while she herself seems completely relaxed and there are no further contractions.

Once all the puppies have been born I check them for defects. The most common points to check are that each has an anus and a penis or vagina. The other important thing to check is that none of the puppies has a cleft palate. This is done by opening the puppy's mouth and looking at the hard palate which is the roof of the mouth. The puppy has a hard palate much like our own hard palate. The puppies may wriggle and cry when the palate is being checked but they will immediately settle down once they have been checked and returned to the bitch. If the hard palate has any holes in it or possibly even a deep cleft in it then this is called a cleft palate. The cleft may affect only the hard palate but in some cases may also affect the nose and lips. If one detects any of these abnormalities the vet should be consulted for advice.

A common concern is that people often will not have seen one foetal sack delivered per puppy delivered. Many people refer to this sack as the 'afterbirth'. There is one foetal sack for each puppy and as discussed earlier the sack may be delivered with the puppy or after the pup has been born. People often try to identify one sack per pup and are concerned that foetal sacks may be retained inside the womb. My experience is that the sacks will always be released without causing complications to the bitch. If you cannot account for all the sacks it may be that that you missed one or that it is delivered long after the pup. I have to date never encountered any problems with a bitch in cases where all the foetal sacks have not been seen.

The bitch will eat the foetal sacks as they appear and she should be allowed to do so. Parts of the foetal sack may have a dark green colour, this is the placenta and this is their normal colour. If the bitch produces green vomit a few hours after giving birth this is because of the green pigment in the placenta.

The umbilical cord is the cord extending from the puppy's belly and it is attached to the placenta part of the foetal sack. The bitch will usually bite this cord off about one centimetre from the puppy's belly when she eats the foetal sack. Once the bitch has bitten through the cord it should not bleed. If the cord bleeds after being bitten off or if the bitch does not bite through the cord then one should cut it off about one and a half centimetres from the puppy's belly. If necessary one can use a thin piece of string to tie around the tip of the severed cord to stop it bleeding. The cord will dry out and shrivel up within a few days after the birth of the pup and then it drops off. The point at which the cord drops off the puppy is then called the umbilicus. In human beings we call this spot the navel or 'belly button'.

Stage three

This is the stage after the pups have been born when one may notice a small volume of ongoing green or red discharge from the vagina. This discharge is the result of the womb contracting and squeezing out the remaining bits of blood clots and foetal fluids. This is normal and provided the bitch is calm, content and comfortable and the pups are content then the birth process is over. The womb takes about forty days after giving birth to reduce down to its normal size. This process is called involution. For the first few days after the birth one may notice that there is a small amount of ongoing green or red discharge from the vagina which the bitch will normally lick away for herself. This discharge is part of the normal cleansing process of the involution.

Problems and complications during mating, pregnancy and giving birth

The process of mating, pregnancy and giving birth is a natural process that has been refined and improved over thousands of years of evolution. The majority of bitches will go through all these processes easily and naturally and their natural instinct will tell them what to do at each stage. There is usually very little need for us to interfere with any of theses processes but occasionally, just as in the case of human beings, you and your vet will need to add a little modern science to the proceedings to ensure the welfare of the bitch and her puppies. I will discuss the most commonly encountered problems and their solutions in the same order that the natural process was discussed earlier.

Problems which may occur during mating, pregnancy, giving birth and after giving birth:

The bitch does not regularly come into season every six to eight months

If a bitch does not seem to come into season every six to eight months there are several possible explanations. The first possible one is that the bitch has 'silent heats'. This means that she does in fact come into season but the outward signs of her season are not very obvious i.e. she may show very little swelling and enlargement of the vagina and very little blood is released from the vagina. This may result in the season not being noticed by us but male dogs will be able to smell that she is in season even if the signs are very faint. These signs may be very faint because the bitch does not produce enough of the appropriate hormones to develop the full-blown changes which should occur at the time of her season. This may often mean that although the male dog realises she is in season, her own hormone impulses are not strong enough for her to encourage or allow male interest and mating. Some dog breeders may respond to this situation by holding the bitch down so that the male dog can mate with her. I feel that this is a dubious moral practice that may be compared to rape but I will concede that this is sometimes the only way that valuable bitches can be bred from if they show faint seasons.

The second possible explanation is that her reproductive cycle is literally not cycling at all. This may also happen in human beings for a variety of reasons whereby women may stop having menstrual cycles. With dogs the most common reason is a hormonal imbalance. I have found that the most common cause for this is too little thyroid hormone in the body. The level of the thyroid hormone may be determined by blood tests but even in cases where the tests are normal I often find that by giving these dogs low doses of thyroid tablets, normal seasons will resume.

The bitch has regular seasons but will not allow mating

The most common cause is that she is still in the pro-oestrus (bleeding) stage of her cycle. During pro-oestrus the bitch will solicit the attention of male dogs but will not allow them to mount her and mate with her. The bitch will only allow mating when she is in the oestrus (ovulation) stage of her cycle. This is the week after she has stopped bleeding. To facilitate the process the vet can be asked to test the bitch to determine when she is due to ovulate and thus be more likely to allow mating. This testing may take the form of blood tests or the tests may be done on smears taken from the vagina.

If she will not allow the male dog to mate with her during the oestrus stage of her cycle it may be simply because she does not like the male dog or it may be that she feels threatened by him. The easiest way to overcome this particular problem is to take the bitch to the male dog's home and not the other way around. If the male dog is brought to the bitch's home she may instinctively be aggressive towards him to protect her territory thus they should meet at his home or on neutral territory. Some breeders may again respond to this situation by holding the bitch down so that the male dog can mate with her but as I said before I feel that this is a dubious moral practice.

The bitch has regular seasons and allows male dogs to mate with her but never becomes pregnant

Here the fault could lie with either the bitch or the male dog. The problem may be that the male dog is infertile meaning that he may have poor quality sperm or that there is a problem with ejaculation of the sperm during mating. These possible problems can be investigated by the vet to determine if the male dog is the problem.

If the male dog is not the cause of the problem then one should investigate the bitch. The first step is to determine exactly when she ovulates and ensure that she is mated at that time. This testing may take the form of blood tests or the tests may be done on smears taken from the vagina. The results may show that she does not ovulate at the usual time in her cycle i.e. at day three of oestrus (which is usually day twelve after the start of bleeding/pro-oestrus). Some bitches may ovulate during the bleeding period or more than three days after the end of the bleeding period. If this is the case, then the usual advice of mating her twelve days after the start of bleeding (i.e. day three of oestrus), will be inappropriate. Thus, if the bitch never falls pregnant when mated, one should determine whether she is ovulating at a different time in her cycle. If this is the case then she should be mated at the time that the tests show she is ovulating even though it may not outwardly seem like the right time.

If the bitch fails to fall pregnant despite being mated at the time that she ovulates then one should investigate the womb (uterus). Once a bitch has been mated and the sperms have fertilized her eggs then the fertilized eggs develop into embryos. These embryos move into the womb (uterus) where they float in a rich fluid produced by the lining of the womb. This rich fluid provides the developing embryos with food and oxygen while the embryo continues to grow and develop a placenta. The placenta is a direct connection between the developing baby and the mother and once this has developed the baby gets all its food and oxygen directly from the mother's blood supply. The placenta is normally fully formed and fully functional within seventeen days of fertilisation. If the developing placenta cannot attach to the lining of the womb then the embryo will die. Thus if one has determined that the bitch was correctly mated at the time of ovulation but then fails to fall pregnant one should investigate whether the problem is that the lining of the womb cannot connect with the embryo's placenta. The most common cause of this problem is called cystic endometrial hyperplasia. This condition causes cysts to develop in the lining of the womb and these cysts cause two possible problems. The first is that the placenta may not be able to attach to the lining of the womb and the second is that the womb cannot effectively fight off bacteria that may be present in the womb. Bacteria in the lining of the womb may prevent the embryo's placenta attaching to the womb. In cases of cystic endometrial hyperplasia one will see no outward signs to tell us that this is the problem. What we will see is simply that the bitch does not become pregnant despite being mated at the right time. The way that this condition is diagnosed as the cause of the problem is by ultrasound scanning of the womb from day eighteen after ovulation. The vet, having diagnosed this as the cause of the problem, may attempt to overcome the problem by using hormone therapy and antibiotics when the bitch is next mated.

The bitch develops a vaginal discharge in the late stages of pregnancy

If a pregnant bitch develops a dark green or bloody vaginal discharge in the late stages of her pregnancy it may be that she is aborting one or all of the puppies. If the discharge develops two or three weeks before the puppies are due to be born then the bitch should have an ultrasound scan to determine whether the puppies are still alive. If the scan shows that all the puppies are still alive then the vet may try hormone therapy and possibly antibiotics to stop her aborting. If one or more puppies is already dead then the best course of action is to allow her to abort the puppies. If she cannot do so naturally and becomes ill then the vet may advise a caesarian surgery to help her do so.

If the bitch develops a dark green discharge a few days before she is due to give birth it may be a sign that she has gone into premature labour. The vet will check her cervix by placing a finger in the vagina and they will also scan the bitch to determine whether all the pups are still alive. Depending on what they find the vet may advise an emergency caesarian birth or medical treatment or it may be best to simply wait for a few days for the premature birth to occur naturally. I would generally recommend an emergency caesarian if the pups were less than one week premature.

If the bitch develops a clear watery discharge a few days before she is due to give birth then it is a sign that she has gone into labour. The vet will check her cervix by placing a finger in her vagina and scanning the bitch to check the condition of the puppies. The vet may then suggest an assisted normal birth or a caesarian birth depending on the condition of the cervix, the puppies and the bitch.

The due date for the birth has arrived but the bitch has not gone into labour

If the bitch does not go into labour on the expected date then one must firstly confirm that the due date is correct. The gestation period in the bitch is approximately sixty-three days from the day of ovulation and the exact day of ovulation is only known if the bitch has been tested at the time of mating. This testing may take the form of blood tests or the tests may be done on smears taken from the vagina. The length of pregnancy from the day of mating may appear to be as long as seventy-two days or as short as fifty-six days. This is because sperm can remain alive in the uterus for as long as a week after mating and thus if the female was mated a week before ovulation, the gestation period from the day of mating would appear longer than the average of sixty-three days. The eggs released from the ovaries can also remain alive for a few days and thus if the bitch is only mated a few days after she ovulated the length of the pregnancy may appear to be less than sixty-three days.

Once we have confirmed that the bitch is between fifty-six and seventy-two days pregnant, or if we know the exact day of ovulation and thus the expected day of giving birth, we can decide on a course of action in the event of the bitch not going into labour on the expected day. The best thing is to examine the bitch by checking to see if she is producing milk, if the vagina has become swollen and the vet will check the cervix to see if it has dilated. I would always recommend seeking advice from your vet if the bitch does not go into labour on the expected day because some bitches may go into labour but not develop any uterine (womb) contractions; this is called primary inertia. In cases of primary inertia the cervix will dilate and the puppies will attempt to be born but the womb will fail to push the puppies out and thus there is a risk that the puppies may die in the womb. Once the vet has examined the cervix they will know whether the pups are due and whether the bitch has a primary inertia. If the cervix is not dilated (open) then the puppies are not due on that day and the advice will be to wait a few days. If the cervix is dilated the vet will determine whether the womb is contracting or not. If the womb is not contracting the vet will attempt to stimulate contractions by rubbing the cervix with their finger and often they will also use injections of oxytocin and calcium and possibly a glucose drip to help the uterus to start contracting. If the vet is unable to make the uterus contract when the cervix is fully dilated then this is called a primary inertia and they will advise a caesarian birth.

The bitch is in labour and is contracting but no puppies are produced

As we have already discussed, the start of stage two of parturition is when one sees the bitch's abdomen contracting in the same way that one would expect if she were constipated and trying to pass faeces. These contractions may however be very subtle initially and sometimes the first sign that stage two has started is that we may see clear liquid pass out of the vagina. This liquid is colourless with little or no smell and this is what people mean when they say 'her waters have broken'. The liquid is called amniotic or foetal fluid and comes from the bag of fluid that the puppy is in. When this fluid appears it means that the bag has broken and the puppy is ready to be born. At this stage the contractions should become more obvious and more frequent. Once the bitch has been straining and has had continuous contractions for about thirty minutes a puppy should be born. If no puppy has been born within thirty minutes of continuous contractions then it would be a good idea to telephone your vet for advice. I set this thirty minute deadline simply because if a puppy is not born within thirty minutes of continuous contractions, it may mean that there is a problem with giving birth to that puppy and this would give me enough time to take action should this be necessary. The actual time that it may take to give birth to the puppy may be as much as two hours of contractions but by asking people to contact me after thirty minutes it means that I would have an hour and a half to get to the bitch to help her before the unborn puppy might be in danger.

The first puppy to be born is often the largest one and generally if the bitch can give birth to the first pup she should be able to give birth naturally to all the pups. If the bitch has been contracting for half an hour and no puppy has been born I would usually perform an internal examination by placing my finger into the vagina. The first thing that I want to confirm is that the cervix is fully dilated. If it were not fully dilated I would advise waiting a few hours to allow it to dilate. If the cervix were fully dilated then I would determine whether or not a puppy has moved into the birth canal in the pelvis. If a puppy is not in the birth canal then I would advise an ultrasound scan to determine that all the pups are well and if that is the case then I would advise waiting a few hours to allow time for a natural birth. If the scan shows that the puppies are distressed then I would advise stimulating contractions with oxytocin injections and stimulate the cervix with my finger. If after thirty to sixty minutes of stimulating contractions no puppies were born then I would consider a caesarian birth.

If the internal examination finds that the cervix is fully dilated and there is a puppy in the birth canal then I would lubricate the inside of the vagina and cervix and stimulate contractions with oxytocin injections and stimulate the cervix with my finger. If, after twenty minutes of stimulating contractions, the puppy has not been born then I would consider a caesarian birth. If the puppy is born within twenty minutes of stimulating contractions then I would give the bitch time to give birth to the remaining puppies naturally even though I may need to stimulate contractions to assist her with each pup. Generally, if the bitch can give birth to the first pup she should be able to give birth naturally to all the pups.

The bitch has given birth to some pups but contractions have stopped

When the bitch stops contracting for more than one hour after the last pup has been born it means either that all the pups have been born or that she is too tired to give birth to the remaining pups. The signal that the bitch has finished giving birth and all the puppies have been born is that she will settle down with them and they will be feeding or sleeping while she herself seems completely relaxed and there are no further contractions. I have however seen cases where, after producing a few pups, the bitch may stop contracting and rest for two to four hours before giving birth to the rest of the puppies. The general rule of thumb is that if the bitch seems completely relaxed and is calmly resting or attending to her puppies then she has most likely finished giving birth.

The bitch may develop secondary inertia if she is in labour for a long period of time. This means that she may be able to give birth naturally to the first few pups but after a while the womb (uterus) may become tired and stops contracting. One would suspect that this is the case if the bitch remains restless and agitated after the birth of the most recent puppy. In these cases it is wise to solicit the advice of your vet who will examine the bitch by feeling her abdomen and possibly taking X-rays to determine whether there are still pups to be born. If the vet finds that there are still pups waiting to be born then one must take action. I would usually try to help the uterus to continue contracting by using oxytocin and calcium injections and possibly also a glucose drip. If these medications are effective then the bitch should be able to give birth to the remaining puppies. If these medications fail to help the uterus then I would consider a caesarian birth for the remaining puppies.

A puppy's head, foot or leg is sticking out of the vagina and seems to be stuck

If a head or a foot or a leg of a puppy is sticking out of the vagina and the bitch cannot deliver the pup within five minutes of the part of the puppy appearing, then try to help her by gently pulling the part of the puppy that is sticking out. One should pull gently but firmly while someone else telephones the vet for further advice. When pulling the puppy I often use a cloth or towel around the exposed part of the puppy as they are usually very slippery. When pulling one should try to pull slightly upwards (towards the tail) and if the puppy remains stuck then try to slide a finger into the vagina next to the pup and try to rotate the puppy a little bit (Fig. 1).

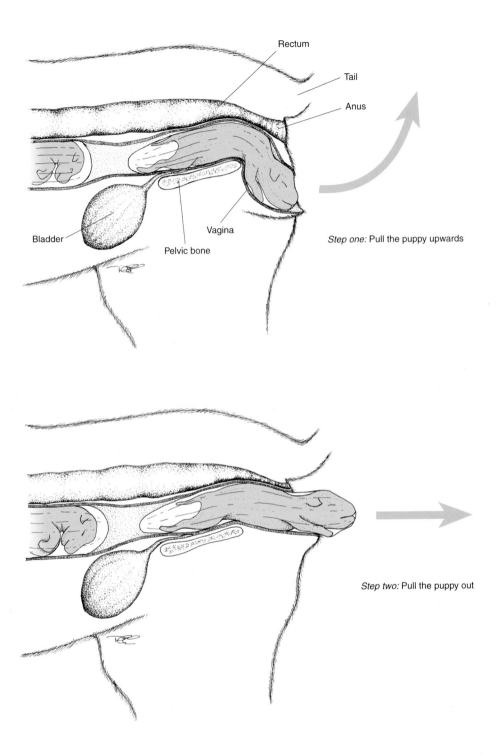

Fig 1 Side view of the rear of the bitch's abdomen during whelping. Assisting whelping: if a puppy seems to be stuck you may assist the bitch by gently pulling the puppy. The diagrams illustrate that the vagina curves downwards over the edge of the pelvic bones. Thus one should not pull the puppy downwards as the bitch's pelvic bones will then act as an obstruction. The puppy should first be pulled upwards towards the bitch's tail to straighten the vagina, then pull the puppy out.

A puppy has been born but it is not breathing

If the pup is still inside its sack then give the bitch a few moments to open the sack and get the puppy out. If she does not do this herself then you should tear the sack open for her. If you need to do this for her then it is important that you tear the sack open, do not cut it open with a knife or a pair of scissors as you may injure the pup. Pups may be born in this sack or without it, both types of birth are quite normal. If the pup is born out of the sack, the sack will normally be squeezed out of the vagina within a few minutes of the pup being born. Once the pup is born and out of its sack the bitch should start to vigorously lick and clean the puppy. The objective of this often quite rough licking is to stimulate the pup to start breathing which it will normally start doing within a few moments of being cleaned. Once the pup has started breathing it will often start shouting and complaining in the same way that newly born human babies do. This loud screaming is nature's way of clearing all fluid from the lungs, throat and nose. If the bitch does not stimulate the pup to breathe or if the pup does not start breathing within a few minutes of being licked, then I tend to help by vigorously rubbing the pup on all sides with a towel. If I need to help I would also first open the mouth and clear away any fluid in the mouth or throat. If the pup does not start breathing within a few moments of rubbing then I would suspend the puppy head downwards while supporting the head, neck and body with my hands to allow any fluid to drain out of the lungs (Fig. 2). While suspending the puppy with their head downwards it is important to keep rubbing all sides of the pup to stimulate breathing. If the pup does not start breathing within ten minutes of this treatment then it is probably stillborn but it is worth telephoning your vet for advice.

Seizures in bitches who have recently had puppies (eclampsia)

Bitches may, within three days of giving birth, develop mild or severe muscle twitching which can resemble a seizure. The muscle twitching or muscle spasms are caused by low calcium levels in the mother's blood stream. Calcium has many functions in the body, one of which is to assist in the function of the nerve cells. If there is insufficient calcium to assist this nerve cell function then the nerves may become unstable and abnormal signs are seen as the nerves discharge impulses spontaneously. This is the situation faced by women and animals when conditions like eclampsia (milk fever) cause a drop in the blood levels of calcium.

Eclampsia may happen shortly after a mother has given birth when she diverts a lot of her own calcium to her milk to go to her baby. The calcium in the mother's bloodstream is transferred to her milk to help the puppies grow strong teeth and bones. If her own blood levels drop too low, then her nerve cells become unstable and may fire impulses spontaneously especially to the muscles. Thus the clinical symptoms of low blood calcium levels are initially twitching and muscle tremors, which may progress to full seizures, convulsions and possible death if treatment is not started quickly. Treatment of low blood calcium is simple and highly effective. The treatment is a simply a matter of injecting calcium into a vein and the patient recovers within minutes.

Once the bitch has recovered, the vet will suggest that you should add a calcium supplement to her diet for a few days and also possibly hand feed the puppies for a few days. There are many specially formulated artificial milk substitutes for puppies and hand feeding them is easy. The reason that the vet may suggest hand feeding the puppies for a few days is that, if they are not drinking

Step 1: Hold the puppy as illustrated. Your hands should support the head, neck and body in a straight line to avoid a "whiplash" injury to the puppy. New-born puppies are very slippery, make sure you have a secure but not tight hold of the puppy.

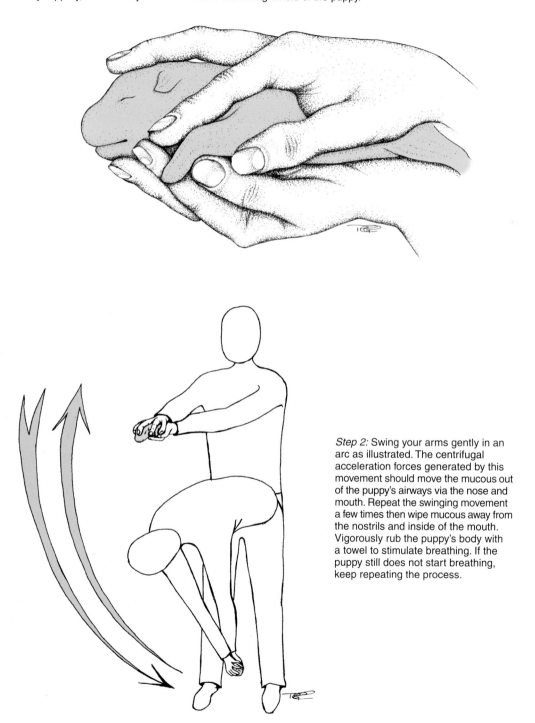

Step 2: Swing your arms gently in an arc as illustrated. The centrifugal acceleration forces generated by this movement should move the mucous out of the puppy's airways via the nose and mouth. Repeat the swinging movement a few times then wipe mucous away from the nostrils and inside of the mouth. Vigorously rub the puppy's body with a towel to stimulate breathing. If the puppy still does not start breathing, keep repeating the process.

Fig 2 Clearing the mucous from the puppy's airways.

milk from the bitch, the milk in the mammary glands will accumulate. As the milk accumulates in the mammary glands, and is not being removed by suckling puppies, so the mother will reabsorb the calcium from the milk back into her own blood stream. Another reason is that, because the puppies are not suckling from the mother for a few days, there is no ongoing loss of calcium via the milk. The puppies usually only need to be hand fed for one to three days and then the mother can continue suckling them. Thus, if one sees muscle tremors or seizure-like symptoms in a bitch who has recently given birth, the diagnosis will almost certainly be eclampsia (low blood calcium levels caused by the production of a lot of milk).

The bitch has swollen, painful mammary glands and will not allow the puppies to suckle (mastitis)

The mammary glands produce milk for the puppies and are equivalent to breasts in human beings. Bitches usually have eight to ten mammary glands each with its own nipple. The process of producing milk is called lactation and the bitch can produce milk for up to ten weeks after the puppies have been born. If the puppies are weaned off milk and start eating solid foods earlier than this, then the bitch will produce milk for less than ten weeks. If you notice that the bitch suddenly stops allowing the puppies to suckle milk from her within six weeks of being born then one should consider the possibility that she has developed mastitis. The word mastitis means inflammation of one or more of the mammary glands and this inflammation is usually caused by an infection. Infections in one or more mammary glands may occur when bacteria from the dog's environment move through the openings in the nipple into the mammary gland. The milk in the mammary gland provides a rich source of food for the invading bacteria and thus an infection may appear very suddenly as the numbers of bacteria multiply very quickly.

The infection in the mammary gland will make it warm, swollen, painful and it may become dark red in colour and thus the bitch will not want the puppies to suckle from her. If the infection is very severe then the bitch may also appear to be unwell. The infection in the mammary gland is like an infection anywhere else in the body in that it can cause a fever and thus the affected individual will appear unwell. The fever will often mean that the affected bitch seems lethargic and may lose her appetite. The infection in the mammary gland may cause pus to develop and thus if one gently squeezes the affected gland, one may notice that a thick yellow or green pus-like material comes out of the nipple.

This condition needs to be treated with antibiotics and sometimes painkillers are also required. The infection is usually very easy to cure and the problem will resolve within five days of treatment. The big question to consider when a bitch has mastitis is whether to remove her from the puppies or not. Some people feel that the bitch should be removed from the puppies if she has mastitis and the puppies should be hand fed while she is being treated. I usually prefer to keep the bitch with the puppies for several reasons. The first reason is that, if the puppies are not suckling from the bitch, all the mammary glands become very full of milk which is uncomfortable for the bitch and increases the chance of infections in other mammary glands. The second reason is that separation from her pups causes distress to the mother and the pups which may make the pups more suscep-tible to other infections because stress reduces the ability to fight off disease. I usually leave the pups with the bitch while treating the mastitis and I find that the presence of pus in the infected mammary gland does not seem to pose a risk to the puppies. If the bitch refuses to let the puppies suckle from her then one should leave them with the bitch but hand feed them every four hours until she will allow them to suckle again. Once the pain of the mastitis is under control, the bitch will allow them to suckle again. Thus if one notices that one or more of the mammary glands appears hot, swollen, painful or an unusual colour, one should consult a vet for advice because, like any infection, it is much easier to treat an infection in the early stages and it is cured more quickly.

2
VOMITING AND DIARRHOEA

One of the most common reasons for taking your dog to the vet is because of vomiting and/or diarrhoea. There are almost one hundred possible causes of vomiting and diarrhoea in dogs. The vet will ask a few simple but very important questions to narrow the list of possible causes. It is very important to answer the questions as accurately as you can and if you do not know the answer to any or all of the questions then it is better to say so than to take a guess. The questions may include some of the following:

- Is he/she suffering from vomiting only, or diarrhoea only, or both?
- If he/she is vomiting and has diarrhoea, which symptom appeared first?
- How long have these symptoms been present?
- How many times has he/she vomited or had diarrhoea in the last twenty-four hours?
- Does he/she seem otherwise unwell or are they as happy and active as normal?
- Does he/she still want to eat or have they lost their appetite?
- Is he/she still drinking water?
- If he/she is still eating and or drinking, are they able to keep the food and water down or do they vomit the food and water back up soon after eating/drinking?
- How old is the dog?
- Has he/she been sterilised (spayed or castrated)?
- Do any other pets at home have the same or similar symptoms?

The purpose of these questions is to guide the vet's thinking which will go something like this: The symptoms of vomiting and/or diarrhoea reveal that there is some sort of problem with the digestive system. The digestive system can be thought of as a long tube which digests food and eliminates waste products from the body (Fig. 3). Any problem which disrupts this long tube will interfere with its ability to move food and wastes from the beginning of the tube (the mouth) to the end of the tube (the anus). Any condition which affects this tube will activate the main defence system of the tube. The main defence system of this tube is to assume that it contains something harmful and it will attempt to reject this harmful material through either end of the tube as quickly as possible. The tube will thus attempt to reject this material through the mouth via vomiting or through the anus via diarrhoea.

  If the problem is situated in the stomach or upper and middle part of the intestine (the small intestine) the symptoms are usually vomiting and diarrhoea although often only diarrhoea is noticed. These cases often start as vomiting and later develop into diarrhoea as the problem moves

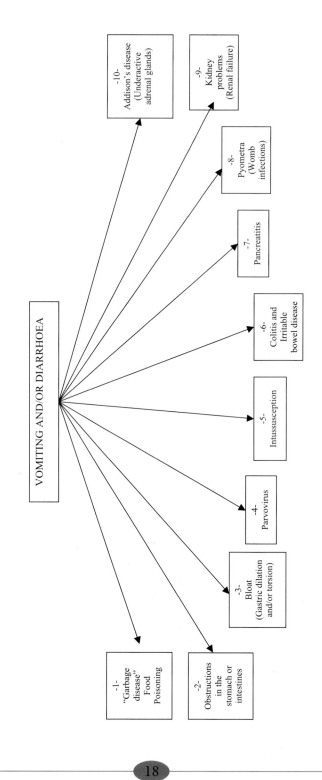

VOMITING AND/OR DIARRHOEA

-1-
"Garbage disease"
Food
Poisoning

-2-
Obstructions
in the
stomach or
intestines

-3-
Bloat
(Gastric dilation
and/or torsion)

-4-
Parvovirus

-5-
Intussusception

-6-
Colitis and
Irritable
bowel disease

-7-
Pancreatitis

-8-
Pyometra
(Womb
infections)

-9-
Kidney
problems
(Renal failure)

-10-
Addison's disease
(Underactive
adrenal glands)

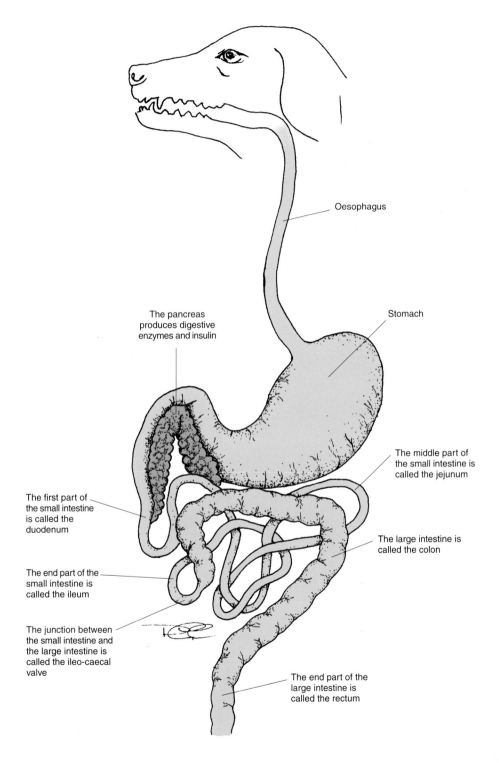

Oesophagus

Stomach

The pancreas
produces digestive
enzymes and insulin

The middle part of
the small intestine is
called the jejunum

The first part of
the small intestine
is called the
duodenum

The large intestine is
called the colon

The end part of the
small intestine is
called the ileum

The junction between
the small intestine and
the large intestine is
called the ileo-caecal
valve

The end part of the
large intestine is
called the rectum

Fig 3   The gastro-intestinal system is simply a long tube or pipe for processing food. Various
parts of the tube are modified into different shapes and sizes to perform different functions.

from the stomach into the small intestine. If the small intestine is the site of the problem then the symptoms often include loss of appetite, the dog feels lethargic and looks very unwell, the diarrhoea is very watery, large amounts of diarrhoea are produced and the dog needs to defecate only slightly more often than normal.

If the problem is located in the lower intestine (the large intestine) the symptom is usually diarrhoea only and no vomiting. These patients produce frequent small amounts of soft faeces and defecate much more often and seem to strain to pass these small amounts of faeces. People often mistake this staining for constipation. The other symptoms associated with a large bowel diarrhoea include a lot of flatulence, slimy or 'jelly-like' faeces, bright red blood in the faeces and the dogs seem bright and alert and active and have a normal appetite. This is in stark contrast to cases of small intestinal diarrhoea where the dogs look very sick and lethargic and lose their appetite.

1 'Garbage disease'/food poisoning

The most common cause of vomiting and/or diarrhoea is that the dog has eaten something which has upset their digestive system. This may be something they have found and eaten in the house, garden or while out on a walk. This is commonly called **'garbage disease'**. This is the same thing that we, as human beings, call food poisoning after eating food that has spoiled. If he/she has recently eaten food that they may not have eaten before, like a different brand of dog food or table scraps, then this may also upset their tummy. The same thing happens to us when we go on holiday and eat foods that we do not commonly eat. The common example is people who develop vomiting and diarrhoea while on holiday in exotic locations like India where it is described as 'Delhi belly'. The reason that we may develop vomiting and diarrhoea while on holiday is not that there is something wrong with the food but rather that our digestive symptoms are not accustomed to that type of food and thus we develop an upset tummy. With time our digestive symptoms will become accustomed to this new food and the symptoms will disappear. If the cause of the tummy upset in your dog is due to something that they have eaten the symptoms will usually start as vomiting and progress into diarrhoea but sometimes diarrhoea is the only symptom.

The treatment for 'garbage disease' is very simple – no food for twenty-four hours and provide only water for drinking. The rationale behind this is that the stomach and intestines are trying to empty themselves out by vomiting and diarrhoea and if we keep feeding more food the stomach and intestines will not reach a point where they are satisfied that they have emptied themselves. Once the digestive system has emptied itself it must be allowed twenty-four hours to rest and thus we withhold food for this period of time. After the twenty-four hour fasting period the dog should be fed a very bland food to start the digestive system working again. This is the same system that we apply to ourselves when we have a tummy upset i.e. we lose our appetite and will eat nothing for a day. When we do start eating again, we tend to eat bland foods like toast and tea until the digestive system resumes normal activity and then we return to our usual foods. The dog should be fed bland food such as boiled rice, pasta or potatoes with boiled chicken, turkey or white fish in small amounts offered three or four times a day i.e. feed small amounts often. This will restart the digestive system without asking it to work too hard. The dog should be kept on this bland diet, feeding small amounts often until the vomiting has stopped and two normal stools have been passed. The dog can then be returned gradually to normal food by mixing their usual food with rice for a few days at about half rice and half dog food proportions. The amount of rice mixed into the usual food is then gradually reduced until the dog is eating entirely their usual food without any further vomiting and diarrhoea. This simple process will solve most cases of vomiting and/or diarrhoea which are caused by eating something which disagrees with the dog and no further treatment will be required. If the problem does not resolve within forty-eight hours or if the symptoms become worse then one should consult a vet for advice.

The vet's next thoughts will progress as follows. If the only symptom is vomiting then the vet will suspect that the problem is situated in the esophagus, stomach or upper intestine. The problem may be simply inflammation as caused by 'garbage disease' and 'unfamiliar' foodstuffs, or infections or obstructions in the esophagus, stomach and upper intestines. Other possible causes of inflammation in the stomach may include primary stomach problems such as excessive acid (heartburn), stomach tumours and non-specific inflammation (gastritis). The inflammation in the stomach may however be due to problems elsewhere in the body such as kidney problems or liver problems. To make sense of this think of the kidneys and liver simply as filters for the body even though they fulfill a great many other functions. If the filters are not removing waste products from the blood then the waste products will accumulate despite the body's attempts to reroute some of them, like urea, to other organ systems for elimination. These waste products, like any other waste products in your car or swimming pool for example, will damage the system if they are not removed. If the kidneys are failing, the level of urea rises in the blood steam and the body tries to eliminate the problem by other routes. The other options for elimination of high levels of urea are via the stomach and intestines or via the lungs. The process via the lungs involves releasing the urea into the air in the lungs thereby allowing its elimination when air is breathed out of the body. The problem with this route is that the exhaled urea is caustic and burns the lining of the mouth and lungs. The other alternative route of urea elimination, via the stomach and intestines, causes much the same problem. The urea released into the stomach and intestines may burn the lining of these organs and cause sufficient pain there to cause the dog to stop eating and in more severe cases the dogs may also vomit and develop diarrhoea. In both of these instances the dogs tend to appear lethargic and depressed as these processes make one feel very unwell in addition to the obvious pain and discomfort.

2 Obstructions in the digestive system

The causes of obstructions in the digestive system are most commonly something indigestible that the dog may have swallowed. These indigestible objects are called 'foreign bodies'. I have seen an enormous range of foreign bodies lodged in the esophagus, stomach and intestines varying from chewed-off pieces of the dog's toys, to stones, golf balls, corn cobs, lumps of swallowed bones. If the foreign body is lodged in the esophagus (the swallowing tube leading from the mouth to the stomach) then the symptoms are: repeated retching (the dog is trying to clear the blockage by vomiting it out), drooling (the dog cannot swallow the normal production of saliva) and the dog is unable to swallow food.

If a foreign body is the cause of the problem it will be identified by careful examination of the abdomen by the vet and by means of X-rays, endoscopy and possibly ultrasound scanning. The foreign body can often be felt in the dog's intestines when the vet is examining the dog. The vet can not usually feel foreign bodies that are present in the stomach or the first part of the small intestine as these organs are situated inside the rib cage and you cannot feel them with your hands. If the vet suspects a problem in this area they will probably suggest X-rays to investigate these areas which are out of reach. The X-rays may not show up all foreign bodies as some of them do not show up on X-rays. The vet may then suggest a barium study. This involves geting the dog to swallow barium liquid (which shows up on X-rays) and repeated X-rays are then taken of the abdomen to follow the movement of barium as it passes through the digestive system. The movement of the barium may then be found to stop flowing at a certain point or it may coat an invisible foreign body which will then show up. Another way of looking for a foreign body is to use an endoscope. This is like passing a camera into the stomach to look around for a foreign body. Ultrasound is another tool which the vet may use to look for a foreign body and it involves the same equipment and procedure that is used when scanning pregnant women to monitor their pregnancy.

If the cause of the problem is that the dog has a foreign body in the stomach or intestines then the symptoms may vary with how the digestive system is able to deal with it. If it is a large foreign body it may remain in the stomach and cause bouts of vomiting which appear randomly and may disappear for a few days only to return later. This happens because some large foreign bodies are too large to pass into the intestine and may float around in the stomach without affecting the dog. When these dogs have eaten and the food is moved from the stomach into the small intestines the foreign body moves with the food and may temporarily block the movement of food into the intestines causing vomiting. When the foreign body then moves away from the valve connecting the stomach to the small intestine the food is once again able to move into the intestine and the vomiting symptoms simply disappear. The foreign body in this instance acts like a ball valve in the stomach and only affects the dog when it is in the wrong position. These cases normally require a surgical operation to remove the foreign body.

If the foreign body is small enough to move through the stomach valve into the small intestines it may then get stuck in the small intestine. If it causes a complete blockage of the small intestine then the symptoms are severe, frequent, repeated, strenuous attempts at vomiting (the dog is trying to remove the object by vomiting it out) with no sign of diarrhoea. These dogs generally feel very unwell and often refuse to eat or drink because the foreign body obstructs all movement of waste products through the intestines and these dogs are at risk of dying from toxic shock if the waste products accumulate and have the effect of 'poisoning' the dog (Fig. 4). If the foreign body gets stuck in the small intestine but only causes a partial obstruction i.e. it does not completely block the intestine, then some food and waste products can squeeze past the obstruction and then move normally through the rest of the intestine. In these cases the same symptoms appear as in a complete obstruction but the symptoms are less severe and the risk of death from toxic shock is less. If the foreign body is stuck, whether it causes a total or partial obstruction, it will require a surgical operation to remove it. If the foreign body is small enough to pass through the entire digestive system them it will cause a range of symptoms as it passes from the stomach (vomiting) to the small intestine (vomiting and diarrhoea) to the large intestine (diarrhoea and straining movements as the dog tries to pass the object out of the body with the faeces).

Thus the most common cause of vomiting and diarrhoea in dogs is that they have eaten some-

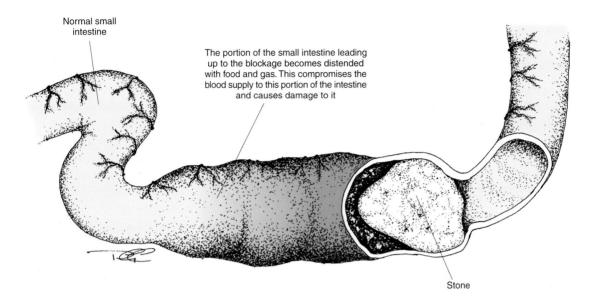

Normal small
intestine

The portion of the small intestine leading
up to the blockage becomes distended
with food and gas. This compromises the
blood supply to this portion of the intestine
and causes damage to it

Stone

Fig 4 An example of a foreign body e.g. a stone, causing a blockage in the
small intestine. The normal flow of food would be from left to right.

thing which disagrees with them. This may be 'garbage disease', 'food poisoning' or solid objects
(foreign bodies).

Many other causes of vomiting and diarrhoea exist and the following discussion will touch on
some of them.

3 Gastric bloat (gastric dilatation and/or volvulus)

This is a condition most commonly encountered in large breeds of dogs and is caused by an
accumulation of gas in the stomach which the dog is unable to get rid of by burping. The exact
cause of this condition is not known and various theories have been proposed. The first theory is
that food in the stomach ferments and produces gas which accumulates in the stomach and causes
the stomach to inflate like a balloon. The second theory is that some dogs, for reasons which are
not understood, swallow a lot of air into the stomach and are unable to burp it out and thus the
stomach inflates. As the stomach inflates it causes pain and the first sign is thus that the dog is
uncomfortable and restless. As more gas accumulates the dog will try to vomit to try to empty the
stomach. These attempts at vomiting are usually seen as non-productive retching i.e. the dog
retches violently and repeatedly without any vomit being produced. As further gas accumulates and
the stomach is inflated further it will start to dilate rapidly. The dilating stomach will start to press
against the organs surrounding it causing further pain and one will see the dog's belly swelling like
a balloon and the abdominal wall becomes very taut. As the stomach dilates further it starts to push

up against the lungs which lie in front of the stomach. The result of this is that the lungs will be compressed forwards and the dog will develop difficulty breathing. The severity, frequency and intensity of the retching will progress as this process unfolds and the dog will rapidly become weaker until they collapse. This entire process develops very rapidly in just a few hours and unless the dog is treated promptly by a vet they will die from shock. A further possible complication that may develop is that the gas-distended stomach may become twisted like a sweet/candy wrapper. This complication is called volvulus and is a serious complication because the twist may cut off the blood supply to parts of the stomach and spleen (Fig. 5b).

There are several ways of treating this condition and each vet may have their own preferences. The point that all vets have in common is that the treatment should be started as soon as possible to ensure the best chance of saving the dog's life. Several years ago this condition was regarded as having a very poor survival rate but as treatments have improved the survival rate has now improved dramatically to the point where ninety percent of dogs with gastric bloat are expected to survive. My advice to people who describe these symptoms to me over the phone is to come to the clinic immediately. The two most common types of treatment are gastric lavage (a stomach pump) to remove all food and gas from the stomach or surgery to deflate the stomach and untwist it if necessary. My biggest concern with dogs who are treated for this condition is that it may happen repeatedly in the same individual with the same life threatening risks every time. The best advice on how to try to avoid a recurrence of gastric bloat is to feed large and giant breed dogs three or four small meals a day rather than one or two large meals and to not exercise the dog for at least one hour after their meals.

4 Parvovirus infections

Parvovirus infections are caused by a virus which attacks the lining of the intestines. It is a very serious infection and is most commonly seen in puppies less than twelve weeks old. The symptoms of parvovirus infection are very severe vomiting and diarrhoea and the affected puppy appears very ill. The affected puppy will vomit and strain very severely to pass diarrhoea frequently throughout the day and night. The symptoms appear very suddenly and the puppy will deteriorate very quickly. The diarrhoea usually appears to be almost pure blood and has a very foul smell. This is a very dangerous condition and is highly contagious to other dogs and puppies. Many puppies die from the infection and thus it is very important to get the puppy to a vet immediately.

The vet will confirm the diagnosis by sending samples of blood and/or diarrhoea to a laboratory for analysis. The condition is caused by a virus and thus the vet cannot cure the infection because there are no treatments to kill the virus. The immune system of the affected individual must kill the virus. This is the same principle as when people develop colds and flu i.e. the treatments we take simply help us feel better. The only way to get over a cold or flu is to wait for the immune system to kill the virus. The objective of treatment for parvovirus is to prevent dehydration using a drip line and most vets will use antibiotics to prevent secondary bacterial infections from developing in addition to the viral infection. The drip line is the most important part of the treatment because dehydration is the most common cause of death in cases of diarrhoea . The second most common cause of death is toxaemia. Toxaemia means that the infection causes toxins to enter the blood

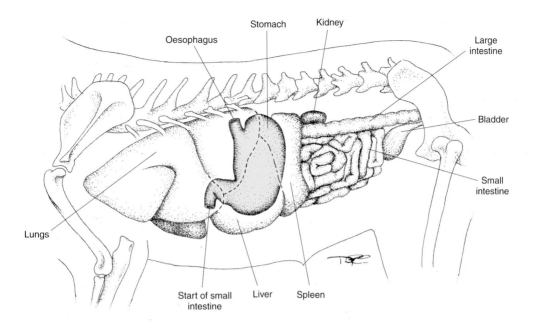

Fig 5a Side view of the body to show the normal size and position of the stomach.

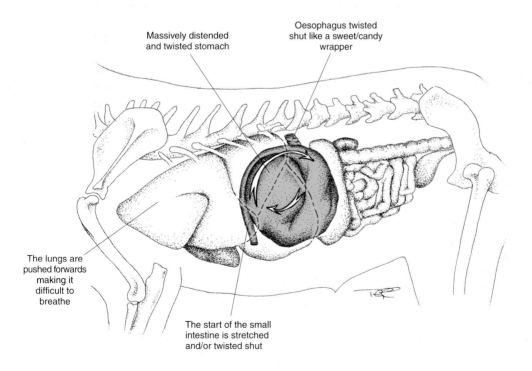

Fig 5b Gastric bloat (gastric dilatation – volvulus – torsion syndrome). The stomach becomes massively distended due to the accumulation of gas. As the stomach distends it presses against the organs around it. The distended stomach presses against the lungs making it difficult to breathe. The distended stomach may twist to shut off the oesophagus and small intestine like the twists in a sweet/candy wrapper.

stream and this has the same effect as a poison on the body. There are treatments available to try to remove these toxins but they are not always effective. Parvovirus is highly contagious to other dogs and puppies and thus all contact with other dogs must be avoided. Most puppies will survive a parvovirus infection if they receive treatment quickly but some puppies will die despite the vet's best efforts.

5 Intussusception

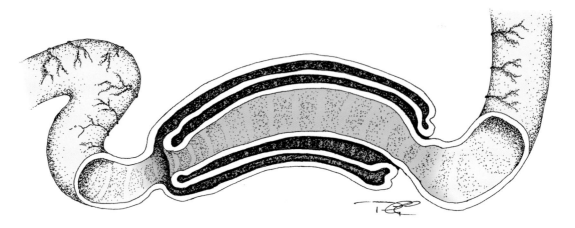

Fig 6 An intussusception occurs when a portion of intestine "telescopes" into itself like a radio aerial.

The intestines, as discussed earlier, can be thought of simply as a long tube for digesting food. In severe cases of vomiting and diarrhoea the forceful contractions of the intestines flow along the intestinal tube in the form of waves of contractions (peristalsis). If a powerful wave of contraction moves very rapidly towards a length of intestine that is stationary then the rapidly moving piece of intestine may slide inside the stationary intestine and get stuck in that position. This is the same effect we see when an extended telescope or telescopic car aerial is pushed closed. The effect of a piece of intestine slipping inside another piece of intestine is referred to as an intussusception (Fig. 6). The effect of the intussusception is that it effectively blocks the movement of food and wastes in the intestine and thus causes the same effect as an intestinal foreign body (blockage). If it causes a complete blockage of the small intestine then the symptoms are severe, frequent, repeated, strenuous attempts at vomiting (the dog is trying to remove the 'object' by vomiting it out) and often also signs of repeated, strenuous attempts at diarrhoea (the dog is trying to remove the 'object' by defecating). These dogs generally feel very unwell and often refuse to eat or drink because the intussusception may obstruct all movement of waste products through the intestines and they are at risk of dying from toxic shock if the waste products accumulate and have the effect of 'poisoning' the dog. If the intussusception only causes a partial obstruction i.e. it does not completely block the intestine then some food and waste products can squeeze past the 'obstruction' and then move normally through the rest of the intestine. In these cases the symptoms are the same as in a complete obstruction (vomiting and/or diarrhoea) but the symptoms are less severe and the risk of death from toxic shock is less.

Intussusceptions tend to occur most commonly in puppies and young dogs. The vet will often be able to feel the intussusception in the dog's belly with their hands. In many cases the vet will want to confirm their suspicion that an intussusception is the cause of the problem by taking X-rays and often also barium X-rays. An ultrasound scan of the belly may also help to confirm their suspicions. Once the intussusception has been confirmed as the cause of the problem then surgery will be required. The surgery may consist of simply pulling the stuck piece of intestine out of the other piece of intestine in the same way that a telescope is extended. However, if there has been a lot of damage to that piece of intestine then it will have to be cut out and the remaining sections of intestine will then be stitched back together. After surgery the patient needs to be starved for about twelve to twenty-four hours to allow the intestine to rest and heal and then one should only feed bland foods. These bland food types should be offered to the dog in several small portions daily for the next week until normal intestinal function has resumed. Once normal stools have been seen for two days then the bland food should be mixed with the dog's normal food for a few days to gradually wean them back onto their normal food.

6 Colitis and irritable bowel syndrome

Colitis and irritable bowel syndrome are well known conditions in human beings. Most of us know someone who suffers from one of these conditions and they will describe a large range of possible symptoms to us. The name colitis is actually only a description of the problem rather than a diagnosis of what causes the problem. The word colitis can be broken down into two parts: 'itis' means simply inflammation and 'col' derived from colon – inflammation of the colon. Irritable bowel syndrome is equally vague and implies simply inflammation and irritation of any part of the bowel (intestine). The large range of symptoms that sufferers will describe is due to the fact that the amount of inflammation that occurs and the portion of the bowel that is affected will determine the symptoms. The most extreme form of this condition in human beings is called Chrone's disease and thankfully this most extreme form does not seem to occur in dogs.

The most common cause of irritable bowel syndrome is a dietary intolerance to certain types of food which produces an allergy-type reaction in the intestines. Colitis is the most common form of irritable bowel syndrome in dogs and by definition the term colitis implies inflammation and irritation in the colon which is the last portion of the bowel leading to the anus. The symptoms of colitis are that these patients produce frequent small amounts of soft faeces and defecate much more often and seem to strain to pass these small amounts of faeces. People often mistake this straining for constipation. The faeces are not only soft or runny but also contains a lot of mucous and appear very slimy. The other symptoms include a lot of flatulence, occasionally bright red blood in the faeces (which may then look like strawberry jam) but the dogs seem bright and alert and active and have a normal appetite. This is in stark contrast to cases of small intestinal diarrhoea where the dogs look very sick and lethargic and lose their appetite. The colitis may be the result of 'garbage disease' as discussed earlier and thus is the result of an isolated incident where a dog has eaten food that has spoiled or simply a type of food, which they have not eaten before. In these cases the same treatment which was discussed for 'garbage disease' will solve the problem i.e. withhold food for twenty-four hours then feed a bland diet until normal stools are passed. If the colitis recurs regularly then one would suspect that the dog has a food intolerance and we would have to either run tests to determine which foods cause the problem or simply experiment with different foods to find which foods the dog can tolerate and which cause diarrhoea.

Irritable bowel syndrome generally implies that the inflammatory/allergic reaction to certain foods occurs in the upper portion of the intestine or in the stomach. If the problem is situated in the stomach or upper and middle part of the intestine (the small intestine) the symptoms are usually vomiting and diarrhoea although often only diarrhoea is noticed. These cases often start as vomiting and they later develop diarrhoea as the problem moves from the stomach into the small intestine. If the small intestine is the site of the problem then the symptoms often include loss of appetite, the dog feels lethargic and looks very unwell, the diarrhoea is very watery, large amounts of diarrhoea are produced and the dog needs to defecate only slightly more often than normal. As with colitis, this may be the result of 'garbage disease' and will be the result of an isolated incident where a dog has eaten food that has spoiled or simply a type of food which they have not eaten before. The treatment is as discussed for treatment of colitis and involves withholding food for twenty-four hours and then feeding a bland diet until normal stools are passed. If the symptoms appear again regularly one would suspect that the dog has a food intolerance and we would either run tests to determine which foods cause the problem or simply experiment with different foods to find which foods the dog can tolerate and which cause vomiting and/or diarrhoea.

The inflammation caused by the food intolerance may cause inflammation affecting only the stomach. This is called 'gastritis'. In these cases the lining of the stomach becomes inflamed and the dog produces more stomach acids than normal which produces the same sensation as 'heartburn' that many people suffer from. The symptoms in this instance would be vomiting and no diarrhoea. Once again this may be the result of 'garbage disease' as discussed earlier and is the result of an isolated incident where a dog has eaten food that has spoiled or simply a type of food which they have not eaten before. Again the treatment is to withhold food for twenty-four hours then feed a bland diet until no further vomiting is seen but if the symptoms recur regularly one would suspect that the dog has a food intolerance and we would have to either run tests to determine which foods cause the problem or simply experiment with different foods to find which foods the dog can tolerate and which cause vomiting. The most common form this condition takes is that the dogs vomit yellow bile usually in the mornings. This is because the increased stomach acids have accumulated in the stomach overnight and thus 'heartburn' will stimulate vomiting to get rid of this acid. These dogs will also often eat grass to stimulate vomiting. I feel that it is a common misconception that normal dogs eat grass. I think that dogs eat grass only when they want to make themselves vomit. The reason that dogs eat grass is the same reason that people take antacids. When a person feels stomach discomfort or heartburn they know that it is due to too much acid in the stomach and thus they take antacids to neutralise the acids. Dogs do not know about the use of antacids and thus nature has evolved to the point where dogs with stomach pain and heartburn instinctively want to empty the contents of their stomach to get rid of the acids and any other stomach contents. Dogs are unable to stick their fingers down their throats to make themselves vomit so they do the next best thing which is to eat something which will irritate the stomach lining enough to stimulate vomiting. Once they have vomited out the excess stomach acids they immediately feel better and continue the rest of the day without any signs of illness or discomfort. This immediate return to feeling well after vomiting is an easy way to differentiate this type of vomiting from more serious causes of vomiting.

As we have seen, the treatment for colitis and irritable bowel syndrome is very simple – no food for twenty-four hours and provide only water for drinking. The rationale behind this is that the stomach and intestines are trying to empty themselves out by vomiting and diarrhoea and if we keep feeding more food the stomach and intestines will not reach a point where they are satisfied that they have emptied themselves. Once the digestive system has emptied itself it must be allowed twenty-four hours to rest and thus we withhold food for this period of time. After the twenty-four hour fasting period the dog should be fed a very bland diet to start the digestive system working again – foods such as boiled rice, pasta or potatoes with boiled chicken, turkey or white fish. Feed this bland food in small amounts three or four times a day i.e. feed small amounts often. This will restart the digestive system without asking it to work too hard. The dog should be kept on this bland diet until the vomiting has stopped and two normal stools have been passed. The dog should then be gradually returned to normal food by mixing the usual food with rice for a few days at about half rice and half dog food proportions. The amount of rice mixed into the usual food is then gradually reduced until the dog is eating entirely their usual food without any further vomiting and diarrhoea. If the problem does not resolve within forty-eight hours or if the symptoms become worse then one should consult a vet for advice. The vet will probably prescribe medication until the problem has resolved.

If the condition recurs regularly the vet will suggest trying different types of food until we can identify which foods cause the symptoms and which foods can be eaten without causing vomiting and/or diarrhoea. Once we have determined which types of food cause the problems we can then avoid the problems by avoiding the food types that the dog is intolerant to. Thus in long term cases of recurrent colitis and irritable bowel syndrome the problem can be solved by simply avoiding the offending types of food rather than repeatedly treating the symptoms without determining the cause. Trialling different types of food can be a long and frustrating process as each type of food should be fed for a minimum of six weeks at a time to determine whether it causes problems or not. The time spent on trialling different types of food is well spent though because this approach focuses on identifying and avoiding the cause of the problem rather than simply treating the symptoms. This principle is more familiar to us than you might think and people who suffer from heartburn will usually identify which foods cause the problem and they will rather try to avoid these foods than simply eating what they like and then suffering the discomfort. During each different food trial it is vitally important that the dog is fed only this food and nothing else otherwise it is impossible to assess the suitability of that particular food.

7 Pancreatitis

The pancreas is a gland which is attached to the stomach and the first part of the small intestine leading from the stomach (the duodenum) (Fig. 3). The pancreas has two functions – it contains cells which produce insulin for the body and it contains cells which produce the digestive enzymes which digest food in the intestines. The pancreas has a tube (pancreatic duct) which connects it to the small intestine and carries the digestive enzymes made by the pancreas into the intestines. The name pancreatitis is actually only a description of the problem rather than a diagnosis of what causes the problem. The word pancreatitis can be broken down into two parts: 'itis' means simply inflammation and 'pancreat' is derived from pancreas. Thus pancreatitis means inflammation of the pancreas. The cause of pancreatitis in dogs is not understood. Some researchers think that it may be due to bacteria in the intestine moving through the pancreatic duct into the pancreas causing an infection in the pancreas but this has not been proven. Most cases of pancreatitis occur for no apparent reason.

The pancreas simply becomes severely inflamed very suddenly and the resulting symptoms vary from just a loss of appetite to severe pain in the dog's belly to severe vomiting and possibly also diarrhoea. The large range of symptoms that sufferers will describe is due to the fact that the symptoms are determined by the amount of inflammation that occurs. The inflammation in the pancreas causes the pancreas to swell and some of the digestive enzymes that it produces leak out of the cells which produce them. These digestive enzymes do not know the difference between the body's own tissues and food that has been eaten and they will start to try to digest the cells of the pancreas. This makes the pain and inflammation in the pancreas even worse and as the pancreas becomes more swollen, more digestive enzymes leak out and the problem becomes progressively worse due to this vicious cycle of events. The pancreas is situated very close to the liver and the inflammation may spread to the liver causing even more pain and discomfort. The typical case of pancreatitis develops very suddenly and is characterised by a sudden and total loss of appetite and severe and profuse vomiting. These patients will look very unwell and lethargic and generally have severe pain when the belly is touched. The diagnosis is confirmed by performing blood tests and possibly also by performing ultrasound scans of the pancreas and taking X-rays.

The treatment for pancreatitis involves withholding food and water for one to three days. The reason for this is that the pancreas is stimulated to release digestive enzymes into the intestine every time food and drink arrives in the stomach. Thus, if these patients are allowed to eat and drink, more digestive enzymes will be released every time they swallow food or drink. The effect of this is that every time they eat or drink more digestive enzymes will leak out of the inflamed pancreas and more damage will be inflicted on the pancreas and the symptoms will become worse. The idea behind withholding food and water is thus to avoid more digestive enzymes being released by the pancreas and thus the pancreas will have a chance to repair itself and stop leaking enzymes. The other benefit of withholding food and drink is that by doing so the pancreas is allowed to rest and this gives it time for the inflammation to subside. If we were to continue feeding these dogs then the pancreas would have to continue working and as it does so it inadvertently keeps damaging itself and thus has no time to heal. These dogs should be maintained on intravenous fluids via a drip line while food and water is withheld to avoid dehydration and shock. The other components of their treatment are painkillers and antibiotics.

I prefer to keep these dogs hospitalised and on a drip until all the symptoms have resolved. After one to three days of not eating and once the vomiting has stopped I will restart the pancreas and intestines by feeding small amounts of bland food types (boiled rice, pasta or potatoes with boiled chicken, turkey or white fish). The dog should be fed this bland food in small amounts offered three or four times a day i.e. feed small amounts often. This will restart the digestive system without asking it to work too hard and the dog should be kept on this diet until the vomiting has stopped and two normal stools have been passed. The dog can then be gradually returned to their normal food by mixing the usual food with rice for a few days at about half rice and half dog food proportions. The amount of rice mixed into the usual food is then gradually reduced until the dog is eating entirely their usual food without any further vomiting and diarrhoea.

Vomiting and diarrhoea as a symptom of diseases/conditions of other organs

Vomiting and or diarrhoea be may symptoms that are seen due to diseases and conditions affecting other organ systems which then cause a knock-on affect in terms of disturbing the normal functioning of the stomach and intestines. In these instances the symptoms of vomiting and diarrhoea are not the primary problem but are one of the symptoms associated with problems in other organs.

Examples of diseases and conditions which may produce a variety of symptoms which may include vomiting and diarrhoea are:

8 Pyometra (womb infections) – see page 64.

9 Kidney failure – see page 57.

10 Addison's disease see page 63.

3

My Dog is Straining to Pass Urine or Faeces

Pet owners will often bring their dog to me because they think the dog is constipated. The reason they think their dog is constipated is that they show repeated straining efforts that appear as if they are constipated and cannot pass any faeces. The medical word for these repeated straining efforts is tenesmus. The most common reasons for this symptom are that the dog is having difficulty passing urine or faeces. The vet, when presented with this symptom, will need to determine whether the problem is due to difficulties passing urine or faeces. Thus the vet must determine whether the problem lies with the urinary system or the intestines and/or rectum. Straining to pass faeces may look exactly like the straining associated with straining due to urinary tract problems. Careful observation of both urination behaviour and defecation behaviour should tell us which activity is occurring normally and thus we will know whether the straining is due to difficulties in passing urine or faeces. If the dog is straining frequently but seems to be urinating normally then we know that the problem is in the intestines, the rectum or the anus. If the dog is straining frequently but is passing normal faeces then we know the problem is in the lower urinary system i.e. the bladder, urethra, prostate, vagina or penis. Even if you are unsure as to which area is causing the straining the vet should be able to determine whether the difficulty lies with urinating or defecating by careful examination of your dog by feeling the bladder and intestines and prostate. Once the vet has determined whether the problem relates to urine or faeces they may recommend further tests to identify the exact site and nature of the problem in that organ system.

If the problem is in the urinary system then the straining movements are called stranguria and if the problem lies in the intestines and/or rectum then the straining movements are called dyschezia. The most common cause of straining attempts is stranguria (straining to pass urine). I will discuss stranguria and dyschezia separately.

Stranguria (straining to pass urine)

The signs of stranguria are that the dog repeatedly attempts to pass urine. When these dogs try to pee one will notice that they are straining much harder than normal and that they produce very little or no urine when they are straining. They will also try to pee much more often than normal. The amount of urine that is passed at each attempt varies from nothing at all to small spots of urine. These small spots of urine are very often tinged with blood.

Stranguria is the result of a problem in the lower urinary tract. The urinary tract consists of a

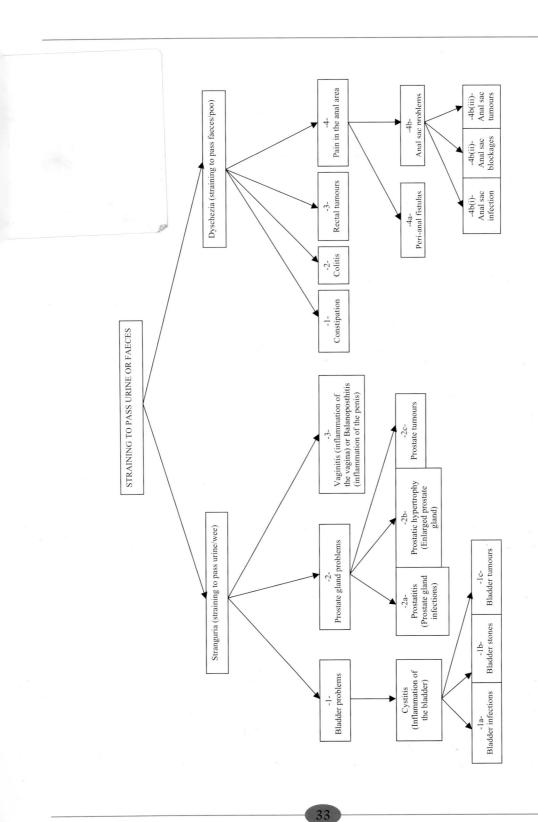

STRAINING TO PASS URINE OR FAECES

Stranguria (straining to pass urine/wee)

-1-
Bladder problems

Cystitis
(Inflammation of
the bladder)

-1a-
Bladder infections

-1b-
Bladder stones

-1c-
Bladder tumours

-2-
Prostate gland problems

-2a-
Prostatitis
(Prostate gland
infections)

-2b-
Prostatic hypertrophy
(Enlarged prostate
gland)

-2c-
Prostate tumours

-3-
Vaginitis (inflammation of
the vagina) or Balanoposthitis
(inflammation of the penis)

Dyschezia (straining to pass faeces/poo)

-1-
Constipation

-2-
Colitis

-3-
Rectal tumours

-4-
Pain in the anal area

-4a-
Peri-anal fistulas

-4b-
Anal sac problems

-4b(i)-
Anal sac
infection

-4b(ii)-
Anal sac
blockages

-4b(iii)-
Anal sac
tumours

number of distinct components. The kidneys are the first part of the urinary tract. Every dog has two kidneys – a left and a right kidney. The kidneys are situated just below the backbone under the last rib on either side of the body. The right kidney is slightly further forward than the left kidney. The kidneys have many functions including the production of urine. The urine produced by each kidney drains into a tube called a ureter which transports the urine to the bladder. Thus the left and right ureter lead from the left and the right kidney to the bladder. The bladder is simply a bag for collecting urine. The bladder is a bag formed by a thin layer of muscle. The function of the bladder is to collect and store the urine produced by the kidneys. When it is full the muscle layer in the bladder wall contracts to push the urine out of the bladder through a single tube called the urethra. In the case of males the urethra passes through the inside of the penis and in the case of females the urethra opens into the vagina. Thus male animals have a much longer and narrower urethra than female animals where it is much shorter and wider. The urinary tract can be divided into two components. The upper urinary tract consists of the kidneys and ureters. The lower urinary tract consists of the bladder and urethra and the vagina or penis.

The symptom of stranguria tells us that the dog is experiencing problems in the lower urinary tract and thus the problem is situated in the bladder or the urethra (and prostate gland) or in the vagina or penis. I will discuss each of these areas individually.

1 The bladder

The most common problems affecting the bladder are cystitis, bladder stones and growths (tumours) in the bladder.

Cystitis

The word cystitis is a very vague term which simply means inflammation of the bladder. This inflammation may be caused by infections, tumours and/or bladder stones.

1a Bacterial cystitis (bladder infections)

The most common cause of cystitis is a bacterial infection in the bladder. Many dogs and human beings, at some stage in their lives, will suffer from a bladder infection. This is called bacterial cystitis. Bacterial cystitis in all species is much more common in females than in males. This is because the bacteria which cause the infection must move up the urethra into the bladder to cause the infection. The female urethra is a much shorter and wider tube than in males and thus it is a shorter and easier journey for bacteria to move into the female bladder (Fig. 7). This journey is much more difficult in male dogs because the urethra is a long and thin tube (Fig. 8). The most common source of origin of the bacteria is the anus. In females the anus is situated close to the vagina. Thus it is once again a shorter journey for bacteria to move from the anus into the opening of the urethra in females than it is in males where the opening is in the tip of the penis, which is much further away from the anus.

Once bacteria have moved into the bladder they need to move into the bladder wall to cause an infection. The natural defence systems of the bladder are the infection-fighting cells in the bladder wall and the acid pH of the urine. Urine in dogs is usually slightly acidic and this acidity tends to kill invading bacteria. Some dogs produce urine which is not acidic enough and these individuals are more prone to infection because bacteria entering the bladder are more likely to survive. If the bacteria are able to penetrate into the bladder wall the bacteria will start to multiply and thus cause infection and inflammation. This process produces an uncomfortable burning sensation in the bladder which makes the muscle layer in the bladder wall contract. The bladder is therefore in a constant state of spasm which makes the dog feel they need to urinate even though there is little or no urine in the bladder and they will make frequent and prolonged attempts to urinate. The bladder however is constantly contracted and thus little or no urine collects there and little or no urine is passed at each attempt to pee. The inflammation in the lining of the bladder may cause microscopic blood vessels in the bladder lining to rupture and thus the urine may contain blood. This blood is sometimes visible to the naked eye giving the urine a pink or red appearance and in mild cases the amount of blood in the urine may be so small that it can only be detected by testing the urine.

When I am presented with a dog who is showing the signs of a bladder infection I will often ask people to bring me a sample of the dog's urine. This is especially important in situations where a particular dog has had several bouts of bacterial cystitis. The immediate tests I can run on the urine include checking for the presence of blood, checking the acidity (pH) and checking for the presence of glucose. These checks can be done quickly and easily by using a urine dipstick. The dipstick is dipped into the urine and within sixty seconds will give me all the above information. This information is important for several reasons. The reason for checking for the presence of blood is to confirm that there is inflammation in the bladder. The reason for checking the acidity (pH) is that if the dog's urine is not acidic enough they will be more prone to repeated infections because they have less protection against bacteria. If the urine is not acidic enough the simple solution is to feed the dog a special diet to produce a more acidic urine which is more likely to kill invading bacteria. This is similar to the wide range of special acidifying drinks available to women who suffer from repeated bouts of cystitis for the same reason viz. if the urine is not acidic enough it is easier for invading bacteria to survive and infect the bladder lining. The reason for checking for the presence of glucose is that if the dog is even mildly diabetic then the glucose in the urine will feed the bacteria, which makes it easier for them to survive in the bladder. This is why diabetic dogs and people are especially prone to bouts of bladder infections. Thus if one finds glucose in the urine it is not sufficient to only treat the cystitis, the vet should also determine why there is glucose in the urine and by correcting this finding there are likely to be fewer episodes of cystitis.

Testing urine with a urine dipstick may be followed by more advanced tests which may include testing for the presence of microscopic bladder stones (crystals), testing for the presence of abnormal cells (tumour cells) and identifying the specific bacteria causing the infection and the most appropriate antibiotic to use. If crystals or abnormal cells are identified then appropriate treatment for bladder tumours or bladder stones must be implemented in addition to treating the infection. This will be discussed in more detail in the next section. Additional tests for investigating bladder infections may also include ultrasound scanning of the bladder, X-rays of the bladder and endoscopy (inserting a small camera into the bladder).

Once the vet has determined that the dog has a bladder infection (bacterial cystitis) and none of the above additional problems are present then the treatment will consist of appropriate antibiotics

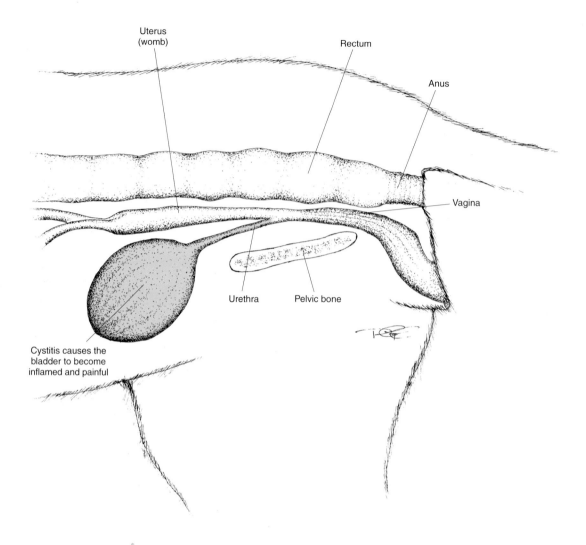

Uterus (womb)

Rectum

Anus

Vagina

Urethra

Pelvic bone

Cystitis causes the
bladder to become
inflamed and painful

Fig 7 Side view of the rear end of the abdomen of a female.

and sometimes also anti-inflammatory treatments to ease the discomfort. If any of the additional
problems discussed above are identified then these must also be corrected to ensure a good recovery
and to reduce or eliminate the risk of recurrent infections.

1b Cystitis with bladder stones (crystals)

The technical name for a bladder stone or bladder crystal is a urolith. Dogs can produce six
different types of bladder stones. Certain types of bladder stones develop in urine which is too

acidic (low pH), other types develop in urine which is not acidic enough (high pH) and other types may develop in any level of acidity (any pH). The urine produced by dogs is usually slightly acidic with a pH of six to six and a half. If an individual dog produces urine with a different acidity then that individual may be prone to developing bladder stones. The most common bladder stones are called struvite stones and these develop in urine which is not acidic enough i.e. the pH is too high.

Many of us grew crystals in jars when we were children. The easiest way to do this is by dissolving the maximum amount of table salt possible in water and then placing a small twig in the water. After a few days you will see small crystals forming on the twig. The twig is necessary to provide a structure for the crystals to form on. Bladder stones (bladder crystals) develop in much the same way. The various types of bladder stones develop from various normal chemicals found in normal urine. The requirement for the formation of crystals from these chemicals is that the acidity of the urine must be correct for the formation of a particular type of crystal and there must be something for the crystal to grow on. In the case of bladder stones the crystals grow on blood cells or bladder lining cells that have become detached and that float around in the urine. The most common reason that red blood cells may be found floating in urine is that the dog may have a bladder infection as discussed earlier. The clumps of blood cells in the urine act like the twig mentioned above and the bladder stone forms around this clump of cells. Thus bladder infections may develop into bladder infections with bladder stones. The cells that line the bladder are like skin cells in that new cells are constantly being formed and old cells are constantly shed. When the old bladder lining cells are shed into the bladder then bladder stones may form around these clumps of shed cells. The bladder stones have sharp edges which scratch the lining of the bladder and this causes inflammation and cystitis symptoms appear. If bacteria enter the bladder then it is much easier for them to invade the bladder wall through these scratches and thus bladder stones may lead to bladder infections. This explanation explains why bladder infections and bladder stones often occur at the same time in one particular individual.

The bladder stone starts off as a microscopic crystal which forms on bladder lining cells or blood cells in the urine. These crystals usually remain so small that they can only be seen when urine is examined under a microscope. In some cases however the crystals may continue to grow until they are as large as grains of sand and in extreme cases the crystals grow as large as a golf ball. The microscopic crystals can be imagined as having a similar appearance to grains of sugar and thus even the smallest crystals have sharp edges which cause irritation and microscopic cuts to the lining of the bladder. The larger the crystal becomes the more irritation it causes and thus any size crystal will cause inflammation of the bladder wall and thus they cause cystitis which may become even more uncomfortable if a secondary bladder infection develops.

The symptoms that one may see in cases of bladder stones/crystals of any size are the same symptoms that one will see with a bladder infection. The bladder stones/crystals produce an uncomfortable burning sensation in the bladder which makes the muscle layer in the bladder wall contract. Because the bladder is in a constant state of spasm the dog feels that it needs to urinate even though there is little or no urine in the bladder and they will make frequent and prolonged attempts to urinate but little or no urine is passed at each attempt to pee. The inflammation in the lining of the bladder may cause microscopic blood vessels in the bladder lining to rupture and thus the urine may contain blood. This blood is sometimes visible to the naked eye giving the urine a pink or red appearance and in mild cases the amount of blood in the urine may be so small that it can only be detected by testing the urine.

When I am presented with a dog showing the signs of cystitis I will often ask people to bring me a sample of the dog's urine. This is especially important in situations where a particular dog has had several bouts of cystitis. The immediate tests I can run on the urine include checking the urine for the presence of blood, checking the acidity of the urine (pH) and checking for the presence of glucose. These checks can be done quickly and easily by using a urine dipstick. The dipstick is dipped into the urine and within sixty seconds will give me all the above information. This information is important for several reasons. The reason for checking for the presence of blood is to confirm that there is inflammation in the bladder. The reason for checking the acidity (pH) is that if the dog's urine does not have the normal level of acidity they will be more prone to develop bladder stones/crystals and/or infections The reason for checking for the presence of glucose is that if the dog is even mildly diabetic then the glucose in the urine will feed invading bacteria which makes it easier for them to survive in the bladder and cause a bladder infection and this in turn may lead to the formation of bladder stones. This is why diabetic dogs and people are especially prone to bouts of cystitis. Thus if one finds glucose in the urine it is not sufficient to only treat the cystitis, the vet should also determine why there is glucose in the urine and by correcting this finding there are likely to be fewer episodes of cystitis.

Testing urine with a urine dipstick may be followed by more advanced tests which may include testing for the presence of microscopic bladder stones (crystals), testing for the presence of abnormal cells (tumour cells) and identifying the specific bacteria causing the infection and the most appropriate antibiotic to use. If crystals or abnormal cells are identified then appropriate treatment for bladder tumours or bladder stones must be implemented in addition to treating the infection. This will be discussed in more detail in the next section. Additional tests for investigating cystitis symptoms may also include ultrasound scanning of the bladder, X-rays of the bladder and endoscopy (inserting a small camera into the bladder), these test will reveal the presence of bladder stones and tumours.

Once the vet has determined that bladder stones/crystals are present they will need to identify what type of stone or crystal it is. The level of acidity (pH) of the urine may give the vet a good idea of what kind of bladder stone/crystal is present as certain stones can only develop at specific pH levels. I feel that direct analysis of the stones/crystals is always necessary because some types of stones/crystals may develop in urine of any pH and in some cases two different types of stone may be present. Microscopic crystals and crystals the size of grains of sand are identified by examining them under a microscope. Larger bladder stones will have to be removed from the bladder by performing an operation to open the bladder and remove the stones. These large stones will then be sent to a specialist laboratory for analysis and identification.

In male dogs small bladder stones may pass out of the bladder and become stuck in the urethra in the penis. The penis of the dog contains a cylindrical bone which is hollow and the urethra runs through this bone. The most common sites for bladder stones becoming stuck is at the back edge of this bone or in the part of the urethra just below the rectum. If male dogs have a bladder stone lodged in the urethra they will be very uncomfortable because the bladder is continually filling with urine which the dog cannot pee out. This leads to severe distention and discomfort of the bladder and the stones must be removed immediately to prevent the bladder from bursting. The second reason that these stones must be removed immediately is that as the urine accumulates in the bladder the waste chemicals in the urine may produce a toxic effect in the body and this may prove fatal if the urine is not removed from the bladder. The first step in these cases may thus be to remove the urine from the bladder using a needle and syringe. The needle is pushed through the abdominal wall and into the bladder and the urine is sucked out with the syringe. The vet will then try to flush the stone back into the bladder by squirting water into the urethra through a catheter. If the vet is able to flush the stone back into the bladder then they will operate to open the bladder and remove the stone. If the stone is stuck in the urethra and cannot be flushed back into the bladder then the vet will operate on the urethra to open it and remove the stone. This operation is less desirable than operating on the bladder because it is more difficult to do and there are more risks and complications possible when the urethra is operated on. The biggest risk is that as the urethra heals after the operation the scar tissue that forms may cause narrowing of the urethra. In the male dog the urethra is a thin tube to begin with and if the scar tissue causes further narrowing the dog may experience permanent difficulty urinating through this narrowing. If the scar tissue does cause narrowing of the urethra the vet will have to operate again to relieve this narrowing but the problem is that further operations may lead to more scarring and further problems. Female dogs do not tend to develop bladder stones becoming stuck in the urethra because the urethra in the female is much shorter and wider than in the male.

Once the bladder stones/crystals have been identified and removed the vet will be able to plan a strategy to try to avoid the formation of new stones/crystals. This is usually achieved by feeding a special type of food to ensure that the dog will produce urine with the correct level of acidity. Thus stones/crystals which can only develop under very high or low acidity levels will not be able to develop again. The vet will also treat the dog with antibiotics if they find that there is also a bladder infection at the same time as the bladder stones/crystals being present as these two problems often go hand in hand for the reasons discussed earlier.

Fortunately most cases of cystitis are simply a 'one off' event caused by a bladder infection and most dogs will not need to have extensive tests and treatments. Most vets will treat first time cystitis patients with antibiotics and possible anti-inflammatories. The vet will often only suggest tests if the problem is not easily cured or if it keeps recurring.

1c Bladder tumours

The bladder is a bag formed by a thin layer of muscle and its function is to collect and store the urine produced by the kidneys. When it is full the muscle layer in the bladder wall contracts to push the urine out of the bladder through a single tube called the urethra. In the case of males the urethra passes through the inside of the penis and in the case of females the urethra opens into the vagina. Thus male animals have a much longer and narrower urethra than female animals where it is much shorter and wider.

Dogs may develop tumours in the wall of the bladder at any stage in their lives. These tumours may be benign growths or malignant (cancerous) growths. The difference between benign and cancerous growths is that a benign growth is not potentially life threatening. A benign growth is not likely to spread to other parts of the body and does not cause a great deal of harm to the tissue it is growing from.

Bladder tumours are very rare in dogs. The most common bladder tumours in dogs are called transitional cell carcinomas and squamous cell carcinomas. These are both highly malignant cancers. Less common tumours are polyps in the bladder wall and these are benign growths. The symptoms of a bladder tumour are very similar to the symptoms of cystitis in that affected dogs are seen to strain to urinate and very often only manage to pass small amounts of urine which may be blood-tinged. The presence of a bladder tumour is confirmed by finding tumour cells in the urine or more commonly by ultrasound scanning or X-raying or by passing a camera into the bladder. Once these tests have confirmed that a tumour is present then a biopsy must be taken to identify what type of tumour it is. Once the tumour has been identified the vet will advise you on the most appropriate course of action.

If the tumour is a polyp then it can be removed. The biggest problem encountered when removing a polyp is the position in the bladder that the polyp is situated. If the polyp has grown from the bladder neck then removal may be very difficult. The bladder neck is the point where the bladder leads into the urethra which is the tube which leads urine out of the body via the penis or vagina. If the polyp has grown from the bladder neck then the success of the surgery will depend on whether the surgeon can save most of the bladder neck or successfully reconstruct it when the polyp has been removed. Even if the surgeon can do this the next possible complication may be that the dog will be incontinent either temporarily or permanently after the surgery.

If the tumour is cancerous then one should X-ray the chest and the abdomen and also scan the abdomen to check for signs of the cancer having spread. I feel that if there is no sign of any spread to other points then one could consider surgery to remove the mass. The surgery involves entering the abdomen and the bladder and removing the mass. If the cancer has grown from the bladder neck then removal may be very difficult or even impossible. Two important points to consider when removing the mass is that not just the mass should be removed but also a margin of normal healthy tissue in every direction to try to ensure that no cancer cells are left behind. The second issue is that the mass can only be removed if vital blood vessels and nerves supplying the bladder and other tissues and organs in the area can be left intact. A very frustrating situation arises when the surgeon finds that the mass cannot be removed in its entirety. In these cases the only remaining option is to try to eliminate the mass by radiation therapy and/or chemotherapy. Many surgeons would want to at least attempt to debulk the mass prior to proceeding with the radiation or chemotherapy. This would involve removing as much tumour tissue as possible without damaging any vital structures trapped in the mass. In many cases, even if the surgeon is able to remove the mass, one might want to follow up on the surgery with radiation and /or chemotherapy to ensure that no tumour cells, which may have spread on a microscopic level to other tissues, are able to grow into a new tumour. There are many different types and ways of using radiation and chemotherapy and the most appropriate protocol will often only be decided after a specialist histopathologist has examined the tumour. For this reason some vets would want to perform surgery in cases where there is more than one tumour mass present or where there is clear evidence of tumour spread to other parts of the body. The object of the surgery in these cases would be to obtain a biopsy of the tumour for analysis by a histopathologist so that the best radiation and/or chemotherapy strategy can be formulated.

Bladder cancers are however highly malignant and often respond poorly to any form of treatment.

Many of my clients may not want to go through all the above steps for any variety of reasons and ask if we could just ' cut to the chase' in terms of trying to help the dog cope with the problem for as long as possible. This would often imply one of two strategies – treat the symptoms of pain or discomfort for as long as possible and when the treatment fails to alleviate the dog's suffering then humanely put him or her to sleep. The most effective way of trying to achieve this is with anti-inflammatory and pain killing treatments. The treatment would involve tablets or injections for the remainder of the dog's life. The treatment is intended only to alleviate the dog's pain and suffering and give them as much good quality, pain free, happy life as possible. I accept that this is not a scientific approach to the problem but many people do not have the financial resources to do more than this or they may not want to subject the dog to any more than this. The overriding consideration must always be the welfare of the dog and if this unscientific approach delivers results in terms of alleviating the symptoms then I have no moral problem with this approach.

People will often request humane euthanasia for their pets with cancer and I feel that this is a reasonable request in the face of a diagnosis with a terminal prognosis. I personally would not deny the request for euthanasia of a cancer patient because we are not all able to cope with the emotional strain of caring for a pet with a terminal condition. Many people, living with this 'sword of Damocles' over their heads, succumb to stress and anxiety and this will often affect the pets living with them to their own psychological detriment. There is never a good time to say goodbye to a pet but sometimes, if they are on a downhill slide, it is better to let them go before they hit rock bottom.

2 Prostate problems

The prostate gland is only found in male dogs. The gland is situated at the point where the bladder leads into the urethra (this is the tube which runs inside the penis which is used to urinate through.) The prostate gland is a spherically shaped gland which lies around the first part of the urethra at the point where it is connected to the bladder (Fig. 8a). The gland is not truly spherical in that it is composed of a left and a right lobe. The function of the prostate gland is to produce the fluid which carries and feeds sperm during ejaculation when dogs mate.

Two common conditions may arise in the prostate gland which may cause a variable amount of pain which causes affected individuals to walk with an arched back and stiff back legs taking shorter than normal steps during walking. The most painful condition is infection and inflammation in the prostate gland which is called prostatitis. The second condition is much less painful and is called prostatic hypertrophy. In the case of prostatic hypertrophy the prostate gland is swollen and enlarged because of the affect of hormones acting on the gland and is not due to infection. The swelling of the prostate gland associated with both of these conditions may also cause the urethra to be compressed at the point where it runs through the prostate gland. The result of this swelling and compression is that affected dogs may find it difficult and painful to urinate through the compressed urethra. These dogs will strain more than normal when trying to pass urine and the urine is often passed in short intermittent spurts. The urine which is passed in this way is often blood tinged.

2a Prostatitis (prostate gland infections)

Prostatitis means infection and inflammation in the prostate gland. This condition is only found in uncastrated male dogs i.e. dogs who have not had their testicles removed by a vet. The reason why the gland becomes infected is not known. The symptoms of prostatitis include walking with an arched back, stiff back legs taking shorter than normal steps during walking, difficulty urinating and lethargy and poor appetite due to the pain and fever associated with this condition. The diagnosis is made by noticing these symptoms and documenting a fever when the temperature is taken with a thermometer. The final step in making this diagnosis is feeling the prostate gland. The vet does this by inserting a finger into the anus and feeling an enlarged and painful prostate gland (Fig. 8b). The treatment for this condition may include antibiotics, anti-inflammatories and hormone injections. If the condition reoccurs often the vet may advise castration as this causes the prostate to shrink and infections in castrated male dogs are very rare. A complication of this condition is that the infection may spread into the backbones which are positioned directly above the prostate gland. This condition is called discospondilitis. The presence of discospondilitis is suspected when there is a great deal of pain and inflammation in the lower back at the level of the lumbo-sacral joint. The lumbo-sacral joint is the joint made by the lowest of the lumbar backbones and the sacrum (the bone forming the roof of the pelvis). If the vet suspects that the dog also has lumbo-sacral discospondilitis the diagnosis can be confirmed by taking X-rays of these bones. The treatment for discospondilitis is very often the same antibiotics and anti-inflammatories that are used to treat the prostatitis.

2b Prostatic hypertrophy (enlarged prostate gland)

The prostate gland may become swollen and painful without being infected (Fig. 8b). This swelling is caused by sex hormones acting on the prostate gland causing it to swell. Two hormones may cause the problem. The first hormone which may cause this problem is testosterone which is the male sex hormone produced in the testicles. This hormone may overstimulate the prostate gland and thus cause it to swell and possibly become painful. The other hormone that may cause swelling of the prostate is the female hormone oestrogen. All male animals normally have very small amounts of female hormone in their body but when there is too much of the hormone it may affect the prostate gland. The effect of too much female hormone is that it causes swelling of the prostate and it can change the structure of the cells in the prostate gland by a process called squamous metaplasia. If this condition develops one should try to determine why there is an increased level of female hormone in that dog's body. The most common source of excess female hormone is from a type of tumour called a sertoli cell tumour that may develop in one of the dog's testicles. The presence of a sertoli cell tumour in a testicle is that the affected testicle is often hard and lumpy and larger than the other testicle which tends to shrink because of the high levels of female hormone produced by the tumour in the other testicle.

The symptoms of walking with an arched back and stiff back legs, taking shorter than normal steps during walking and difficulty in urinating are far less severe than in cases of prostatitis. The affected dog will generally not be lethargic or lose their appetite, as they do not develop a fever with this condition. Thus when the temperature is taken it will be normal and when the prostate gland is touched during the rectal examination by the vet, the prostate will be found to be

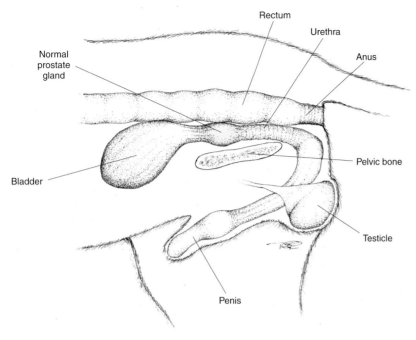

Normal
prostate
gland

Rectum

Urethra

Anus

Pelvic bone

Bladder

Testicle

Penis

Fig 8a   Side view of the rear end of the abdomen to show the normal size and position of the male urinary system.

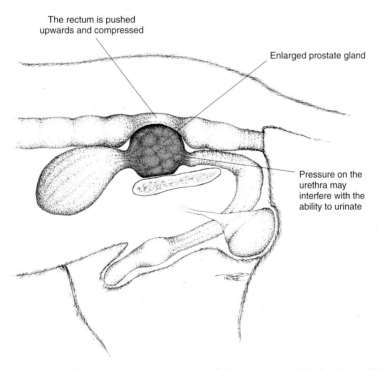

The rectum is pushed
upwards and compressed

Enlarged prostate gland

Pressure on the
urethra may
interfere with the
ability to urinate

Fig 8b   The prostate gland may become enlarged due to prostatic hypertrophy or infection (prostatitis). The enlarged prostate pushes against the rectum making it difficult and/or painful to defecate (poo). The enlarged prostate may also exert pressure on the urethra making it difficult to to urinate (wee).

enlarged and swollen but there is little or no pain when it is touched. The treatment for this condition depends on which hormone is causing the prostate gland to swell. If too much testosterone (male hormone) is the problem the dogs may be treated with injections to lower the levels of this hormone. If these injections do not solve the problem or if the problems keeps recurring then castrating the dog will solve the problem because this removes the 'factory' which produces the male hormone. If the cause of the problem is too much oestrogen (female hormone) the solution to the problem is also to castrate the dog because this will remove the tumour in the testicle which is producing the female hormone. In cases where one cannot determine which hormone is causing the problem the vet may advise tests to investigate the problem. These tests may include blood tests, ultrasound scans of the prostate and testicles and possibly also biopsies from the prostate gland.

2c Prostatic tumours

Prostate cancer is the most common cause of prostate problems in human beings. Prostate cancer or benign prostatic tumours are very rare in dogs. When prostate tumours do occur they produce the same symptoms seen with prostatitis and prostatic hyperplasia. The presence of a prostatic tumour is confirmed by performing ultrasound scans of the prostate and taking a biopsy from the prostate gland. Once the type of tumour has been identified the treatment options and considerations are the same as in the case of bladder tumours as discussed earlier.

3 Infections and inflammation in the penis and vagina

Infection and inflammation in the vagina is called vaginitis and in the penis is called balanoposthitis. Infection and inflammation in these organs are very rare but if they do arise then the symptoms and treatment will be the same as in the case of cystitis (bladder infection) as discussed earlier.

Dyschezia (Straining to pass faeces)

Straining to pass faeces may look exactly like the straining associated with the urinary tract problems discussed earlier. Careful observation of both urination behaviour and defecation behaviour should tell us which activity is occurring normally and thus we will know whether the straining is due to difficulties in passing urine or faeces. If the dog is straining frequently but seems to be urinating normally then we know that the problem is in the intestines, the rectum or the anus. Even if you are unsure as to which area is causing the straining the vet should be able to determine whether the difficulty lies with urinating or defecating by careful examination of your dog by feeling the bladder and intestines and prostate. Once the vet has determined that the problem relates to passing faeces they may recommend further tests to identify the exact site and nature of the problem in that organ system.

Straining to pass faeces may be the result of problems in the lower intestine, the rectum or the anus. The most important point to make at this stage is that straining attempts to pass faeces do not necessarily mean simply that the dog is constipated. The straining efforts (dyschezia) may be the result of constipation, 'obstructions' in the rectum, inflammation in the rectum (colitis), growths in the rectum or pain, infection and inflammation in the anal area. These possible causes of dyschezia will be discussed individually in this order.

1 Constipation as a cause of dyschezia

Constipation may occur in dogs for the same reasons that it occurs in human beings. Most cases happen for no obvious reason but occasionally it may be because there is too little fibre in that individual's diet. The treatment for simple constipation is simply an enema to soften the hard mass of faeces in the rectum. Once the faeces have been passed one should carefully examine them to try to identify why the constipation occurred. Most commonly no reason is apparent and this event may be regarded as a 'one off' event and no further action or treatment is required. If one finds a large amount of the dog's fur binding the faeces together then one should determine why so much fur is present in the faeces. This may be because the dog is very itchy and is grooming more than normal. If this is the case one should identify and treat the cause of the itchiness and thus no further episodes should occur. Please refer to the chapter on itchy dogs for more details. If one determines that there is too little fibre in the dog's diet then this is easily corrected by feeding more fibre.

Constipation in male dogs may occur due to difficulty in passing faeces. The difficulty may be the result of an enlarged prostate gland pressing against the rectum or it may be due to a condition called a rectal diverticulum. If the problem is that the prostate is enlarged and pressing against the rectum thus obstructing the movement of faeces, the cause of the prostatic enlargement should be determined and treated. Please refer to the prostate section dealt with earlier in this chapter. A rectal diverticulum may be the cause of the straining and apparent constipation. I will explain what a rectal diverticulum is: the rectum is simply the last part of the large intestine that leads to the anus. The rectum is effectively just a long tube for collecting faeces and holding them until the individual is ready to pass the faeces (defecate). The walls of the rectum may become stretched just before the rectum attaches to the anus and as the walls stretch outwards they form a bulge in the rectum. Imagine this bulge to be similar to the bulge in a car tyre when it develops a weak spot. Once this bulge has developed it tends to start stretching and becomes progressively larger. Once it has enlarged sufficiently it forms a blind ending pocket which opens into the rectum. This pocket forms because as faeces are passed every day they are pushed into this pocket. While the pocket is still shallow this does not affect the dog but once this pocket has stretched and become deeper, the faeces which are inadvertently pressed into the pocket when the dog defecates are unable to move back into the rectum. This process continues every time the dog passes faeces and thus more and more faeces are pushed into the pocket which has formed. As the amount of faeces accumulates the dogs will become more uncomfortable and they tend to strain more to try to pass the faeces in the pocket. With time this impaction of faeces tends to dry out and the faeces become very hard.

The way to alleviate this discomfort is to give the dog an enema to soften the faeces and then the faeces needs to be scraped out of the pocket. This pocket from the rectum is called a rectal diverticulum. The dog may develop a diverticulum to the left and/or to the right of the anus. When the diverticulum is full of faeces one can see the bulge that it forms next to the anus. The rectal diverticulum develops as a result of increased straining to pass faeces due to prostatic enlargement or colitis or due to a weakness or hernia in the muscles surrounding the rectum. The initial treatment for this condition is to alleviate the constipation by giving the dog an enema and removing the faeces from the rectal diverticulum with a gloved finger inserted into the anus. The dog should be fed a special diet to keep the faeces soft enough to stop them becoming trapped in this blind ending pocket. If the faeces have a sloppy texture then they will not get stuck in the pocket as easily. The next step is to stop the dog from straining, as this is what has caused the pocket to develop. If the straining is due to prostatic enlargement the prostate should be treated as discussed earlier in the chapter. If the straining is due to colitis then the colitis should be treated as discussed in the chapter on vomiting and diarrhoea . If the straining has caused a weakness or a hernia in the muscles surrounding the rectum (the perineum), this should be repaired with an operation. Once all the factors which have caused the pocket to develop have been treated the pocket should shrink over a period of time. If the pocket does not shrink then one should maintain the dog on a diet that will keep their faeces very soft for the rest of their lives.

'Obstructions' in the rectum will cause the symptoms of straining. The most common cause of an apparent 'obstruction' is the presence of undigested bone shards in the rectum. These bone shards have very sharp edges and cause a lot of pain in the rectum and this leads to staining. When a gloved finger is inserted into the anus the vet can feel the bone shards in the rectum. The reason I refer to this as an 'obstruction' is that it is not a true obstruction (blockage) but appears to be so because the dog finds it very painful to pass these bone shards. Thus even though they want to try to pass the shards they stop the attempts as soon as they feel the pain. Most of these cases can be relieved by administering an enema but many dogs are in so much discomfort that a sedative will be required for the enema.

2 Colitis as a cause of dyschezia

Colitis causes significant inflammation and irritation in the large intestine and rectum to cause the symptoms of severe straining with no apparent faeces being passed. For a full discussion on colitis and its treatment please refer to the chapter on vomiting and diarrhoea .

3 Rectal tumours/growths as a cause of dyschezia

Growths called rectal polyps may develop in the rectum. These are usually benign growths i.e. they are not a cancer. These growths may cause the symptom of straining and when faeces are passed they may be streaked with blood from the growth. The vet will identify the presence of rectal polyps by inserting a gloved finger into the anus. Once the presence of rectal polyps has been confirmed as the cause of the problem they can usually be removed with a simple operation.

4 Infection, pain and inflammation in the anal area

Conditions which cause pain and inflammation in and around the anus may cause the straining symptoms of dyschezia because the process of defecating is painful and the affected dog will try to avoid defecating for as long as possible. When the dog can wait no longer they will show pain and strain as faeces are passed. The most common causes of pain in the anal area are peri-anal fistulas and anal sac problems. I will discuss each of these conditions individually.

4a Peri-anal fistulas as a source of pain causing dyschezia

Peri-anal fistulas are seen as small holes in the skin at any point around the edge of the anus. These holes may vary from one millimetre in diameter to several millimetres in diameter. There may be only one hole visible or a great many holes may appear. These holes may appear severely inflamed or not inflamed at all. The holes that develop in the skin each lead into a 'tunnel' which extends into the tissues around the anus. Some of these 'tunnels' may be a single 'tunnel' and others may branch off into several other 'tunnels'. These tunnels are called fistulas. The fistulas generally cause a great deal of pain because of the inflammation they cause in the anal area. This inflammation makes defecation very painful and often dogs will cry out when straining and attempting to defecate. The pain in the area often results in the anus not relaxing when faeces are passed and thus the faeces may have a thin ribbon-like appearance. German shepherd dogs are the breed most commonly affected by this condition and it is rare in other breeds.

The cause of peri-anal fistulas is not understood. Some researchers suspect that the tunnels start from the wall of the rectum and extend to the skin and other researchers suspect that the fistulas start from the skin and extend into the tissue around the rectum. The fistulas are inflamed and painful tunnels and may discharge a clear or pussy fluid. Because the exact cause of these fistulas is not known a great many treatments are available but no one single treatment is guaranteed to cure the problem. The various treatments may be purely treatment with medication or may be surgical treatment or a combination of both. The medications that have been trialled include antibiotics, cortisone, cyclosporin and a variety of treatments to suppress the immune system. The surgical operations that have been trialled include scraping out the inside of the fistulas, removing the fistulas entirely and amputating the end portion of the rectum with the creation of a new anus. This condition is frustrating for the vet and distressing for the dog and their owner because there is not a guarantee that any of the treatments will cure the problem. The conditions may not respond at all to treatment or it may only improve with treatment or it may reccur after treatment has appeared to cure it. Many vets have different opinions on the best course of action when treating this con-dition and I would encourage dog owners to discuss all the treatment options regarding their success rates and possible complications before embarking on treatment for their dog. Referral to a specialist centre with the latest treatments and technology may offer the best hope for success but I advise all people that the problem may be incurable in some individuals. This means that in some cases the best we can hope for is to control the pain caused by this condition to the extent that the affected dog can lead a normal and pain free life despite the presence of the fistulas.

4b Anal sac problems as a source of pain causing dyschezia

The anal sacs (anal glands) may become blocked, infected or may develop tumours and this may result in sufficient pain in the area of the anus to cause pain and straining when affected individuals defecate. The various anal sac conditions and their treatments are fully discussed in chapter 12.

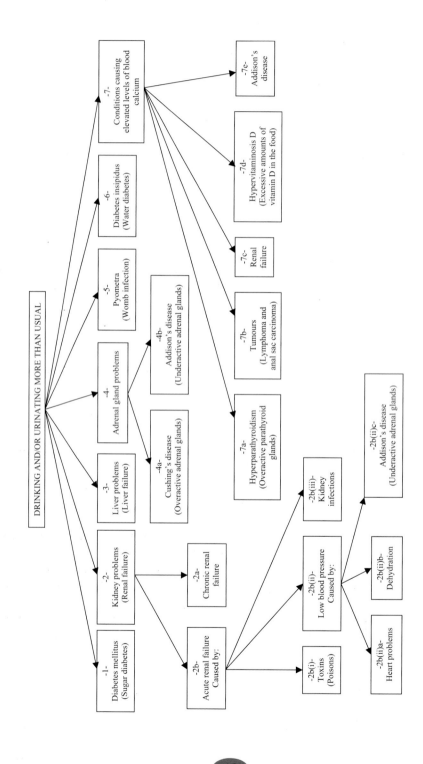

DRINKING AND/OR URINATING MORE THAN USUAL

-1-
Diabetes mellitus
(Sugar diabetes)

-2-
Kidney problems
(Renal failure)

-2a-
Chronic renal failure

-2b-
Acute renal failure
Caused by:

-2b(i)-
Toxins
(Poisons)

-2b(ii)-
Low blood pressure
Caused by:

-2b(ii)a-
Heart problems

-2b(ii)b-
Dehydration

-2b(ii)c-
Addison's disease
(Underactive adrenal glands)

-2b(iii)-
Kidney infections

-3-
Liver problems
(Liver failure)

-4-
Adrenal gland problems

-4a-
Cushing's disease
(Overactive adrenal glands)

-4b-
Addison's disease
(Underactive adrenal glands)

-5-
Pyometra
(Womb infection)

-6-
Diabetes insipidus
(Water diabetes)

-7-
Conditions causing elevated levels of blood calcium

-7a-
Hyperparathyroidism
(Overactive parathyroid glands)

-7b-
Tumours
(Lymphoma and anal sac carcinoma)

-7c-
Renal failure

-7d-
Hypervitaminosis D
(Excessive amounts of vitamin D in the food)

-7e-
Addison's disease

4

My Dog is Drinking and/or Urinating a Lot More Than Usual

A common comment I hear from my clients is ' I think he/she is drinking more than normal' or 'He/she is weeing (urinating) more than normal'. Technically this is referred to as a polyuria (urinating more)/polydipsia (drinking more) syndrome. The first step in investigating this is to determine whether in fact the dog is drinking or urinating excessively. The general expectation is that a dog will drink and urinate an approximate amount determined by their size and weight. The formula used to calculate the amount of water a dog will require daily is sixty to eighty ml per kg per twenty-four hours. Thus if a dog weighs twenty kilograms then their daily water requirement is about 1.4 litres (approx. 2.5 pints) of water every twenty-four hours. In reality most dogs are not seen to drink this amount every day because some of this water is taken in with their food which contains water. Thus dogs on dry food will be seen to drink more water than dogs on tinned or moist food. However, this is an approximation of the daily fluid requirement and if the individual is suddenly seen to be drinking much more than usual, even if this increased amount is within the calculated requirement, the phenomenon should be investigated. The amount of urine normally produced is about twenty-five to forty ml per kg per twenty-four hours. Thus the same twenty-kilogram dog would be expected to produce up to 800ml of urine daily.

These calculations are not absolute and if one suspects that the individual is drinking and/or urinating more than normal some investigation is merited even if the increased quantities are within the calculated amounts. The next issue to try to determine is whether the primary problem is an increased thirst or an increased urine production. Simply put, one needs to determine whether the dog is peeing more because he is drinking more or whether he is drinking more to replace the increased fluid loss due to peeing more.

There are many causes of a polyuria/polydipsia syndrome. The old axiom that 'the common things occur commonly' is again very appropriate in this situation and the most usual causes of this syndrome are:

- Diabetes mellitus (sugar diabetes)
- Conditions affecting the kidneys or liver
- Adrenal gland disorders

- Pyometra (uterine/womb infections)
- Diabetes insipidus (water diabetes)
- Conditions causing elevated levels of calcium in the blood

The starting point in investigating this syndrome is to perform a complete physical examination and to run some routine tests on blood and urine samples. If these initial tests fail to give us a diagnosis then the investigation is continued with more specialised blood and urine tests and possibly X-rays and ultrasound scans.

1 Diabetes mellitus (sugar diabetes)

The most common symptoms of diabetes mellitus are a sudden increase in thirst and urinating with increased appetite and sometimes weight loss. There are two types of diabetes mellitus – insulin dependant and non-insulin dependant diabetes. To discuss this we first need to understand what diabetes mellitus is. Insulin is produced in a gland called the pancreas, which is situated along the first part of the small intestine. The pancreas has two functions – it produces a number of digestive enzymes which are led along ducts into the intestine where they digest the food we have eaten and it produces insulin, which is released into the blood stream. Insulin circulates in the blood stream and its function is to move glucose from the blood into the cells. Think of insulin as a man stoking a furnace. The man is the insulin, the furnace represents the body's tissues and the wood being thrown into the furnace is the glucose. If the pancreas fails to produce insulin, then the man in this analogy is eliminated from the equation and the result is that although there is sufficient wood (glucose) to stoke the furnace (the body's tissues), none of this wood is being thrown into the furnace which will then be unable to function. The additional effect is that as more wood is being transported to the site, the amount of wood (glucose) accumulates in the transporting mechanism (the blood stream.)

The effect on the body is that the tissues (furnace) are being deprived of their food/energy source and call out for more glucose (wood). The body responds by eating more to raise the blood glucose levels but because the glucose is not being thrown into the cells by the insulin, the blood glucose level increases and the cell's ability to function is compromised because, like the furnace, they are not being fed. The clinical effect is a dog who is hungry and eating more to try to feed their hungry cells but, because there is no boilerman (insulin) to move the wood (glucose) into the furnace (the cells), the dog will lose weight despite the increased appetite. An important point to make at this time is that, in advanced cases of diabetes, the period of increased appetite may not have been noticed. In these long term or more severe cases the presenting sign may be weight loss in the face of a loss of appetite. These dogs may feel too unwell to eat because of prolonged starvation of their body tissues and a condition called diabetic ketoacidosis whereby toxic chemicals called ketones accumulate in their bodies.

The basic principle in treating a diabetic dog is to inject insulin every day to move glucose from the blood stream into the cells of the body. There are many different kinds of insulin available and they are classified as ultra-short acting, short acting, intermediate acting and long acting insulin. This classification is based on how long a single insulin injection will work. The ultra-short acting insulin may only work for eight hours and thus it needs to be injected three times daily and the long acting insulin works for about twenty-four hours and thus needs to be injected once a day. The most effective and thus the most commonly used insulin in dogs is the short acting insulin which works for about twelve hours and thus needs to be injected twice daily. This is more inconvenient than using a once a day type of insulin but the once a day type of insulin does not control the blood sugar levels well enough for the dog to live a comfortable normal life.

A very important point to make at this stage is that the treatment for diabetes is aimed at 'controlling' the diabetes. This means that the insulin does not cure the diabetes in the true sense of the word because if the diabetes could be cured then there would be no need for ongoing treatment. The principle of the treatment is to artificially (by injection) give the body insulin which it is unable to produce for itself. Thus, by injecting insulin, we are artificially controlling the glucose levels in the blood by artificially moving the blood glucose into the body's cells to feed them so that they can function normally. This process is referred to as controlling the diabetic and implies controlling the movement of glucose from the blood into the cells. The amount of glucose required by each cell in the body is different every day and every hour. This is because our level of activity is always changing and we eat different types of food each of which provides a different level of glucose (energy) for our bodies to use. Think about the day you are having today as compared to yesterday. You may have been at work yesterday and have the day off today doing different things. Thus the amount of glucose (energy) your body needs today is different to yesterday and every other day of your life. The food you have eaten today is different to what you ate yesterday and thus provides your body with a different level of glucose (energy). This is why people with diabetes need to check their blood glucose levels by pricking their fingers and testing the drop of blood to decide how much insulin they need to inject themselves with throughout the day. They can also check their glucose levels by testing their urine.

People with diabetes do not just rely on the test results from the drop of blood or urine but also on how they feel. If, for example, they feel tired and know that they have not eaten much that day, they will be fairly sure that they need to eat something high in energy to boost their blood sugar levels. By the same token, if they know they have eaten enough that day then they will know that they probably just need a bit more insulin to help move the blood glucose into their body's cells. These people will test a drop of their blood or urine just to be sure that their assumption is correct and will either eat something or inject a bit of insulin or both so that they feel fine again. The amount of insulin they need to inject or the amount of food they need to eat will vary according to the kind of day they are having. Thus human diabetics are constantly fine tuning their blood glucose levels and the amount of glucose being moved into their cells based on how they are feeling at the time. Dogs are unable to speak and thus cannot tell use when they need to eat a bit more or when they need more or less insulin at any particular time on any particular day. Thus we treat them according to their blood and urine glucose levels at the time that we think they need another insulin injection.

In practical terms we would inject the diabetic dog with insulin twice daily. Just like every human diabetic, every dog diabetic will need a different kind of insulin and a different dosage. When a dog is first diagnosed as having diabetes mellitus the first stage of their treatment is called the 'stabilisation' phase. This is the phase where we need to determine which insulin they need, how much insulin they need and how often they need it. The starting dose of insulin that I use is a half a unit of short acting insulin per kilogram of body weight given twice daily. Thus for a dog weighing twenty kilograms I would start the stabilisation phase with ten units of short acting insulin injected twice daily. Insulin is measured and dosed as units rather than as millimetres and insulin syringes are thus calibrated as units. The next point to consider during the stabilisation phase is that we need to control how much food the dog eats and when they eat it. This is because we need to know how much energy (glucose) they will have moving from their stomach and intestines into their blood supply. This is important because we need to know that a specific amount of glucose will move into their blood stream and thus we know how much insulin we need to give them to move that amount of glucose into their cells.

The most common protocol used during the stabilisation phase is to calculate how much food the individual will eat in one day. We then divide that food into two portions. The first portion is fed in the morning and the second portion is fed eight hours later. The insulin dose, calculated according to the dog's bodyweight, is injected about thirty minutes after they have eaten their food. This is because we must first see them eat so that when we inject the insulin we know that there will be glucose in the bloodstream for the insulin to work on. The traditional approach during the stabilisation phase is to follow this protocol and then measure the blood glucose levels every two hours over a twenty-four-hour period. The blood glucose levels are measured as mmol/l. This is just a measurement similar to measuring distance in yards or weight in kilograms. These blood glucose levels are then plotted on a graph and we can then check that the amount of food and the amount of insulin used is able to maintain the dog at normal blood glucose levels all day every day. If the levels are too high then the insulin dose must be increased or if the levels are too low the insulin dose must be reduced. We will also be able to see from the graph how long each insulin injection lasts and this will tell us whether we should change the dose or the type of insulin. This process can also be done by testing the level of glucose in the urine but it is less accurate and it is difficult to ask a dog to wee every two hours.

When the blood glucose graph (the glucose curve) has been drawn up we want all the points on the graph to be between three and nine mmol per litre. When the level of blood glucose goes above nine mmol/l then glucose starts to move into the urine. The glucose moving into the urine pulls a lot of water with it and this is why diabetics will urinate more than normal. If urine is tested and we find glucose in it then we know that the blood glucose is above the normal level of nine mmol/l. We can approximate from the amount of glucose in the urine just how high above nine the blood glucose is likely to be. Thus a person or a dog with diabetes can monitor their condition by regularly testing their urine but this is not as accurate as blood testing. The further problem with monitoring according to urine glucose levels is that if there is no glucose in the urine we can say that the blood glucose level is below nine mmol/l but we cannot say how low below nine the level is. This is important because if the blood level drops below three then the diabetic person or dog has had too much insulin and this can be life threatening.

Once we have determined the type and amount of insulin the patient needs by drawing up a normal glucose curve for that patient, they are then called a 'stabilised' diabetic. Further monitoring and further adjustments can be made over the rest of their lives by once or twice weekly urine or blood tests. We should find that when the diabetic dog has been 'stabilised', their thirst, appetite and urinating should return to normal. Any future increases in thirst, appetite or weeing will alert us that their diabetes is no longer controlled and that we need to redetermine the dose and type of insulin that they require.

The best food for a diabetic is a high fibre food. There are many commercially produced high fibre diets available specifically for diabetic dogs. By feeding these foods the diabetes will be much easier to control and often a lower dose of insulin will be required to stabilise and control the diabetes over the long term. These foods ensure a slower release of glucose from food after the dog has eaten and thus the blood glucose levels do not rise and fall as rapidly during and after eating. This slower rise and fall of blood glucose makes it easier for the injected insulin to move the glucose into the cells throughout each day. It is important that the two portions of food are given at the same amount and at the same time every day to ensure that we always know how much food is being digested. The same amount of insulin will therefore be required at the same time every day to ensure that the blood glucose levels are constantly and predictably between three and nine mmol/l at any time. No other food or treats should be fed during or between meals as this will result in variations in the daily blood glucose levels which may not be controlled by the previously calculated insulin dose. The dose of insulin would have been calculated to manage only the normal meals fed at regular times and if additional food or treats are fed at different times then the blood glucose levels may become erratic, elevated and uncontrolled.

This protocol for stabilising the diabetic dog has several potential flaws. The problems we may encounter are that the dog may refuse to eat the special food, many people are unable to feed the second meal eight hours after the first due to other commitments and the dog will have been stabilised under hospitalisation conditions at the veterinary clinic which are different to the conditions that they live in at home. This last point implies that a hospitalised dog is likely to be more stressed in the clinic than they are at home and thus their glucose (energy) requirements are higher than they are at home. This may mean that the dose of insulin required to control their diabetes is different when they are at home and feeling more relaxed.

These potential flaws with the traditional approach to stabilising a diabetic dog have led me to take a slightly less rigid approach. The main reason for this is that we can never control a dog's diabetes as well as a human being could control their own diabetes. This is because human diabetics are constantly able to fine tune their blood glucose levels by assessing how they feel at any moment in time and by testing themselves at any time of the day and they can make very subtle and accurate adjustments. Dogs cannot speak to let us know that they may need any of these subtle adjustments and thus we dose them according to their blood and urine glucose levels and according to their symptoms. Thus if we see that a diabetic dog starts to drink and pee more we know that we need to increase their insulin but the human diabetic would have made the adjustment before these symptoms appeared. This does not imply that diabetic dogs suffer as a result of less tightly controlled blood glucose levels but demonstrates that humans control their blood sugar levels more quickly and more efficiently.

The approach that I take with my diabetic patients is that the object of treatment is to have a happy dog living a normal life despite being a diabetic. The way I decide whether their diabetes is controlled is that they should not show any symptoms of being diabetic. The object of my approach is to have a happy and energetic dog who has a normal appetite, who will drink and urinate normal amounts and who has a normal and stable bodyweight. I find that I can achieve this despite bending a number of the rules of treatment as described earlier. The first rule that I bend is the interval between meals and insulin injections. I find that most of my clients are working people who cannot be home to feed the second meal eight hours after the first. I suggest to these people that they feed half the dog's daily food in the morning when they get up for work and inject the insulin dose when the dog has started eating or as soon as they have finished eating. The second half of the daily food is the feed twelve hours after the first and the second insulin dose is also given when the dog is eating or when he has finished his meal. I also tell them that if they are out for a meal or at a movie when the second meal and insulin dose is due, that they do not have to rush home to do this. No harm will come from the second meal and insulin dose being a few hours late or early. The next rule I bend is that I suggest feeding the special diabetic food but if the dog refuses to eat it then try mixing the diabetic food with the usual food. If the dog still refuses to eat the special food then simply continue feeding the normal dog food. The third rule I bend is that I rely mostly on the symptoms rather than on blood and urine tests to control the diabetes. I try to stabilise these patients at home and adjust the levels of insulin according to how well the symptoms of increased appetite, thirst and urination are resolving. Once these symptoms have resolved I accept that we have found the correct insulin dose for that individual. I accept that this approach is less scientific than it should be but I find that is the only approach that many people can accommodate in their lives and the results are as good as the more regimented approach I described earlier as documented in most textbooks. If this more relaxed approach does not resolve all the symptoms then I will suggest to my clients that we revert to the more academic system of blood and urine tests to draw up a glucose curve to identify why the diabetes is not being controlled.

Once the diabetic dog has been stabilised and the symptoms of diabetes have resolved then we will have determined the dose and frequency of insulin required by that individual. The dog will be maintained on this dose permanently. This is called the maintenance phase. There may however be a need to adjust the dosages at various times in the dog's life for various reasons. My advice to people is to monitor the symptoms of their dog and adjust the insulin dose accordingly. It takes time for people with a diabetic dog to become confident in their own assessment of their dog's overall condition and initially adjustments will often only be made after a conversation with their vet to confirm their observations and proposed insulin dose adjustments. A tool for people to use to confirm their suspicions regarding the need to adjust the insulin levels is a urine dipstick test. Urine glucose dipsticks are cheaply and freely available from pharmacists and are very easy to use. The dipstick is dipped in urine and will change colour according to the amount of glucose in the urine. This colour change is compared to the whole range of possible colour changes on a chart and each colour change is representative of a specific amount of glucose in the urine. The higher the glucose level is, the higher the insulin dose will need to be. These dipsticks should be regarded only as a tool to confirm what we already suspect according to the symptoms we see in the diabetic dog. Thus if we notice that at some point the dog starts to drink more we would suspect that their insulin dose needs to be increased slightly. This suspicion is confirmed using a urine dipstick test which will show an elevated amount of glucose in the urine. The dose of insulin is then increased.

The primary indication for reducing the dose of insulin is if the diabetic dog suddenly seems unwell in any way. They may appear unwell either because they have picked up another unrelated condition or infection or they may have been given too much insulin. They may have been given too much insulin because of an accidental overdose or their diabetes may have altered and they simply need less insulin. If they have been given more insulin than they need they initially appear drunk. The signs of being drunk i.e. they seem weak, uncoordinated and unsteady or wobbly on their feet is due to the insulin dose dropping the blood glucose levels too low and thus the treatment in this situation is to get glucose (energy) into them immediately. When human diabetics experience this they will simply eat chocolate to boost their glucose levels until they feel better. Chocolate however is poisonous to dogs and thus I advise people to use syrup or honey in this situation. This is easily done by smearing the syrup or honey into the dog's mouth until the signs of 'drunkenness' disappears which should be within an hour. If the signs do not disappear then one should consult a vet to consider further intervention. The vet will often use a glucose drip to correct low blood glucose levels if this is required. The effects of too much insulin are far more serious and potentially life threatening than the effects of too little insulin and thus if the dog suddenly seems drunk immediate action in the form of high-energy foods like syrup is warranted. If one is unsure whether the dog has had too much or too little insulin and they appear drunk, it is better to assume that too much insulin has been given and to use syrup or honey to try to resolve the problem on the assumption that too much insulin has been given as this is the more serious possibility.

The golden rule regarding adjustments of the insulin level is to increase or decrease the dose by no more than two units per dose. Once this adjustment has been made it will take about five days for the dog to adjust to this new dose thus one must wait five days before adjusting the dose again. These minor adjustments can be made by the owner at home without first consulting the vet but if the adjustment fails to control the symptoms then it is wise to consult the vet regarding any further dose adjustments. The second golden rule in the maintenance phase of diabetes is never stop the insulin. If the dog is ill and loses their appetite or if they simply do not want to eat a meal at any time for whatever reason the insulin dose should still be given but half the normal dose. The vet should then be consulted to determine why the dog is ill or has lost their appetite. If they have simply picked up an unrelated illness like a chest infection or an upset stomach then this should be treated and half the insulin dose should be given until the illness has been cured by the appropriate treatment and the appetite has returned to normal. The third golden rule is that it is better to give too little insulin than to give too much. Thus if one is uncertain as to whether to increase or decrease the insulin dose it is safer to decrease the dose until a vet has been consulted. The basic principle is to increase the insulin dose if the dog starts to eat, drink or wee more and to reduce the dose if the dog appears to feel unwell.

Most dogs with diabetes will stabilise within about two weeks of starting treatment and the insulin dose remains fairly constant once they are in the maintenance phase. Occasionally we encounter the 'problem diabetic' – dogs who are difficult to stabilise or maintain despite all the appropriate steps and treatment described earlier. These dogs will require more intensive investigation and treatment of their condition to find out why they are not performing as expected. It may be a simple matter of determining their individual response to various types or doses of insulin or they may be experiencing insulin resistance or insulin antagonism.

Insulin resistance means that the body's cells are unable to receive glucose from the blood supply despite adequate levels of insulin trying to move glucose into the cells. This may happen for a variety of reasons which need to be identified and treated by your vet. Insulin antagonism means that the body is producing substances which interfere with insulin thus preventing the insulin from moving glucose from the blood into the cells. The most common form of insulin antagonism is the effect of some female hormones which interfere with insulin. Some female dogs will develop diabetes around the time of coming into heat (coming into season) because at this time the female hormones which interfere with insulin are at their highest levels. In these cases the diabetes may be permanently cured by sterilising the dog (spaying). The process of sterilisation is technically called an ovariohysterectomy. This operation involves removing the ovaries and the uterus (the womb). The ovaries produce the female hormones which interfere with insulin and thus this operation may permanently cure the diabetes if this is the sole cause of the diabetes. For this operation to cure successfully the diabetes it must be done very soon after the diabetes has appeared around the time of the season. The second most common form of insulin antagonism is much rarer and is the result of the body producing antibodies against insulin. These antibodies function just like antibodies which fight against disease and have the effect of attacking and inactivating the insulin. Thus these patients will not stabilise because even if high doses of insulin are injected the body's antibodies simply inactivate the insulin. This condition is diagnosed with special blood tests and is very rare.

2   Conditions affecting the kidneys

There are many conditions which may affect the kidneys and result in an increased amount of urine production. The primary problem here would be polyuria (peeing more) and as a result the dog would drink more (polydipsia) to replace the excessive amount of water lost in the urine. The kidneys have three primary functions in the body. The first function is that they act as filters which take out waste products from the blood supply so that they can be eliminated from the body in the urine. The second function is to regulate the amount of water in the body. The amount of water which is eliminated by the kidneys will directly affect the concentration of the urine which is assessed as the specific gravity (SG) of the urine. The concentration of the urine varies from day to day depending on the overall amount of water in the body. To understand this concept consider your own urine – sometimes it is more concentrated (more yellow) and other times it is more dilute (less yellow). This is because the kidneys are constantly adjusting the amount of fluid in our bodies. When the urine is more concentrated the kidneys are actively reabsorbing water in the process of producing urine and when the urine is less concentrated the kidneys are actively allowing more water to be passed from the body in the urine. The third primary function of the kidneys is the production of a chemical called erythropoetin. The function of erythropoetin is to stimulate the bone marrow to produce red blood cells.

When kidney conditions develop, one or more of these functions may be affected to varying degrees and as the particular function is diminished or lost it will produce specific clinical signs which the dog owner or the vet will notice. The most common clinical sign which is noticed is a dog which starts peeing more because the kidneys' ability to retain water is lost and thus more water is lost in the form of dilute urine. The dog then starts to drink more to replace these losses. The most common cause of this loss of ability to conserve water is loosely called kidney failure and this may be acute (develops very suddenly) or chronic (develops over a long period of time).

2a Chronic (long term) kidney failure

Chronic renal failure (long term kidney failure) is far more common than acute kidney failure. The most common cause of chronic kidney failure is simply old age. Ultimately the reason we all die is because one or more organ fails. The reason for this is simply that our organs are only able to function for a fixed period of time and then will fail due to long term wear and tear just as various parts of our cars will start to break down after years of use. Chronic renal failure is a slow, gradual process and often it has started long before we see any signs which may signal that this process is underway. This is because the body will activate many compensatory mechanisms to compensate for the reduced efficiency of the kidneys. I would loosely categorise chronic kidney failure as having three phases – mild (early) kidney failure, moderate kidney failure and severe end stage kidney failure. Each of these phases can be further defined as being compensated or uncompensated. If the stage is compensated, few or no clinical signs will be present because the body's other systems are compensating for the reduced or lost kidney functions. In the event of the stage of kidney failure being uncompensated then clinical signs will be present. The most common clinical signs in uncompensated kidney failure are urinating and drinking more, lethargy, poor or no appetite and pale mucous membranes.

If the dog is eating less or nothing at all and there is no sign of pain in the mouth then kidney failure is a possibility. Kidney failure may cause weight loss and loss of appetite by simply making dogs feel unwell due to the accumulation of urea and other waste products in the blood stream. To make sense of this think of the kidneys simply as filters for the body even though they fulfill a great many other functions. If the filters are not removing waste products from the blood then the waste products will accumulate despite the body's attempts to reroute some of them, like urea, to other organ systems for elimination. These waste products, like any other waste products in your car or swimming pool for example, will damage the system if they are not removed. Other kidney functions will also be lost, for example the kidney's ability to produce a chemical called erythropoetin. Think of erythropoetin as a messenger chemical normally produced by the kidneys to tell the bone marrow to produce red blood cells. If this function is lost or reduced there will be fewer red blood cells in the blood supply and the affected dog will appear pale in addition to the other possible symptoms of kidney failure as discussed above. This is often described as anemia which implies a reduced number of red blood cells in the circulation which may occur for other reasons besides kidney failure but the other possibilities will be discussed in the section under pale mucous membranes. The way the vet will initially assess whether your dog is pale is by looking at the mucous membranes, typically in the mouth and eyes. The general rule of thumb is to check the colour of the dog's eye and mouth mucous membranes and compare them to your own.

The most common and most obvious clinical sign of chronic kidney failure is the 'drinking and weeing more' syndrome. This happens because the kidneys' ability to reabsorb water is reduced or lost and once the body has realised that an excessive amount of water is being lost, then the individual will start drinking more to replace this excessive loss.

The presumptive diagnosis of kidney failure, based on the clinical signs described above, is confirmed by performing blood and urine tests. One of these tests involves testing the level of urea accumulating in the blood stream as the kidneys slowly fail to filter it out. The term kidney failure does not imply total loss of kidney function. Broadly one can categorise old age kidney failure as mild, moderate or severe. Think about this in terms of our own ageing process. After about the age of seventy we can expect to have to get out of bed once or several times during the night to have a pee. This is because we have lost some of our kidneys' ability to conserve and reabsorb water. I would categorise this state as mild compensated kidney failure. The reason I call it compensated kidney failure is that the body will compensate for the other kidney functions which are impaired, and we show no other symptoms than producing more urine and drinking more water to replace this loss. The loss of kidney function (kidney failure) happens because all our organs have a limited life span and start to deteriorate in old age as we approach the end of our lives. As the kidneys continue to deteriorate and function less efficiently, the body's compensatory mechanisms cannot cope and other symptoms of kidney failure will appear and we will move into moderate compensated kidney failure. We still do not necessarily feel unwell because the compensatory mechanisms will reduce the overall impact on the rest of the body. We will however start to lose weight and hence we become frail in old age. This is because the kidneys start to lose their ability to reabsorb proteins and we lose a lot of protein in our urine. Ultimately we will enter into severe kidney failure and the compensatory mechanisms will be unable to cope and we enter the phase of severe decompensated kidney failure. At this point the impact of the severe loss of kidney functions includes the loss of the chemical erythropoetin as discussed earlier with resultant pale mucous membranes, and the accumulation of urea in the blood stream which makes us feel unwell by its presence and as a result of the body's attempts to eliminate it via the alternative pathways of the lungs and intestines as discussed earlier. The deterioration from this point tends to be rapid and ultimately we die of 'old age'.

Dogs follow the same process of gradual kidney failure and what we can do to help depends on the stage at which they are presented to the vet. In the initial compensated stages, treatment is aimed at trying to maintain body weight by using anabolic agents and trying to reduce the kidneys' workload by feeding specially formulated diets. At this point, just as in human beings, the dogs will feel fine in themselves but will lose weight despite apparently normal appetites. Feeding specially prepared commercially available dog food designed for the older dog will significantly extend the lifespan and equally importantly will yield a good quality of life in their golden years. Once dogs have entered the severe decompensated stage of kidney failure, the treatment is much the same but predictably the benefits are much diminished. Occasionally dogs may be prematurely pushed into the next phase of their progressing kidney failure by the strain of other illnesses and they may be pulled back to the earlier phase of their kidney failure by the use of a saline drip. The effect of the drip is to flush out the accumulating waste chemicals, like urea, which make us feel unwell. Consider the scenario of a dog who is actually only in moderate kidney failure but as a result of a respiratory infection for example, refuses food and water for a few days. These dogs are urinating more as they fail to replace this loss of water by drinking, they rapidly dehydrate and thus the chemicals such as urea in the blood stream become more concentrated and blood tests will suggest that the dog is in more advanced severe kidney failure. By replacing the lost fluid with a drip the true situation is reinstated and effectively the dog is pulled back into compensated kidney failure and should feel much better as the symptoms of severe kidney failure are resolved. Dogs who are genuinely in severe advanced kidney failure will also be improved while on a drip line but will relapse when the drip is disconnected. It is obviously not a practical or feasible option to consider maintaining a drip line permanently in a dog but as a short-term treatment will often significantly improve the dog's condition. At this stage, just as in human beings, the only thing that will save the individual is a kidney transplant and our best efforts in the absence of a kidney transplant will only serve to delay the process of decline. I feel that we should continue all feasible treatment for as long as the dog is able to live a happy, functional, comfortable life at home. Realistically this implies that when the dog reaches the point where the treatment is ineffective we have no option but to consider humanely putting him or her to sleep.

2b Acute (sudden) kidney failure

Kidney failure may be acute (develops very suddenly) or chronic (develops over a long period of time). Acute kidney failure most commonly develops due to one of three causes – toxins taken in by the dog, conditions which cause a sudden drop in blood pressure or kidney infections.

2b(i) Toxins

Various common chemicals in and around the home may be taken in by dogs and have a toxic effect on the kidneys which damages them and affects their ability to function normally. The most common chemical which may cause this is ethylene glycol which is found in car engine coolant which may have been spilt or leaked onto the floor. Ethylene glycol has a sweet taste and many dogs will lap it up because of this sweet taste. The ethylene glycol, once in the body, may have a toxic effect on the kidney and induce sudden (acute) renal failure. This initially manifests as a reduced production of urine as the kidney is so swollen that no urine can be produced and later, as the swelling subsides, an excessive amount if urine is produced because some of the ability to reabsorb water has been lost. Fortunately most dogs will recover from this poisoning effect and the kidneys will repair themselves adequately to return to normal function. The treatment for these cases is largely supportive care. This, in real terms, means using intravenous fluids via drip lines to flush the toxins out of the kidneys. The potential for recovery depends on the amount of toxin drunk by the dog, if very large amounts have been taken in, the dog's kidneys may be permanently and irreversibly damaged and some dogs may die despite our efforts at saving them.

2b(ii) Low blood presure as a cause of acute renal failure

The second most common cause of acute kidney failure is a sudden severe drop in blood pressure. The drop in blood pressure is most commonly due to heart failure, dehydration or adrenal gland failure (Addison's disease). In these cases, treating the cause of the sudden drop in blood pressure treats the acute kidney failure. In the case of dehydration, the treatment consists of slow re-hydration with a drip and intravenous fluids. If the cause is heart failure then the heart must be treated and in the case of Addison's disease this specific condition must be treated. At the same time we must again use intravenous fluids to rinse the kidneys and get them working while the underlying cause is being treated. The specific treatments for heart failure and Addison's disease will be discussed later. A discussion on heart failure is on page 192 and a discussion on Addison's disease is on page 63. The reason that these two conditions cause kidney failure is that both will cause a drop in blood pressure. This drop in blood pressure means that less blood is reaching all the tissues and organs in the body. The kidneys are very greedy organs and require a very good blood supply to function. Twenty-five per cent of the blood pumped by each heartbeat goes to the kidneys. The remaining three-quarters of the blood pumped by each heartbeat is shared by all the cells of the rest of the body. Thus, the kidneys have a very high requirement in terms of blood supply and are the first organs to fail when the blood supply to the body's tissues is reduced. The most common causes of reduced blood supply to the body's tissues are conditions which cause low blood pressure and the most common causes of low blood pressure are heart failure and Addison's disease.

2b(iii) Kidney infections
The third condition causing acute kidney failure is infection in the kidneys. This is the least common cause of kidney failure in dogs and the treatment consists of intravenous fluids and antibiotics.

Other kidney conditions which may produce the syndrome of 'drinking and weeing more' include renal medullary solute washout, nephrotic syndrome, nephrosis and glomerulonephritis. These conditions are much less common than those previously discussed conditions and may require more specialised tests to diagnose them.

3 Conditions affecting the liver (liver failure and liver disease)

Conditions and diseases which affect the liver may result in the same clinical signs caused by kidney failure. The most obvious additional symptom which would suggest the liver as the cause of the problem, rather than the kidneys, is the presence of jaundice (icterus). This is a yellow discolouration of mucous membranes and in severe cases of the skin. Jaundice usually only develops in severe or advanced cases of liver diseases but may also be caused by other diseases. Blood tests are usually required to differentiate between liver and kidney conditions as the cause of drinking and urinating more and also to determine the cause of the jaundice.

The most common causes of primary liver disease in dogs are liver tumours and old age liver failure. Dogs who develop clinical symptoms as a result of primary liver tumours usually have a poor prognosis. This means that there is often very little we can do to cure the problem and treatment is aimed at supporting the liver by feeding specially designed liver support diets and using medical treatments to help the dog to feel better until they deteriorate to the point where we have no option but to let them go by painlessly putting them to sleep.

Old age liver failure, just like old age kidney failure, is usually a gradual process. Treatment again consists of feeding specially designed liver support diets and a variety of medical treatments to help the dogs feel better and to slow down the process of weight loss.

4 Adrenal gland disorders

Adrenal gland disorders may result in increased thirst and urination. The problem with the adrenal glands may be that they are overactive (Cushing's disease) or underactive (Addison's disease).

4a Cushing's disease
Cushing's disease is the most common disorder of the adrenal glands. The adrenal glands are small glands situated at the front edge of each kidney. There are two adrenal glands in the body, one on

the left and one on the right. The primary function of the adrenal gland is to produce a chemical called glucocorticoid. The adrenal glands are controlled by the pituitary gland in the brain. Think of the pituitary gland as the head office and the adrenal gland as the factory. The head office will send messages to the factory to tell the factory how much to produce. In the case of Cushing's disease the factory is producing too much. The product produced by the factory is the chemical glucocorticoid. The factory may be overproducing this chemical. The cause of this overproduction is either that there is a problem at the head office (which is sending out too many messages asking the factory to produce), or that there is a problem with the factory (which is overproducing even though the head office is not asking for increased production).

The most common problems with the head office (pituitary gland) is that it is either just over-active or that there is a tumour in the pituitary gland. The pituitary gland tumour is composed of the cells which produce the messages to tell the adrenal glands to produce their chemicals. Thus, as the pituitary tumour grows, more messages are being sent to the adrenal glands (the factory) and thus the factory production is increased and there will be an excessive amount of the product in the body. The most common problem with the factory is that there may be a tumour in the adrenal glands which causes the adrenal glands (the factory) to be larger than normal. Thus, when a normal amount of messages are received from the normal head office (the pituitary gland) asking the factory to function at, for example, eighty per cent of maximum production, the factory, being much larger than normal, will produce more chemicals than normal. The clinical problems seen with over-production from the adrenal glands are generally the same irrespective of whether the problem is located in the head office (pituitary gland) or the factory (the adrenal gland). The ultimate outcome will be an excessive amount of glucocorticoid in the body. This glucocorticoid is the same as the synthetically produced cortisone or steroid that people with asthma are treated with. Thus the symptoms seen in Cushing's disease are the same symptoms that we see in people and animals which are treated with high doses of cortisone over long periods of time.

The earliest symptom of Cushing's disease is often an increased thirst and urination. The other common clinical symptoms associated with this condition are an increased appetite, a fat body and thin legs, a thinning coat with thin skin and secondary bacterial infections causing 'acne' and black-heads. This combination of symptoms will prompt your vet to include special blood tests for Cushing's disease in the set of other tests to investigate the syndrome of increased thirst and urinating. The most common test to check for Cushing's disease is called the ACTH stimulation test. Once Cushing's disease has been diagnosed as the cause of the problem, further specialised tests including a dexamethasone suppression test can be performed to identify whether the primary problem is in the pituitary gland (the head office) or in the adrenal gland (the factory). Eighty per cent of cases of Cushing's disease are due to problems in the pituitary gland. Most of the pituitary gland problems are simply that this gland is overactive for no apparent reason but occasionally the cause of the problem is a pituitary gland tumour.

The aim of treatment in Cushing's disease is usually the same irrespective of where the primary problem is situated i.e. in the pituitary or in the adrenal gland. The treatment is aimed at reducing the size of the adrenal gland (the factory), thereby restricting the production of the chemical gluco-corticoid. The size of the adrenal gland/s can be reduced by surgically cutting away some of the gland or by destroying some of the adrenal gland using medical treatments. My preference is to destroy some of the adrenal gland tissue using medical treatment. The only time I would consider surgery is if there is a tumour in one of the adrenal glands. The object of the surgery would be to remove the tumour. In most cases of Cushing's disease there is no underlying tumour and thus the best treatment would be to shrink the adrenal glands using medication. The old type of treatment is called Lysodren which is available in tablet form. Lysodren tablets have the effect of destroying the cells of the adrenal gland. The new method of treating the condition with medication is by using a new treatment called Vetoryl tablets. This new treatment is far superior to the old system of using Lysodren tablets because Vetoryl works more quickly, it has virtually no side effects and it is not toxic to the rest of the patient's body. The major problem with a decision to use Vetoryl tablets is that they are very expensive and the dog being treated will need to stay on treatment permanently with regular repeated blood tests. I will discuss the treatment of Cushing's disease with these two treatment options individually.

The objective when using Lysodren is to shrink the adrenal gland (the factory) down to a size where it is only able to produce the normal amount of glucocorticoid required by the body. When treatment for Cushing's disease is started the Lysodren is given daily for one or two weeks until the patient starts to lose their appetite. It is generally at this point that enough adrenal gland tissue has been destroyed and the remaining adrenal gland tissue will be unable to overproduce gluco-corticoid. The concern in this initial stage of treatment is that too much of the adrenal gland will be destroyed thus too little glucocorticoid can be produced. This is easily rectified by supplementing the natural glucocorticoid with tablets called prednisolone for a short period of time. If this situation arises then the Lysodren tablets are stopped until the patient stabilises. The reason the patient will stabilise is that the adrenal gland tissue will regrow when the Lysodren tablets are stopped. Once enough adrenal gland tissue has regrown then the adrenal gland will produce enough glucocorticoid for the body and the prednisolone tablets can be stopped. Once we have determined that the Lysodren tablets have shrunk the adrenal glands down to the correct size then the tablets are only given once weekly. This once weekly dose is too low to shrink the adrenal glands any further and the object of the once weekly dose is simply to stop the adrenal gland from regrowing and overproducing again. If the Lysodren tablets are stopped entirely, the adrenal gland (the factory) will enlarge again and the symptoms of Cushing's disease will reappear. The Lysodren tablets must be continued at a once weekly or once every other week dose for the rest of the dog's life to keep the condition under control. The frequency and dose of the long term Lysodren dose is established by repeating blood tests to measure the function of the adrenal glands to determine that they are functioning at the correct level of production of glucocorticoid.

Lysodren tablets are very powerful and we, as vets and pet owners, must protect ourselves from their effects by using gloves and facemasks when administering the treatments. When I discuss this fact with my clients many will, quite naturally, be anxious about using such a powerful and poten-tially dangerous treatment. The next question they will ask me is 'What will happen if we don't treat this condition?' The answer is that the symptoms will continue as they are or will become more severe. The important point to make at this stage is that the treatment will not extend the life span of the patient. The objective of the treatment is merely to eliminate the symptoms of Cushing's disease. If the symptoms are mild and the patient and the owner can comfortably live with the symp-toms then we do not have to treat the condition. In the untreated patient the long-term plan will be to ensure that the dog always has access to water to allow them to drink more and to control the secondary skin infections with occasional courses of antibiotics. If the symptoms of Cushing's disease are severe enough to be affecting the quality of life of the dog or their owner then Lysodren testament is the only option. The decision which determines the best course of action hinges on whether the condition is affecting the quality of life of the patient. If the dog can live quite happily and comfortably with the symptoms then Lysodren treatment is not necessary.

Vetoryl tablets have recently become available for the treatment of Cushing's disease in dogs. This new treatment is fantastic in terms of how quickly it cures the symptoms of this condition and the fact that it almost never produces side effects. Using the tablets at home is not dangerous for the people in the household and dogs do not feel unwell while on treatment. The tablets are administered every day for the rest of the dog's life. The tablets work by reducing the total amount of glucocorticoid produced by the adrenal glands. At the time of writing Vetoryl is a new product and not everything is known about the potential for side effects after long term use but the cases I have treated with this product have done spectacularly well on the treatment and have shown no side effects. I would have no hesitation in using this product rather than Lysodren.

4b Addison's disease

Addison's disease is the opposite of Cushing's disease – the adrenal glands are underactive. The result of this is that there is insufficient production of glucocorticoid and mineralocorticoid which are essential for the normal functioning of the body. Patients with Addison's disease may be under-producing both of these chemicals or underproducing just the glucocorticoids. The adrenal glands are small glands situated at the front edge of each kidney. There are two adrenal glands in the body, one on the left and one on the right and their primary function is to produce glucocorticoid and mineralocorticoid. The adrenal glands are controlled by the pituitary gland in the brain. Think of the pituitary gland as the head office and the adrenal gland as the factory. The head office will send messages to the factory to tell the factory how much glucocorticoid ad mineralocorticoid to produce. In the case of Addison's disease the factory is producing too little. The factory may be underproducing one or both of these chemicals. The cause of this underproduction is either that there is a problem at the head office (which is sending out too few messages asking the factory to produce), or that there is a problem with the factory (which is underproducing even though the head office is not asking for decreased production).

The function of mineralocorticoid is to regulate the levels of sodium, potassium and water in the body. Glucocorticoid is essential for the normal functioning of every cell in the body in that it is required for producing energy for the cells and helps the cells to use this energy.

Most cases of Addison's disease are the result of the adrenal glands (the factory) being under-active for no obvious reason. When Addison's disease develops due to underactive function of the adrenal glands (the factory) the body develops a deficiency of mineralocorticoid and glucocorticoid. If the cause of the Addison's disease is an underactive pituitary gland (the head office) then there is usually only an underproduction of glucocorticoid.

Often the only symptom of Addison's disease is an increased thirst and increases urination. The other symptoms which may occur are lethargy, vomiting and diarrhoea , weakness and trembling. These symptoms are often episodic which means that they appear for short periods then disappear for a while only to reappear at a later date. These waxing and waning symptoms are generally very vague and very mild and often these dogs are only diagnosed as having Addison's disease when they suddenly collapse and are presented to the vet in a critical condition. The diagnosis is made by performing routine and specialised blood tests. The definitive test is the same as for Cushing's disease i.e. the ACTH stimulation test which measures the level of function of the adrenal glands.

The treatment for Addison's disease is simply a matter of supplementing the low levels of gluco-corticoid and/or mineralocorticoid with tablets. If the dog is presented collapsed they will however also require a drip and intravenous fluids in the initial stage of the treatment. The treatment with tablets will be a life long therapy but the long-term outlook for these patients is very good and most will live entirely normal active lives with daily treatment with one or two types of tablets. Prednisolone tablets are used to supplement the glucocorticoid levels and Florinef tablets are used to supplement the mineralocorticoid levels. Most dogs will only require both types of tablets for the first month of treatment and then lifelong daily treatment with Florinef tablets. The required treatment and dosage is monitored by occasional follow-up blood tests.

5 Pyometra (uterine/womb 'infections')

When a female dog suddenly starts to drink more water one of the questions the vet will ask you is whether or not she has been spayed (sterilised). If she has not been sterilised then the vet will ask when she had her most recent season. If her most recent season was less than two months ago the vet will consider the possibility of a pyometra being the cause of the increased thirst.

Pyometra is often called a uterine/womb infection. This common name is not entirely accurate because, although the condition results in an accumulation of pus in the womb, there may, occasionally, be no infection in the womb. This may sound like a paradox and to explain this we need to understand what pus is. Pus is primarily an accumulation of white blood cells. The white blood cells are the cells which fight infections. When there is inflammation or damage anywhere in the body, the body will send white blood cells to that site just in case the cause of the problem is an infection. If there is an infection such as bacteria invading that area, the white blood cells will call more white blood cells to the area and they will attack the bacteria. In the process of killing the bacteria most of the white blood cells will also die and this accumulation of white blood cells is called pus. If there were no bacteria at the site of infection then the white blood cells will still patrol the area to ensure that no infection starts in the area of inflammation. This will also result in an accumulation of white blood cells and thus pus will still accumulate but to a lesser extent. To make sense of this explanation consider cuts and grazes you may have had on your own body. The presence of a large amount of pus will suggest that the cut has become infected and you may need antibiotics to help the white blood cells kill the bacteria causing the infection. If there is only a small amount of pus accumulating in the cut then it is possible that there is no infection and the pus that you see is simply a small accumulation of white blood cells patrolling the area until it heals. Thus pus may be due to infection or it may be 'sterile' pus if there is no infection. We can tell the difference by testing the pus for the presence of bacteria.

In the case of pyometra large amounts of pus may accumulate in the womb (uterus). This pus may be due to infection or it may be 'sterile' pus. The vast majority of cases of pyometra are, however, due to a bacterial infection in the womb. There is no need to differentiate between these two types of pus in this situation because the treatment is the same i.e. remove the womb by spaying the dog.

Pyometra may occur in any female dog of any age and any breed. The vast majority of cases are however seen in middle aged and older dogs. The condition develops as a sequence of events starting at the time of the dog's season (in heat). When the dog is in season eggs are released from the ovaries for fertilisation. If the dog is mated and sperm fertilises the eggs then in embryo will develop and the bitch becomes pregnant. These embryos move into the womb and start to develop into foetuses. When the embryos first arrive in the womb they do not have a placenta attaching them to the mother's womb for food and oxygen. The placenta may take as long as seventeen days to fully develop and in that time the embryos need food and oxygen. The womb provides this by producing a fluid from the cells lining the womb. The embryos float around in this fluid using it for food and oxygen while they grow and develop a placenta. Once the placenta develops then the embryo is connected to the mother's blood supply and they get their food and oxygen directly from the mother's blood supply. The placenta is commonly called the afterbirth because it is expelled after the baby/puppy is born.

Pyometra develops when the cells which line the womb are overactive and produce a lot of this nutrient fluid which is intended to feed the embryos. This may happen irrespective of whether the dog was mated or not. This rich fluid accumulates in the womb even if there are no embryos to feed. The problem starts when bacteria in the body enter this fluid. The nutrient-rich fluid is the ideal environment for bacteria to grow in and soon a severe infection starts with a large accumulation of pus in the womb.

The symptoms of pyometra usually develop within two months of the bitch's season ending. The symptoms are caused by the accumulation of pus in the womb. The pus in the womb is toxic to the body and the only thing the body can do is to try to flush them out of the body. The way the body does this is to drink more so that more urine is produced so that the kidneys can filter out the toxins. This is the same principle that vets and doctors use in a case of poisoning i.e. they will use intravenous fluids via a drip line to try to flush the poisons or toxins out of the patient's body. Thus the clinical symptoms that we see first are an increase in the amount of water being drunk and an increase in urinating. The pus has a toxic effect on the body so that as the amount of pus in the womb increases the toxins in the body increase and the second symptom that appears is a poor appetite because these dogs start to feel ill because of the toxins. The next symptoms to develop are vomiting and diarrhoea and these develop because of a further rise in toxins in the body as still more pus is being produced in the womb. These symptoms usually develop in this order as the amount of pus accumulates in the womb. The symptoms may be very subtle in the initial stages and often these dogs are only brought to the vet when they are very ill, often at the point of collapse, as the pus is poisoning the body.

There are two types of pyometra commonly seen – open cervix and closed cervix pyometra. The cervix is the tube connecting the womb to the vagina. and is usually sealed off or closed except when the bitch is in season or due to whelp. If the cervix is open at the time of the pyometra then we often see pus coming out of the vagina from the womb. This pus may be seen caught in the fur around the vagina or on the underside of the tail. Most dogs suffering with pyometra with an open cervix will however frequently lick these areas clean and thus remove the evidence of pus discharging from the vagina. If pus is seen in, on or around the vagina within two months of a season and in association with the other symptoms discussed in the previous paragraph, then we have confirmation of the diagnosis of pyometra causing the increased thirst and appetite. In the cases of closed cervix pyometra the diagnosis may be much more difficult to make as the cervix is sealed off and no pus discharges from the vagina. In the event of a closed cervix pyometra there tends to be much more pus in the womb as none of it is draining out through the cervix and vagina. The large amount of pus in the womb in these cases may even give these dogs a distended, pot-bellied appearance. The larger amount of pus also means that these dogs tend to be far more toxic and ill when they are presented to the vet. The cases of closed cervix pyometra are often more difficult to diagnose. In these cases it is the combination of symptoms discussed in the previous paragraph coupled with the fact that the bitch had a season within the last two months that will prompt the vet to consider pyometra as a possible diagnosis. This suspicion will prompt the vet to X-ray or scan the belly to look for an enlarged womb. If an enlarged womb is seen on the X-ray or scan in the presence of all the other symptoms then we have the diagnosis of closed cervix pyometra.

The treatment of pyometra has two components. The first component is to correct the dehydration and toxic effect on the body by using antibiotics and intravenous fluids through drip lines. As soon as the bitch is well enough for surgery the second component is to remove the womb which is full of pus. The operation is similar to a routine sterilisation in that the womb and the ovaries are removed, but the big difference is that the operation is being carried out on a very diseased womb in a very sick dog. The next immediate concern after the operation has been done is to ensure that the toxins and bacteria are completely flushed out of the body to avoid damage to the kidneys or infection in the kidneys. I will often want to continue with the intravenous fluids and antibiotics for a few days after the operation especially if the dog was very toxic and very ill. If the bitch is eating and drinking well after the operation I may simply send her home with antibiotics to recover in a home environment.

The treatment of choice for this condition is as described above but sometimes we may be faced with pyometra in a very valuable breeding bitch and we may want to try to cure the condition without removing the womb so that the bitch may be bred from in the future. This may be attempted by using antibiotics and a treatment called prostaglandin to try to make the womb contract to expel the pus. This approach will often fail to cure the problem and thus the bitch may become more unwell and the prostaglandin therapy may cause many side effects. I am of the opinion that this treatment approach has a high failure rate and a high complication rate and thus would only attempt this treatment approach in exceptional circumstances.

6 Diabetes insipidus (water diabetes)

Diabetes insipidus is sometimes called water diabetes and is completely different to diabetes mellitus (sugar diabetes) which has just been discussed. Diabetes insipidus occurs when the pineal gland in the brain is not producing enough of the chemical ADH (anti-diuretic hormone). This chemical is produced by the pineal gland in the brain and is carried by the blood stream to the kidneys where it stimulates the kidneys to reabsorb water in the process of producing urine. Water is a precious commodity for the body and thus the water in the body is constantly being purified and recycled by the kidneys. Very little water is released from the body by the kidneys in the form of urine. The ADH is produced by the pineal gland in the brain which acts like a control centre for regulating the amount of water in the body. The ADH is simply a messenger chemical which is produced by this control centre (the pineal gland) to tell the water-recycling factory (the kidneys) how much water should be recycled and reabsorbed. If the body has too much water (overhydrated) less ADH is sent to the kidneys which then produce more urine and thus the excess water is expelled. If the body needs to conserve water or is starting to dehydrate then more ADH is sent to the kidneys which then produce less urine and water is conserved. In the case of diabetes insipidus, the pineal gland does not produce enough of this chemical and thus the kidneys think that they are being told to recycle less water and allow more of it to leave the body in the urine. Most human beings experience this same effect when drinking alcohol. This is because alcohol interferes with the messenger chemical ADH and thus the ADH does not tell the kidneys to recycle water. The kidneys then release more water in the urine and thus we have to urinate more often when drinking alcohol.

The symptoms of diabetes insipidus are simply drinking more and weeing more. The affected dog will feel fine and act normally. The primary problem is that the kidneys are producing too much urine because the body wants to avoid becoming dehydrated and thus needs to replace the lost water, this will increase the patient's thirst levels. Some dogs may even seem to become incontinent and start wetting indoors and even start wetting their beds. This is not true incontinence as there is no problem with their bladder control. The problem is that there is just too much urine accumulating in the bladder and the bladder was not designed to hold onto that much urine and as a result they may have 'accidents' indoors.

The diagnosis is made by testing their urine on at least two separate occasions. If the urine concentration is the same on both tests then the diagnosis is confirmed. At least two tests must be done as the urine concentration does vary from day to day. If both tests show a urine specific gravity (urine concentration) below 1.008 then we have our diagnosis. This can be further confirmed by doing a water deprivation test where the patient is deprived of water for up to twenty-four hours and blood and urine tests over this period show that water loss in the urine continues despite the fact that no water is being drunk. This tells us that the body is unable to produce ADH to tell the kidneys to conserve and recycle water when there is no water available to drink to maintain the normal water balance in the body.

The treatment for diabetes insipidus is very simple. Artificial ADH is available in the form of tablets called Vasopressin. The average dose of Vasopressin is one mg given once daily. The specific dose to control the problem may vary from one individual to another and some dogs may require a higher dose but this does not present a risk in term of side effects. The treatment is simple, cheap and effective and most dogs will return to normal thirst and urination levels very soon after the treatment is started. The treatment will need to be continued throughout the dog's life.

7 Conditions causing elevated levels of calcium in the blood stream

When tests are performed to identify the cause of increased drinking and urination in dogs, often the only abnormality which is identified is an elevated level of calcium in the blood. This elevated level of blood calcium will cause increases in the amount of urine produced and subsequently the body will want to drink more to replace the lost water. Although the high level of blood calcium causes these symptoms, the objective is to identify the cause of the raised calcium level. The most common causes of elevated blood calcium are:

- Hyperparathyroidism (overactive parathyroid glands)
- Tumours
- Kidney problems
- Excessive amounts of calcium or vitamin D in the diet
- Addison's disease (underactive adrenal glands)

7a Hyperparathyroidism (overactive parathyroid glands)

Hyperparathyroidism (overactive parathyroid glands) is a very rare condition. The dog has four small parathyroid glands found at the front of the neck associated with the thyroid glands. There are two thyroid glands. One thyroid gland is found on either side of the windpipe (trachea). Associated with each thyroid gland are two small parathyroid glands. The function of the parathyroid glands is to regulate the amount of calcium in the body and hence the amount of calcium in the blood stream. One or more of the parathyroid glands may become enlarged and overactive. The result of this enlargement and overactivity is that there will be an excessive amount of calcium in the body. This excessive amount of calcium may be deposited in any of the body's tissues turning them to bone and thus affecting their specific functions but the most common clinical symptom seen with this condition is increased weeing and drinking due to elevated levels of calcium in the blood stream. The condition is confirmed by specialised blood tests which measure the level of activity of the parathyroid glands and by ultrasound scans of the parathyroid glands. The treatment for this condition is surgical removal of the enlarged parathyroid gland/s. Usually only one parathyroid gland is enlarged and overactive and once it has been removed the remaining glands function quite adequately at regulating the blood calcium levels and the symptom of increased weeing and drinking will disappear.

7b Tumours (causing elevated blood calcium levels)

Some types of tumours or cancers may cause elevated blood calcium levels. The two most common tumours which may do this are anal sac tumours and lymphoma. The anal sacs are two small scent glands situated on either side of the anus. If one imagines the anus to be a clock then the glands are situated at the four and eight o' clock positions (Fig. 15). These small sacs produce a foul smelling liquid which is released when the dog passes faeces. The reason for these scent glands is to scent the faeces as a means of using faeces to mark out the dog's territory. This is exactly the same concept as the more familiar process of dogs weeing on lamp-posts as a means of scent marking their territory. Anal sac tumours are tumours which develop from these anal sacs and tend to be cancers called apocrine gland carcinomas. These tumours are identified by careful examination of the anal sacs by feeling through the skin overlying them and by means of rectal examination with a finger in the anus. The treatment is surgical removal of the tumour and the anal sac. These tumours may infiltrate very deeply in the tissues around the anus and rectum and may regrow after having been removed.

The second type of tumour which may cause an elevation in blood calcium levels is a very malignant type of cancer called lymphoma. This cancer may develop anywhere in the body and may often be very difficult to find. The search for the possible presence of this cancer as the cause of the elevated blood calcium level may require repeated physical examinations, X-rays and ultrasound scans. In some cases it may be very easy to find and in other cases it may be very difficult as the cancer could be hiding anywhere in the body. There are two common lymphoma presentations – multicentric lymphoma where the cancer may be found at many sites in the body or single lymphoma where it is found only at one site. The concern with finding only a single site of lymphoma is that there may have already been a microscopic spread of the cancer to other sites which will only become apparent when the tumour starts to grow at these other sites. Lymphoma is usually spread along the lymphatic system of the body and thus in the case of multicentric lymphoma, many lymph nodes are found to be enlarged due to the prescience of the rapidly growing tumour. Any (and often all) of the lymph nodes throughout the body may be found to be affected at the time of the initial examination.

I feel that if there is only one tumour present and there is no sign of any spread to other points then one would consider surgery to remove the mass. The way to check for spread to other sites is by X-rays, ultrasound scanning and blood testing. If one can confirm that there has been no identifiable spread of the cancer then the option of surgery may proceed. The surgery involves entering the body and removing the mass. Two important points to consider when removing the mass is that not just the mass should be removed but also a margin of normal healthy tissue in every direction to try to ensure that no cancer cells are left behind. The second issue is that the mass can only be removed if vital blood vessels and nerves supplying other tissues and organs in the area can be left intact. A very frustrating situation arises when the surgeon finds that although the mass can be removed in its entirety, it would involve sacrificing the blood supply to other vital areas. This is often due to the fact that the blood vessels or nerves of other organs are trapped in the tumour mass and cannot be freed from the mass. This means that one then cannot remove the mass because it would cause the death of the dog. In these cases the only remaining option is to try to eliminate the mass by radiation therapy and/or chemotherapy. Many surgeons would want to at least attempt to debulk the mass prior to proceeding with the radiation or chemotherapy. This would involve removing as much tumour tissue as possible without damaging any vital structures trapped in the mass. In many cases, even if the surgeon is able to remove the mass, one might want to follow up on the surgery with radiation and/or chemotherapy to ensure that no tumour cells, which may have spread on a microscopic level to other tissues, are able to grow into a new tumour. There are many different types and ways of using radiation and chemotherapy and the most appropriate protocol will often be decided after a specialist histopathologist has examined the tumour. For this reason vets would want to perform surgery in cases of multicentric lymphoma where there is clearly more than one tumour mass present or where there is clear evidence of tumour spread to other parts of the body. The object of the surgery in these cases would be to obtain a biopsy of the tumour for analysis by a histopathologist so that the best radiation and/or chemotherapy strategy can be formulated.

Many of my clients may not want to go through all the above steps for any variety of reasons and ask if we could just ' cut to the chase' in terms of trying to help the dog either cope with or overcome the problem. This would often imply one of two strategies – treat the symptoms of pain and loss of appetite for as long as possible and when the treatment fails to alleviate the dog's suffering then humanely put him or her to sleep. The most effective way of trying to achieve this is with a category of medication called glucocorticoids. These treatments are the same as for treating asthma in human beings with the difference being one would employ larger doses in treating these dogs. In addition to this I would often use anabolic treatments to help the dog gain weight. The treatment would involve tablets or injections for the remainder of the dog's life. The treatment is intended only to alleviate the dog's pain and suffering and give them as much good quality, pain free, happy life as possible. The second option is to remove the tumours that are found during the clinical examination and follow up the surgery with the lifelong glucocorticoid therapy as described above. The glucocorticoid therapy is only started when the dog has recovered from the surgery as these treatments may slow down the rate healing of the operated site. Once again I accept that this is not a scientific approach to the problem but many people do not have the financial resources to do more than this or they may not want to subject the dog to any more than this. The overriding consideration must always be the welfare of the dog and if this unscientific approach delivers results in terms of alleviating the symptoms then I have no moral problem with this approach.

7c Kidney conditions (causing elevated blood calcium levels)
Many of the kidney problems discussed earlier may cause elevated blood calcium levels by stimulating the parathyroid glands to become overactive. Treating the primary kidney condition as described earlier treats this cause of elevated blood calcium level with its resultant increase in thirst and urine production. Successful treatment of the kidney condition will stop the stimulation of the parathyroid glands and thus the blood calcium levels will return to normal.

7d Excessive dietary calcium and/or vitamin D
Excessive amounts of calcium and/or vitamin D in the dog's diet will also cause elevated blood calcium levels with the resultant increase in thirst and urinating. Correcting the diet will resolve the problem.

7e Addison's disease (underactive adrenal glands causing elevated levels of blood calcium)
Addison's disease has been discussed earlier in the chapter as a possible cause of increased thirst and increased urination. This condition may be revealed as the cause of the problem during the investigation of increased levels of blood calcium.

5

My Dog is Leaking Urine or Wetting in Their Bed or on the Floor Overnight

This is a very common problem that I encounter and sometimes people tell me that pee is leaking out when the dog is walking around but most commonly the problem is that the dog is wetting their bed or urinating on the floor overnight. Female dogs are more likely to develop these symptoms than male dogs and they can be the result of several conditions. The way the vet will try to narrow down the possible causes is to ask you to bring a urine sample from the dog and they will ask you a number of questions. Your answers to the questions are very important and it is important not to try to guess the answer. It is better to answer a question with 'I don't know' rather than to guess as the details that you give the vet will very often give them enough information to make the diagnosis without expensive tests. The questions will include some or all of the following.

- If the dog is female, has she been spayed (sterilised) and if so when was she spayed?
- How old is the dog?
- How long have you been aware of the problem?
- Is the dog drinking more than normal, less than normal or about the same?
- Is the dog eating more than normal, less than normal or about the same?
- Is the pee leaking out when the dog is awake and active or only when they are asleep or resting?
- Is the dog peeing outside more than normal, less than normal or about the same as they normally do?
- When they do go outside for a pee do they seem to be straining to pee or are they peeing normally?
- When they do go outside for a pee are they producing more pee, less pee or about the normal amount of pee?
- Does the pee look and smell normal?

Once you have answered these questions the vet's thoughts will go something like this: If a dog is leaking urine the cause of the problem is either that they are producing more pee than normal or that they are producing a normal amount of pee but the bladder is unable to hold onto the normal

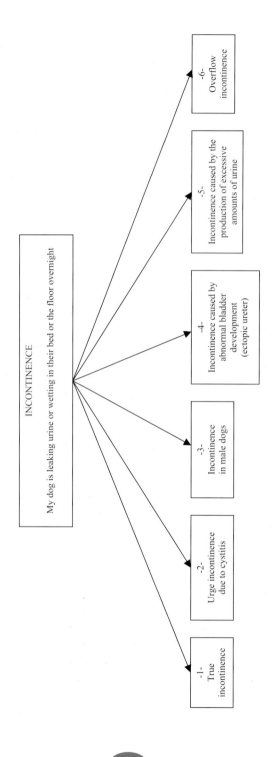

INCONTINENCE

My dog is leaking urine or wetting in their bed or the floor overnight

-1-
True
incontinence

-2-
Urge incontinence
due to cystitis

-3-
Incontinence
in male dogs

-4-
Incontinence caused by
abnormal bladder
development
(ectopic ureter)

-5-
Incontinence caused by the
production of excessive
amounts of urine

-6-
Overflow
incontinence

amount of pee. If the bladder is unable to control the normal amount of pee the cause of the problem may be that the bladder is not properly developed, or that the bladder 'valves' are not working properly or that the bladder is inflamed. If the dog is very young or has had the problem since a young age the cause of the problem may be that the bladder has not developed normally. If the dog is a middle-aged or older female then the problem is very likely that the bladder valves are not working properly especially if the problem developed soon after she was spayed. If a female dog is attempting to pee more often, seems to be straining to pee and is only producing small amounts of pee at a time then the problem is very likely that the bladder is inflamed and/or infected. If a male dog is attempting to pee more often, seems to be straining to pee and is only producing small amounts of pee at a time then the problem is very likely that the bladder is inflamed and/or infected or that there is a prostate gland problem or that the urethra is blocked.

The vet will test the urine to check for:

- signs of infection or inflammation in the bladder
- to check the concentration of the urine (this is a rough test to check whether the dog is producing more pee than normal)
- to check for glucose in the urine (this is a test to check for diabetes)
- to check the acidity of the urine (if the acidity is not normal then there is a possible risk of infection or bladder stones)
- to check for microscopic traces of blood (if blood is present then one would look for conditions which cause inflammation in the bladder like infections, bladder stones or tumours)
- to check the amount of protein in the urine (if there is protein in the urine it may be because of kidney problems or because there is blood in the urine)

Once the vet has asked their questions and tested the urine they will examine the dog thoroughly and pay special attention to the urinary tract especially how the bladder and kidneys feel and how the genitals look and feel. The urinary tract consists of a number of distinct components. The kidneys are the first part of the urinary tract. Every dog has two kidneys viz. a left and a right kidney. The kidneys are roughly situated just below the backbone under the last rib on either side of the body. The right kidney is slightly further forward than the left kidney. The kidneys have many functions including the production of urine. The urine produced by each kidney drains into a tube called a ureter that transports the urine to the bladder. Thus the left and right ureter lead from the left and the right kidney to the bladder. The bladder is simply a bag for collecting urine. The bladder is a bag formed by a thin layer of muscle. The function of the bladder is to collect and store the urine produced by the kidneys. The urine that collects in the bladder is stored there until the individual consciously decides to have a pee. The reason that pee does not simply leak out of the bladder even when it is very full is that there are two 'valves' which control the movement of pee from the bladder into the urethra. One of these valves is controlled by our 'conscious mind' and the other is controlled by our 'subconscious mind'. When the bladder is full and the individual decides to urinate, the muscle layer in the bladder wall contracts to push the urine out of the bladder through a single tube called the urethra. In the case of males the urethra passes through the inside of the penis and in the case of females the urethra opens into the vagina. Thus male animals have a much longer and narrower urethra than female animals where it is much shorter and wider. The urinary tract can be divided into two components. The upper urinary tract consists of the kidneys and ureters. The lower urinary tract consists of the bladder and urethra and the vagina or penis.

Once the vet has collected all the information that they need they will make one of the following diagnoses:

1 True urinary incontinence

The symptoms in this diagnosis will typically include some or most of the following.

The affected dogs are usually middle aged or older female dogs who have been spayed but young females or unspayed females may also be affected. These individuals will have normal thirst and appetite levels and they seem to urinate normally during the day. They tend to leak small or large amounts of pee only when they are sitting or lying down when they are resting or sleeping. They do not realise when they are leaking pee and may sometimes seem surprised when they notice a puddle of pee after they have been sitting or lying down. The pee looks and smells normal and when the vet tests the urine nothing abnormal is found.

To explain true urinary incontinence I must first explain again roughly how the bladder works. The bladder is simply a bag for collecting urine. The bladder is a bag formed by a thin layer of muscle. The function of the bladder is to collect and store the urine produced by the kidneys. When one wants to have a pee, the muscle layer in the bladder wall contracts to push the urine out of the bladder through a single tube called the urethra. In the case of males the urethra passes through the inside of the penis and in the case of females the urethra opens into the vagina. The urine that collects in the bladder is stored there until the individual consciously decides to have a pee. The reason that pee does not simply leak out of the bladder even when it is very full is that there are two 'valves' which control the movement of pee from the bladder into the urethra. One of these valves is controlled by our 'conscious mind' and the other is controlled by our 'subconscious mind'.

Thus, when you are fully awake the reason that we do not wet ourselves when the bladder is full is that both valves are held shut until we decide to pee. When we are asleep (and the 'conscious mind' and its valve are asleep) only the valve controlled by our subconscious mind holds the pee in the bladder and thus we do not wet ourselves when we sleep. When an individual develops true urinary incontinence it means that the valve controlled by the 'subconscious mind' loses the ability to work and hold urine in the bladder. The loss of this valve does not affect us when we are awake and alert because while we are alert the valve controlled by the 'conscious mind' can keep the urine in the bladder until we decide to have a pee. However, when we are asleep the 'conscious mind' and the valve it controls are also 'asleep'. This means that when an individual with true urinary incontinence is asleep or resting, neither of the valves function and thus they may wet themselves if the bladder is full. This is a very simplistic explanation of the problem and strictly speaking not an accurate explanation but it gives one an idea of why the urine only leaks out when the individual is asleep or at rest.

The first question to ask when this diagnosis is made is 'Why did the valve controlled by the subconscious mind suddenly lose its ability to function?' There are two common possible explanations for why this valve has stopped working. The first explanation is that the valve may stop working properly because the dog has been spayed and the second explanation is that the valve simply stops working as efficiently as we grow older.

If the symptoms of true urinary incontinence develop soon after the dog was spayed, then we can assume that the act of spaying the dog has caused the incontinence. There are two common explanations for why the valve stops working after the dog has been spayed i.e. either the valve has been inadvertently damaged by being stretched during the operation or that after being spayed the level of female hormones drops so low that the valve cannot work properly because it needs a minimum level of female hormones to work. The first explanation stems from the fact that some surgeons have a higher incidence of incontinent patients after spaying than other surgeons. This has led to the theory that the technique of the individual surgeon may inadvertently damage the valve. The second explanation stems from the fact that if the incontinence develops soon after the dog has been spayed, the symptoms may often be cured by treating theses patients with low doses of female hormone tablets. These are both unproven theories but the important message is that if the incontinence develops soon after the dog was spayed the vet should try to resolve the problem by treating the dog with female hormone tablets. This is not a guaranteed treatment but if it is effective then it will often be a life-long treatment. An interesting point to consider at this stage is that certain breeds seem to have a higher risk of becoming incontinent after being spayed. Doberman pinschers seem to have the highest risk of becoming incontinent after being spayed and at this stage researchers have not been able to explain why this is so.

If the symptoms of true urinary incontinence develop in a dog which has not been spayed, or if the symptoms develop in a dog which was spayed a long time before the symptoms developed, then we can assume that the problem has not been caused by the act of spaying the dog. The explanation for the condition in these individuals is the same as in human beings. The accepted theory is that, with advancing age, the valve simply starts to work less efficiently. This may be because the valve simply starts to 'wear out' or it may be because the shape and position of the bladder has changed as the individual has grown older. If the changes in the shape and position of the bladder have caused the problem then one may consider trying to correct the problem by performing the same operation that is offered to women with urinary incontinence. The operation is not guaranteed to correct the problem and can sometimes be associated with complications that may require further surgery. The conventional approach to treating incontinence in cases not suspected to have been caused by spaying is by using medication and often the vet will have to try various treatments at various doses to cure the problem. Most individuals will have to stay on the medication for the rest of their lives to control the problem. My preference is to treat the problem with medication rather than surgery.

2 Urge incontinence

This type of incontinence may happen when the urge to pee is so great that the bladder valves are unable to stop urine from being passed even though they are fully functional. The diagnosis of urge incontinence implies that there is no problem with the functioning of the valves of the bladder.

Urge incontinence may be seen in severe cases of cystitis when the bladder is contracting so force-fully that the bladder valves have no hope of holding the urine in the bladder. Urge incontinence is seen most commonly in females of any age and may occur in spayed or unspayed individuals.

Human beings who have experienced cystitis will confirm that it is a very uncomfortable condition. Cystitis means inflammation of the bladder and may be caused by infections, tumours or stones. These processes produce an uncomfortable burning sensation in the bladder which makes the muscle layer in the bladder wall contract. Thus the bladder is in a constant state of spasm which makes the dog feel that they need to urinate even though there is little or no urine in the bladder. This sensation of burning and contraction of the bladder makes dogs feel like they need to urinate all the time and thus they will make frequent and prolonged attempts to urinate. The bladder however is constantly contracted and little or no urine collects in the bladder and thus little or no urine is passed at each attempt to pee. The inflammation in the lining of the bladder may cause microscopic blood vessels in the bladder lining to rupture and thus the urine may contain blood. This blood is sometimes visible to the naked eye giving the urine a pink or red appearance and in mild cases the amount of blood in the urine may be so small that it can only be detected by testing the urine.

The symptoms seen with a diagnosis of urge incontinence are that the dog constantly strains to pee many times a day. Each time they try to pee one will notice that they seem to be straining very hard to pee but very little urine comes out. The small amount of urine that does come out may be blood tinged. These dogs will ask to be let out for a pee as often as every ten to thirty minutes throughout the day and one will often notice that they seem to be uncomfortable and distressed. When these patients try to sleep at night the constant spasm of the bladder means that they may have 'accidents' in their beds or cannot wait until the morning and may pass small amounts of pee on the floor. The reason that they may have 'accidents' in their beds is because the bladder is in a constant state of contraction. Thus if they fall into a deep sleep the spasms of the bladder may be too strong for the bladder valves to hold the urine in the bladder and thus small amounts of pee may leak out.

When the vet examines the dog they will often feel that the bladder is contracted and painful and that the urine contains traces of blood. The different types of cystitis and their treatments are described in detail in the chapter on straining to pass urine.

3 Incontinence in male dogs

Male dogs very rarely develop urine incontinence because the design of the lower urinary tract is very different to that of females. Male dogs who drip urine from their penis during the day or night should be promptly examined by a vet, as this apparent 'incontinence' may be the result of a blockage in the urethra. This blockage may be caused by bladder stones getting stuck in the urethra or by problems with the prostate gland. Careful observation of these cases will usually reveal that the affected dog is not actually incontinent but will frequently strain to pass urine with very little success.

If there is a blockage in the urethra, the bladder will be severely overfilled because it is unable to empty itself despite the fact that the kidneys are constantly pouring more urine into the bladder.

The severe overfilling of the bladder is initially very uncomfortable. If the problem is not quickly identified and resolved the bladder may be so overstretched that it is permanently damaged and unable to contract normally in the future. If the bladder remains severely overfilled and unable to empty for more than about two days the dog's life is at risk. Dogs can, and indeed do, die from untreated urethral obstructions so always have the condition checked by a vet who will determine the cause of urine dripping from the penis. One the vet has determined whether the dripping urine is due to a blockage or incontinence they will advise you on the best treatment. If the vet confirms that the cause of the problem is incontinence they will consider all the possible causes discussed in this chapter. If the vet thinks that the problem is a suspected blockage they will consider all the possible causes discussed in the chapter on straining to pass urine.

4 Incontinence due to abnormal bladder development (ectopic ureter)

The basic anatomy of the urinary system has been discussed at the beginning of this chapter. The urine produced by each kidney moves from the kidney into the bladder via a tube called the ureter. The ureter pours urine into the bladder for collection until the individual decides to have a pee. One may encounter rare cases where one or both of the ureters has developed abnormally. This condition is called an ectopic ureter. In this condition the ureter leads from the kidney but instead of draining urine into the bladder it drains the urine into the vagina. The vagina was not designed to collect urine and thus urine is seen to be leaking from the vagina whether the dog is awake or asleep. This condition is usually noticed at an early age in young puppies and most people will notice that the pup is leaking urine when playing and walking around without realising that they are doing so. The vet will confirm the diagnosis by taking X-rays and the condition can be usually be rectified by surgery to move the ureter to the correct position. This is a very rare condition seen in young female dogs.

5 'Incontinence' due to excessive urine production

Dogs which have a medical condition which causes excessive production of urine will have to urinate more often than normal. When they do have a pee one will notice that there are no signs of straining or discomfort and that large puddles of urine are produced each time the individual has a pee. These individuals will also very often eat and/or drink more water than normal. There are many conditions which may cause an excessive production of urine and the most common ones are discussed in the chapter on drinking and peeing more than normal. If a dog is producing more urine than normal they will have to empty their bladder more often than normal and thus, if they are unable to go outside at night, they may have 'accidents' on the floor overnight. When one notices the puddles in the morning one may assume that the dog is simply 'being naughty' or that they have become incontinent. By careful observation of all of their symptoms one should realise that this apparent 'incontinence' is not truly incontinence but rather an excessive production of urine which cannot be held in the bladder for extended periods of time. The examination and tests run by the vet should explain the reason for the excessive urine production and confirm that the accidents on the floor are not due to genuine incontinence.

6 Overflow incontinence

If the bladder is paralysed it will be unable to contract and thus the individual will be unable to urinate of their own free will. If the bladder valves are also paralysed then the bladder will simply 'overflow' when it is full. This overflow is seen as urine leaking from the dog both when they are awake and when they are asleep. The bladder is kept full because the kidneys are constantly producing urine but because it is unable to contract there is a constant overflow effect and the bladder is never emptied. The bladder may become paralysed if the nerve supply to the bladder is damaged. This damage may be caused by many factors e.g. trauma such as car accidents, internal tumours, and spine and nerve conduction problems. Most of these causes of damage to the nerves supplying the bladder will have other obvious symptoms which will tell us what the cause of the problem is and what needs to be done to correct the bladder problems and any other problems present at the same time.

6

MY DOG IS HAVING SEIZURES/CONVULSIONS

Most people think of epilepsy when they think of seizures. The classic image of an epileptic fit (seizure) is of a person who suddenly falls to the ground unconscious and has violent muscle spasms. This is called a grand mal seizure. A common misconception is that one should try to help someone who is having a seizure by pulling their tongue forwards to prevent him or her from 'swallowing their tongue'. This is not the correct thing to do because the individual having the seizure may clamp their jaw tightly shut as part of the muscle spasms of the seizure. If you have your fingers in their mouth when they clamp their jaws shut, they may very seriously damage your fingers and dogs especially might even bite your fingers off.

One can think of the brain as being a computer. Computers may occasionally 'jam' or 'crash' for no apparent reason. When the computer crashes it may scramble the information contained in the computer and the way to remedy the situation is to re-boot the computer. When it then comes back on line, most computers will unscramble themselves and function normally again until the next time they 'jam' or 'crash' or they may in fact never do so again. The computer may also crash if, for example, someone accidentally unplugs it while you are working on it. In this case the computer will also 'crash' and it may scramble or lose the document you were working on at the time. When you then plug it back in, the computer will then re-boot and unscramble itself. Thus a computer may 'crash' because of a problem inside the computer or it may 'crash' because of external problems.

The brain is very much like a computer in that it controls and processes all the information in the body. When an individual has a seizure it is very similar to a computer 'crashing'. The brain, like the computer, may seizure (crash) either because of a problem in the brain, or because of external problems affecting the ability of the brain to function normally. Once a seizure has happened, the brain may correct the fault within a few minutes but if the brain is unable to correct the fault, then the seizure may continue for several hours. If the seizure is very short then the brain will usually 're-boot' itself but if the seizure continues for more than ten minutes then the brain may need to be 're-booted' by a vet or doctor. The vet will 're-boot' the brain by using medications which stop the seizures and 'knock the dog out' for one or several hours. When they wake up, the brain will have been 're-booted'. A grand mal seizure is the equivalent of a computer 'crashing' and a petit mal seizure is the equivalent of a computer 'jamming'.

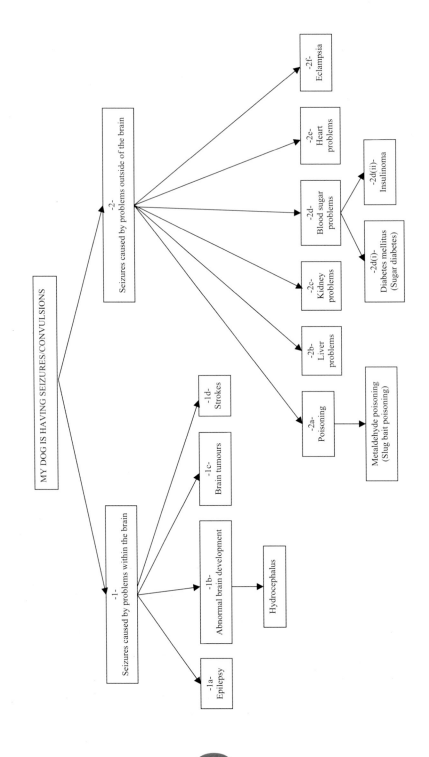

MY DOG IS HAVING SEIZURES/CONVULSIONS

-1-
Seizures caused by problems within the brain

-1a-
Epilepsy

-1b-
Abnormal brain development

Hydrocephalus

-1c-
Brain tumours

-1d-
Strokes

-2-
Seizures caused by problems outside of the brain

-2a-
Poisoning

Metaldehyde poisoning
(Slug bait poisoning)

-2b-
Liver problems

-2c-
Kidney problems

-2d-
Blood sugar problems

-2d(i)-
Diabetes mellitus
(Sugar diabetes)

-2d(ii)-
Insulinoma

-2e-
Heart problems

-2f-
Eclampsia

Grand mal seizures

These are the classic seizures most people think about when I discuss seizures or convulsions. When a grand mal seizure happens it usually strikes very suddenly and the dog will fall to the ground, either on their chest or their side. They may yelp or cry out as the seizure strikes them. Their eyes may seem to be 'rolling in the eye sockets' and they may drool and salivate. They may then have muscle twitching or violent muscle spasms affecting any or all of the muscles of the body. They may defecate and urinate onto themselves or the floor. During the seizure the dog may or may not seem unconscious. Even if they seem conscious during the seizure, they usually do not seem to be aware of other people or things around them. The muscle twitching or spasms will continue for anything from a few seconds to a few hours. When the seizure ends you will notice that they may seem confused or disorientated. They will then either return to normal within a few minutes to a few hours or another seizure may strike within a few minutes or hours.

Petit mal seizures

These have also been called 'fly-gazing' or 'star-gazing'. Petit mal seizures do not involve most of the symptoms of a grand mal seizure i.e. there are usually no muscle spasms and the dog usually does not fall over. The only symptom that the dog is having a mild seizure is that they seem to watch an invisible fly flying around their head or gaze at invisible stars over their heads. This vacant staring may go on for a few seconds to a few minutes. When it stops, the dog may seem a bit confused for a few minutes but then usually they seem completely normal again.

Thus grand mal and petit mal seizures appear very different but both reflect abnormal brain activity. The time before the seizure is called the pro-drome and the time after the seizure is the recovery phase. The pro-drome is a very important concept. During the pro-drome many dogs will seem anxious and unsettled. These dogs will often go up to their owners during the pro-drome and seek reassurance, as they seem to realise that something is about to happen to them. The pro-drome may last for a few minutes or even a few hours. If we learn to recognise the symptoms of the pro-drome it gives us the opportunity to try to stop the impending seizure by either giving medication and/or stimulating the dog. This stimulation simply takes the form of talking to them and focusing their attention on yourself while reassuring them. This is a concept employed by some doctors. We have all heard of guide dogs for blind people but few of us have heard of seizure dogs for people with epilepsy. These are dogs who are able to recognise when a person is about to have a seizure i.e. they know when a person is in the pro-drome even though the people do not realise it themselves. No one knows how some dogs can do this; but if they can, then they can be used to warn an epileptic person that they are about to have a seizure. This gives that person the opportunity to quickly take their medication and possibly also to try to activate and focus their minds with an activity to try to prevent the seizure from happening.

The recovery phase is the time after the seizure has stopped. Some dogs will recover within a few minutes and then continue as if nothing had happened. Other dogs may seem disorientated and shaken by the experience and they may take several hours to 'get over it' and return to normal.

Once you have witnessed a seizure, take careful note of the time of day and all the symptoms associated with the seizure. There is nothing you can do at home to stop the seizure once it has started. The only help you could offer is to place a pillow under the dog's head to stop them hurting themselves during the muscle spasms. You should not even attempt this if there is a possibility that the dog may accidentally bite you. You definitely should not reach into their mouth to pull their tongue forwards because they may accidentally severely injure you and you might even lose your fingers. The only thing you can do during the seizure is to watch all the stages carefully so that you can answer the vet's questions about it later. If possible, get someone to phone the vet for advice while you watch the dog. Once the seizure is over you should reassure the dog and then it would be wise to phone the vet for advice.

Emergency treatment for grand mal seizures

If the grand mal seizure does not stop within five minutes you should phone your vet for advice. The vet will almost certainly want to examine the dog immediately. The most suitable place to examine a dog having a seizure is at the veterinary clinic because the vet may not be able to bring all the equipment they need to your house. If the seizure has not stopped naturally within five minutes the vet will probably advise that they have to use medication to stop the seizure. The vet will usually use two types of medication to do this. The first thing they will do is to sedate the dog with an injection. If one or more sedative injections do not stop the convulsions then the vet will have to administer a full general anaesthetic. Once the dog is under the general anaesthetic the vet will need to keep them asleep for as long as several hours. While they are sleeping under the general anaesthetic the vet may also start anticonvulsive treatment. This is because, although the general anaesthetic stops the muscle spasms, the seizure in the brain may continue without any obvious outward signs. The anticonvulsive treatment thus stops the abnormal activity in the brain and the anaesthetic stops the muscle spasms. While the dog is under the anaesthetic and asleep, these treatments will 'reboot' the brain just like a computer. Once the vet has administered the treatment and has stopped the seizure they will ask you several questions and may start running some tests. The questions and tests are discussed in the next few paragraphs.

When the vet is presented with a dog who has had one or more seizures, they will initially try to determine whether the cause of the problem is inside the brain or whether it is due to external factors affecting the brain. The vet will ask you a wide variety of questions. Some of the questions will relate directly to the seizure and others will be directed to other symptoms that may have been developing before the seizure occurred. Your answers to the questions are very important and it is essential not to try to guess the answer. It is better to answer a question with 'I don't know' rather than to guess, as the information that you give the vet will very often give them enough information to make the diagnosis without expensive tests. The questions will include some or all of the following.

- What time did the seizure occur?
- What was the dog doing when the seizure occurred?
- Did the dog realise that something was wrong before having the seizure (was there a prodrome)?
- When the seizure occurred, did the dog fall over and if they did, did they fall onto their chest or onto their side?

- Did the dog lose consciousness during the seizure?
- How long did the seizure last?
- How long after the seizure did it take the dog to seem normal again (how long was the recovery period)?
- Has the dog had seizures before?
- How old is the dog?
- Have you used any pesticides e.g. snail or slug poison in or around your house and garden?
- In the days or weeks before the seizure, was the dog's appetite increased, decreased or normal?
- In the days or weeks before the seizure, was the dog drinking more, less or the same amount of water as normal?
- In the weeks before the seizure was the dog coughing and/or do they get tired and out of breath more quickly than normal when going for a walk?

The purpose of these questions is to guide the vet's thinking which will go something like this:

If the seizures happen in a very young dog (less than one year old) one might suspect a birth defect in the brain or elsewhere in the body.

If the seizures happen soon after the dog has eaten a meal then one might suspect that a liver problem is affecting the brain.

If the seizures happen during exercise then one might suspect that a heart condition or a blood glucose disorder is affecting the brain.

If the seizures happen when the dog is resting or sleeping then one might suspect primary epilepsy.

If the dog had an altered thirst or appetite in the days or weeks prior to the seizure then one might suspect that a problem elsewhere in the body is affecting the brain.

If the dog is very old one might suspect that they have had a stroke.

If there was a clear pro-drome period then one might suspect primary epilepsy.

If pesticides have recently been used at home the dog may have eaten some of it and poisoning is affecting the brain.

If the dog has recently given birth to puppies then the seizures may be caused by eclampsia.

Once the vet has thoroughly examined your dog and asked you some or all of the above questions, they may be able to make a specific diagnosis but in most cases they would need to run some tests to be sure of the diagnosis. The tests would include some or all of the following: blood tests, X-rays, ECG heart monitor, ultrasound scans, brain scans. The vet uses all this formation to determine whether the seizures are caused by a problem within the brain or a problem in another part of the body which is affecting the brain.

If the problem is within the brain, the most common diagnoses are primary epilepsy (young or middle age dogs) or abnormal brain development (young dogs) or brain tumours (middle age or older dogs) or strokes (older dogs). If the seizures are caused by problems outside of the brain, the most common diagnoses are poisoning or problems with other organs in the body (liver, kidneys, pancreas or heart) or eclampsia.

1 Seizures caused by problems within the brain

1a Primary epilepsy

Epilepsy is most commonly first noticed when the dog is between six months and three years old but it may develop at any age. The symptoms are usually grand mal seizures which occur when the dog is resting or sleeping. There is often a distinct pro-drome and a fast and full recovery after the seizure has ended. The seizures may occur as a single episode or several seizures may happen in a row. The are no other abnormalities besides the seizures i.e. the seizures occur occasionally but at all other times the dog appears absolutely normal in every respect. Not all dogs with epilepsy will have grand mal seizures. Dogs with mild epilepsy may have 'fly gazing' as the only symptom.

There is not a specific test for epilepsy in dogs. Epilepsy means that the brain suffers seizures for no apparent reason the same way that some computers will frequently crash for no apparent reason. This is the same as epilepsy which occurs in human beings. Because there is no specific test for epilepsy, the vet can only make this diagnosis by running enough tests to prove that none of the other causes of seizures exist in that individual. This is called making a diagnosis by exclusion i.e. the vet will exclude all of the other possible causes of seizures and thus the only remaining diagnosis is epilepsy.

If the dog is presented to the vet during a grand mal seizure, the vet may have to use sedative injections or a general anaesthetic to stop the muscle spasms. They will usually start anticonvulsive treatment at the same time. The emergency treatment for a grand mal seizure is discussed at the beginning of this chapter.

Once the diagnosis has been made, the vet may use tablets to prevent seizures from happening in the future. Not all cases of epilepsy need to be treated. If the dog only suffers two or three very short seizures a year with a rapid full recovery within a few minutes of each seizure, then the vet may suggest that no treatment is required. This is because most epilepsy treatments will strain the liver and thus one must decide which is the least damaging to the dog viz. the added strain on the liver or an occasional non-life threatening seizure which does not significantly affect the dog before or after. I would usually only start treatment for epilepsy if the individual had more than one seizure a month or if each seizure lasts more that two minutes.

The decision to treat or not to treat the condition should be discussed with your vet on an individual case basis. If the decision is that treatment is required, the treatment consists of tablets that the dog will probably need to take for the rest of his or her life. The most common treatment used to control epilepsy in dogs is called phenobarbitone. Phenobarbitone works on the brain by 'lowering the seizure threshold'. This effectively means that the treatment calms and stabilises the cells in the brain and thus the cells are unlikely to function abnormally. Abnormally functioning brain cells cause seizures by causing a 'short circuit in the wiring of the brain'. This is similar to a computer where a short circuit in the electronics causes the computer to crash. The treatment usually does put some strain on the liver but normally we have no signs of this other than the fact that blood tests will reveal that the liver becomes slightly inflamed when this treatment is used. There is no specific dose of treatment which suits all dogs and thus the vet will start the treatment at an average dose and then adjust the dose up or down. The decision to increase or decrease the dose will be determined by how effectively the treatment is working to stop the seizures from happening and by using blood tests to measure the level of the treatment in the blood supply. This treatment is intended to stop all seizures from happening without producing side effects. Thus, although blood tests may show that the treatment strains the liver, the patients should show no signs or symptoms of side effects to the treatment. Most epileptic dogs can be expected to live long, happy, normal lives once the diagnosis has been made and treatment has been started.

1b Abnormal brain development in young dogs
The most common brain abnormality that a puppy may be born with is called hydrocephalus. This is a very severe abnormality and most puppies will show obvious symptoms of abnormal brain function within a few months of being born. One of the symptoms may be grand mal seizures. Many other symptoms will also be present i.e. the affected puppy seems dull and lethargic, is smaller than the other pups and is not able to walk, eat and play normally. There are currently no effective treatments for these patients and most of them will die. The vet will often make the diagnosis basis on the age, the symptoms and the size and shape of the puppy's skull. The diagnosis can be confirmed by taking skull X-rays and brain scans. The vet may, if you request, try to treat the condition for as long as possible by using phenobarbitone to prevent seizures if they are occurring in the affected individual. The use of phenobarbitone is discussed in the paragraph on epilepsy.

1c Brain tumours
Brain tumours are very rare in dogs and occur most commonly in old dogs. The symptoms caused by the brain tumour depend on which part of the brain is affected. If the tumour causes seizures then they are usually grand mal seizures. The diagnosis of a brain tumour can only be made by performing a brain scan. Some brain tumours may respond to radiation therapy and others are untreatable. This also applies to brain tumours in human beings. Any treatment for brain tumours should only be undertaken by an oncologist (tumour specialist).

1d Strokes in older dogs
Dogs may suffer a stroke just as people do. Strokes usually only occur in old dogs and fortunately most dogs will recover completely within one week after having the stroke. The word 'stroke' means that a blood vessel in the brain has burst or become blocked. Once this happens a small piece of the brain that relies on blood from that blood vessel will die off. The stroke usually does not cause seizures but I have included it in this section because the affected dog will often not be able to stand or walk after a stroke and when they try to do so they have very jerky movements and often fall over. They usually have their head tilted to one side and their eyes will often twitch from side to side or up and down. This twitching eye movement is called nystagmus. The dog may appear very disorientated or they may be fully aware of their surroundings. With severe strokes the affected dog may not be able to walk for anything up to three days. In the case of a mild stroke the dog may be able to walk immediately after the stroke and will be unsteady on their feet to varying degrees i.e. some will repeatedly fall over and others might just seem a bit 'wobbly'. Once they are able to walk they will often tend to walk in circles either to the left or to the right. These dogs will usually recover completely within seven days of the stroke.

The vet will often be able to make the diagnosis of a stroke based on these symptoms, but for confirmation will have to take a brain scan. There is no treatment to 'fix' a stroke. The various treatments that vets may use are intended to help the brain to repair itself. The brain is similar to a computer and it will repair itself by 're-wiring' around the damaged part of the brain. Dogs are able to do this 're-wiring' much more effectively than human beings and thus most dogs will recover much better from a stroke than people do.

2 Seizures caused by problems in the rest of the body outside of the brain

The brain is a very sensitive structure and can be severely effected by lack of oxygen or various different types of chemicals. A good example of the effect of chemicals on the brain is alcohol. If one drinks alcohol it will affect brain function e.g. slurred speech, loss of balance and staggering. In severe cases excessive alcohol will cause unconsciousness and possibly death. Lack of oxygen will also affect brain function e.g. if a person stands still for long periods of time they may not pump enough blood and oxygen to the brain and thus they may faint. A lack of energy (food) may also affect brain function. If you do not eat for a long period of time there is not enough glucose in your blood to feed your brain and you may pass out (faint). These are just everyday examples of how a lack of oxygen or blood glucose or excessive amounts of specific types of chemicals can affect brain function. I have used these everyday examples to illustrate that abnormal brain function does not mean that there is necessarily a problem with the brain. These examples demonstrate that abnormal brain activity may be caused by factors (problems) in the rest of the body outside of the brain. These factors (problems) can cause a normal brain to function abnormally and thus result in seizures in an individual who actually has a normally functioning brain.

2a Poisoning as a chemical cause of seizures

The most common poison which may be eaten by dogs and cause seizures is metaldehyde – used in gardens to kill snails and slugs. The symptoms of metaldehyde poisoning are drooling and muscle twitching which may become more severe with spasms and seizures developing after a short time. The treatment is to make the dog vomit to get rid of the poison from their stomach. If you cannot make them vomit then they should have their stomach pumped out by a vet. If the dog has progressed to the point where they are having grand mal seizures then they will require sedatives and/or a full general anaesthetic and anti-seizure treatment. The emergency treatment for a grand mal seizure is discussed at the beginning of this chapter. Most dogs will survive metaldehyde poisoning if they are treated quickly but dogs can and do die from this chemical if they have eaten large amounts of it or if they do not get medical attention soon enough.

2b Liver problems as a cause of seizures (Hepatic encephalopathy)

If a dog has a problem which damages the liver or interferes with its ability to function normally, one of the symptoms that may develop is seizures. Seizures develop in these cases because the liver has lost its ability to remove dangerous chemicals from the bloodstream. The liver has many functions and one of these functions is to remove harmful chemicals from the body. Most of these harmful chemicals are normal waste products produced by other organs in the body. The liver normally filters out and detoxifies these naturally occurring chemicals in the body. Provided the liver is working normally, these chemicals are only ever present in the body in very small amounts because the liver is constantly detoxifying them. If the liver is unable to function normally then these naturally occurring chemicals will start to accumulate in the body. Once too much of these chemicals has accumulated in the bloodstream they will start to affect the brain in a similar effect to alcohol. If the blood levels continue to accumulate, these chemicals may cause the brain to have seizures because these chemicals effectively start to 'poison' the brain. The treatment is to fix the liver problem and then the seizures will stop once the liver starts removing the waste chemicals from the body efficiently again.

The liver will be identified as the problem when the vet performs the tests mentioned earlier i.e. blood tests, X-rays and ultrasound scans. The most common liver problem in young dogs that may cause seizures is an abnormally developed liver which causes an abnormality called a hepato-portal shunt. Once this has been diagnosed, the vet will treat the problem either by operating on the liver or using medication and switching the dog onto a special diet to help the liver. The most common liver problems causing seizures in older dogs are tumours in the liver and scirrosis of the liver. These are serious conditions and the vet may not be able to significantly help the dog. Each case must however always be considered individually and some cases will respond well to various treatments.

2c Kidney problems as a cause of seizures (Renal encephalopathy)

The kidneys, like the liver, remove naturally occurring chemicals from the bloodstream. If the kidneys lose their ability to function properly then these chemicals will start to accumulate in the body. Once too much of these chemicals has accumulated in the bloodstream they will start to affect the brain in a similar way to alcohol. If the blood levels continue to accumulate, these chemicals may cause the brain to have seizures because they effectively start to 'poison' the brain. The treatment is to fix the kidney problem and then the seizures will stop once the kidneys start removing the waste chemicals from the body efficiently again. Please refer to chapter 4 for a full discussion on different types of kidney problems and how to treat them.

2d Abnormal blood sugar levels as a cause of seizures

2d(i) Diabetes mellitus (sugar diabetes)

This may cause seizures. Please refer to chapter 4 for a full discussion on diabetes and how to treat it.

2d(ii) Insulinoma

Very low blood sugar levels may be caused by a condition called insulinoma. This condition is caused by a tumour in the pancreas gland where insulin is produced. The diagnosis is made when the vet runs blood tests as discussed at the beginning of the chapter. The tumour must be removed to cure this very rare condition.

2e Heart problems as a cause of 'seizures'

Heart problems that affect the dog's blood pressure, or the ability of the heart to pump blood containing oxygen to the brain, may cause abnormal brain activity. This happens because, if the brain cells are not receiving enough oxygen, the brain cannot function normally. The result of insufficient oxygen supply to the brain is usually that the individual will faint rather than have a seizure, but I have included it in this section because fainting may look like a seizure. The technical word for fainting is syncope. When an individual faints they fall to the ground unconscious and may show mild muscle twitching movements, they usually recover within a few moments and may then seem dazed or disorientated for a short time. This may make it difficult for a pet owner to determine whether the dog has fainted or has had a true seizure. The primary difference between fainting and epileptic seizures is that fainting usually occurs during exercise or exertion and epileptic seizures usually happen during sleep or rest. The vet will however investigate the possibility of a heart problem when they examine the dog and this is done during the routine testing. The vet will then be able to determine whether the incident was a seizure or a faint and will be able to prescribe the appropriate treatment.

2f Seizures in bitches who have recently had puppies (Eclampsia)

Bitches may, within three days of giving birth, develop mild or severe muscle twitching which can resemble a seizure. The muscle twitching or muscle spasms are caused by low calcium levels in the mother's blood stream. Calcium has many functions in the body, one of which is to assist in the function of the nerve cells in the body. If there is insufficient calcium to assist this nerve cell function then the nerves may become unstable and abnormal signs are seen as the nerves discharge impulses spontaneously. This is the situation faced by women and animals when conditions like eclampsia (milk fever) cause a drop in the blood levels of calcium.

Eclampsia (milk fever) may happen shortly after a mother has given birth when she diverts a lot of her own calcium to her milk to go to her baby. The calcium in the mother's bloodstream is transferred to her milk to help the puppies grow strong teeth and bones. If her own blood levels drop too low, then her nerve cells become unstable and may fire impulses spontaneously to the muscles. Thus the clinical symptoms of low blood calcium levels are initially twitching and muscle tremors, which may progress to full seizures, convulsions and possible death if treatment is not started quickly. Treatment of low blood calcium is simple and highly effective. The treatment is a simply a matter of injecting calcium into a vein and the patient recovers within minutes.

Once the bitch has recovered, the vet will suggest that you should add a calcium supplement to her diet for a few days and also possibly hand feed the puppies for a few days. There are many specially formulated artificial mild substitutes for puppies and hand feeding them is easy. The reason that the vet may suggest hand feeding the puppies for a few days is that, if they are not drinking milk from the bitch, the milk in the mammary glands will accumulate. As the milk accumulates in the mammary glands, and is not being removed by suckling puppies, the mother will then re-absorb the calcium from the milk back into her own bloodstream. The second reason is that, because the puppies are not suckling from the mother for a few days, there is no ongoing loss of calcium via the milk. The puppies usually only need to be hand fed for one to three days and then the mother can continue suckling them. Thus, if one sees muscle tremors or seizure-like symptoms in a bitch who has recently given birth, the diagnosis will almost certainly be eclampsia (low blood calcium levels caused by the production of a lot of milk).

7
THE ITCHY DOG

Dogs who itch and scratch various parts of their bodies are one of the more common situations vets will be asked to solve. There are an enormous number of possibilities to consider with an itchy dog but the old axiom of 'the common things occur commonly' is very true in this situation. The first points to consider are the breed, the age and the lifestyle of the dog. The breed will often make one consider conditions commonly found in that breed, for example golden retrievers and Labrador retrievers often suffer from skin allergies, terriers often have skin mites, German shepherds are susceptible to deep bacterial infections. Young dogs are susceptible to skin mites; middle age dogs are more susceptible to endocrine problems (problems with their 'glands'). Dogs working or walking in areas with various types of wildlife may be susceptible to the skin conditions spread by the wildlife. One must always consider the 'big picture' and not simply just focus on the affected portion of skin.

The vet will ask a few simple but very important questions to narrow the list of possible causes of itchy skin. It is very important to answer the questions as accurately as you can and if you do not know the answer to any or all of the questions then it is better to say so than to take a guess. The questions may include some of the following:

- How old is the dog?
- How long has the dog been itchy?
- Is the dog very itchy i.e. scratching all the time or moderately itchy i.e. scratching only occasionally?
- Does the dog itch all over or are certain parts of the body more itchy than others?
- Are other pets or people at home also itchy?
- Has the dog had the same symptoms before?
- Are there any other symptoms i.e. changes in thirst or appetite or does the dog seem ill?
- Have you seen fleas on the pets at home or have people at home been bitten by fleas?
- Have you changed the environment at home e.g. new carpets, recent building or redecorating work etc?

The vet may ask many more questions in addition to the ones mentioned above. The aim of these questions is to guide the vet's thoughts which will go something like this: The three most common categories of problems causing itchy skin are allergies, skin parasites and endocrine disorders. If the itching is caused by an allergy, the other pets in the household will probably not be itchy and the affected dog will often have a history of being itchy on previous occasions, often at the same time

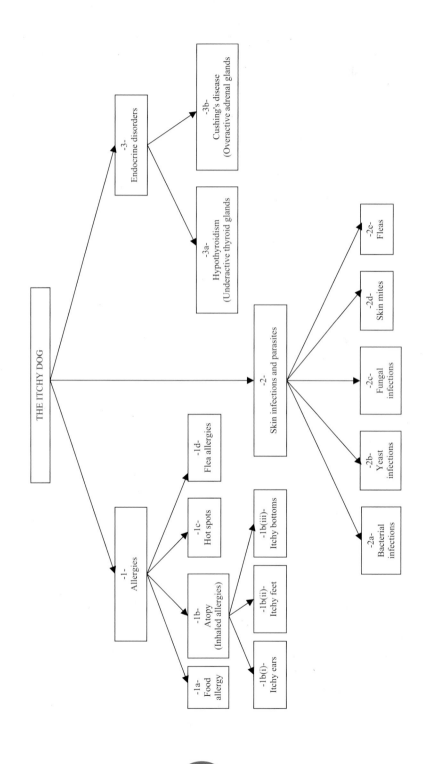

THE ITCHY DOG

-1-
Allergies

-1a-
Food allergy

-1b-
Atopy
(Inhaled allergies)

-1b(i)-
Itchy ears

-1b(ii)-
Itchy feet

-1b(iii)-
Itchy bottoms

-1c-
Hot spots

-1d-
Flea allergies

-2-
Skin infections and parasites

-2a-
Bacterial infections

-2b-
Yeast infections

-2c-
Fungal infections

-2d-
Skin mites

-2e-
Fleas

-3-
Endocrine disorders

-3a-
Hypothyroidism
(Underactive thyroid glands

-3b-
Cushing's disease
(Overactive adrenal glands

every year if the allergy is associated with the seasons. If the itching is caused by an allergy the most itchy areas may be the ears, the feet, the bottom or the lower back at the base of the tail. If the itching is caused by skin parasites, the other pets at home or even the people may also be itchy if the parasite is contagious. If the itching is caused by an underlying endocrine problem e.g. thyroid or adrenal gland problems there will usually be a range of other symptoms in addition to the itching.

Once the vet has asked all the appropriate questions and has examined your dog they may be able to make a specific diagnosis. In most cases of itchy skin the vet will recommend some tests to determine the exact cause (or in some cases several causes) of the itching. These tests may include analysis of hair samples, skin scrapings, blood tests and possibly skin biopsies. Once the vet has determined whether the skin itching is caused by an allergy, a skin parasite or an endocrine problem (or any combination of these problems) they will advise you on the best course of action. I will discuss each category of skin condition individually.

1 Skin allergies

The most common types of allergies affecting dogs' skin are atopy and flea allergies. Atopy means that the allergy is caused by substances in the air such as pollen. The symptoms of atopy are usually itching all over but the ears, the feet and the bottom are often the most itchy areas. Flea allergy typically causes severe itching over mostly the lower back just above the base of the tail. This area is often scratched so much that there is very little hair left and the skin is covered in many small scabs caused by the scratching.

When discussing skin problems/disorders, the affected parts of the skin are referred to as the lesions. One must consider the way the lesions have evolved since the condition first started. Consider dogs with skin allergies like atopy. These dogs are generally mildly itchy all over but the most itchy areas are the ears, the feet or the anal region. Some dogs may show only itchy ears or only itchy feet or only itchy bums or any combination of these areas. The unfortunate ones will lick or scratch all these areas. The licking and/or scratching that these dogs do may be only occasional or they may be so itchy that they are doing it all the time. The dogs who lick or scratch the area severely enough will often damage the skin to the point where secondary infections develop and mask the underlying problem. To make sense of this consider someone who scratches a mosquito bite to the point where they break the skin and a scab develops. If they then continue scratching, the scabby area may become infected. If they then showed the lesion to a doctor without telling him or her anything about the lesions, the doctor would not be in a position to know that the scabby infected skin lesion is not the actual problem and that the initial cause of the problem was a mosquito bite. Vets are in the same situation in that our patients are unable to explain how the lesion started and we are presented with the end result which may be a non-specific, infected, itchy, scabby area. The further complicating factor is that the more the area is scratched the itchier it becomes and the more infected it becomes the itchier it gets. As it itches more the dog scratches more, as they scratch more it itches more. The result is the sudden appearance of a scabby, itchy area that often rapidly expands as the dog continues to aggravate it. This vicious circle of itching and scratching may lead to the original problem being obscured by the secondary infections. Thus in these cases the vet will often want to treat the secondary infection until it resolves and then the underlying problem will be revealed.

People will often bring their dog to me and ask me to treat the patch of eczema that the dog has developed and has been licking and scratching over the last few days. I will suggest that we treat the eczema for a few days and then reexamine the lesions to try to establish an underlying cause. The reason for this is twofold. The first is that I feel that the word 'eczema' is used so loosely that it means nothing more than a scabby, oozing patch of skin or areas of dry flaky skin. With this in mind I feel that it is not appropriate to make a diagnosis of 'eczema' because it is so non-specific as to be almost meaningless. It would be the same as examining a lame dog and making a diagnosis of a limp. Yes, the dog may have a limp, but the point of the diagnosis is to identify why there is a limp, for example is there a broken bone, a sprained tendon, an injured muscle etc. The second reason for wanting to reexamine the lesion after a few days is that if we treat only the secondary infection caused by the scratching then we have not solved the problem. If the underlying cause of the itching is still there then the problem will simply recur later when the treatment is finished. Thus it is important that we treat the symptoms and the cause. Sometimes the original cause may have disappeared by the time the secondary infection has been resolved, as in the case of a mosquito bite which has been severely scratched, and no underlying cause can be identified but it is always worth looking for the underlying cause because if it is due to a long term allergy then this must be treated to avoid or minimise further episodes of secondary infections.

I have used the word allergy very loosely thus far and at this point it is worth discussing in more depth. Dogs develop allergies just as people do and the most common causes seem to be house dust and house dust mites, grasses and pollens, insect bites (e.g. fleas) and various types of food. The way that we manifest our allergies is to develop hay fever, asthma or skin eczema. Dogs only rarely develop asthma or hay fever; most dogs with allergies will develop itchy skin. The thing that causes the allergy is called the allergen. The route by which the allergen is taken into the body does not necessarily affect where in the body the allergy effect will be produced. Consider people with an allergy to nuts or bee stings, if they are exposed to the nuts in their food or a sting in their skin they will often develop severe swelling in their airways which may cause suffocation. This demonstrates that the site of the allergy reaction does not necessarily have to be the same as the route of exposure to the allergen. The same concept applies to dogs in that they generally manifest their allergies as inflammation and itching in the skin. This applies to food allergies; inhaled allergies like pollens and house dust mites and injected allergies like fleabites.

1a Food allergies

Dogs who are itchy all over their bodies will sometimes improve when they are fed a different kind of food i.e. the degree of itchiness will reduce or disappear entirely. This raises the concept of the individual being allergic to certain types of food or certain specific food ingredients. The same phenomenon occurs in human beings who are often able to alleviate their allergy symptoms e.g. hay fever or asthma, by avoiding certain types of food. The most common types of food associated with allergies are wheat products, dairy products and beef. We have found that by eliminating one or more of these ingredients from a dog's diet, their itchiness will reduce or resolve.

The concept of individuals being truly allergic to certain types of food or food ingredients has raised a lot of speculation. The current thinking is that true allergy to certain types of food is in fact very rare and that most individuals thought to have a food allergy are actually only intolerant to certain types of food. This change in thinking has come about as a result of increased research into food allergy. It may seem to be pedantic but one should try to differentiate between a true food allergy and a food intolerance. In the case of a true food allergy one should be able to fully resolve the dog's itching by feeding what are called novel foods. Novel foods are simply types of food made from ingredients that the dog has never eaten before. Because they have never eaten these ingredients before they cannot be allergic to them because allergies develop only after repeated exposure to a specific allergen (an allergen is the thing that triggers the allergy). If the itching resolves when the dog is fed a novel food, then one should try feeding the original food again. If the itching immediately reappears it suggests that the dog is truly allergic to that type of food. Thus, if a dog is truly allergic to a certain type of food, we should be able to trigger the allergy (itching) every time we feed this food and the allergy should resolve every time we withhold this food. In research trials this is often not the case i.e. the itching may resolve or reduce when a certain type of food is withheld, but when it is then fed to the dog at a later time the allergy is not triggered. These dogs would then be regarded as simply intolerant to that food rather than allergic to it. Food intolerance thus implies that feeding certain ingredients simply makes the individual more susceptible to all their other allergies.

If one suspects that an itchy dog is itchy because they are allergic or intolerant to a specific type of food, then one would investigate this by elimination food trials. Simply put this involves feeding the dog a novel food for eight weeks. If the symptoms resolve on the novel food but reappear when the original food is fed, then the dog has a true food allergy and the itching can be resolved by feeding the dog the novel food exclusively for the rest of their life. If the itching either does not resolve completely on the novel food, or does not recur when the original food is fed, then one can conclude that the dog is simply intolerant to that type of food. In these cases one may have to continue the search to identify the food to which the dog is allergic. In practical terms, it is not always essential to continue the search i.e. if the itching resolves when the dog is fed the novel food and their other allergies no longer cause any symptoms, then one can simply feed the novel food exclusively for the rest of their life.

The reality is that most itchy dogs can be improved by feeding novel foods specifically prepared for dogs with allergies. Even if these foods only reduce the level of itching without curing the problem entirely, they do make it easier to control the other allergies the dog may suffer from. Most of the well-known dog food manufacturers produce a novel food for dogs with allergies and vets have different personal preferences as to which type of novel food they may recommend.

1b Atopy

Inhaled allergies are called atopy and animals with atopy are called atopic individuals. Atopy and allergy to flea bites are the most common types of allergy diagnosed in dogs. The most severe sites of itching in response to allergy reactions are the ears, paws and the anal region as mentioned before. Some dogs may have only itchy ears or only itchy bottoms or only itchy feet or any combination of these three. The classic form of allergy in dogs are ones with itchy 'ears and rears'.

1b(i) Itchy ears

Dogs suffering from allergies, especially atopy, very commonly present with itchy, inflamed ears or even infected ears. The cases where the dog's allergies have caused the inflammation and itching in the ears are called allergic otitis externa. The lining of the ear canal down to the level of the ear drum is the same type of skin that covers the rest of the body; thus inflammation due to allergic reactions extends all the way down the ear canals. The ear canal is basically a tube of cartilage lined with skin. When the skin layer becomes inflamed, the cartilage will not allow the skin layer to swell outwards as cartilage is not pliable enough. The result is that the swelling of the skin lining is inwards and this means that the ear canal becomes narrowed when it is inflamed and air movement in the ear canal is reduced and the ear canal becomes a warm, dark, moist place. Bacteria, yeast and fungi love warm, dark, moist places and thus one will often see a secondary infection in an ear canal that is inflamed due to allergies.

The inflammation that develops in one or both ear canals can be demonstrated by comparing the colour of the skin in the ear canal with a piece of skin elsewhere on the body. The skin at the opening of the ear canal is generally pinker that the skin elsewhere (Fig. 14b). The result of long term low grade inflammation in skin is that the skin thickens. To make sense of this consider people who work with their hands a lot and who develop calluses on their hands. This is because the long-term abrasion and irritation causes long term inflammation in the skin of the hand. The body attempts to protect the hand by thickening the skin, and in the places where it is most thickened we identify calluses. The ear canal responds in much the same way in that long term, low grade inflammation will result in thickening of the skin lining the ear canals. The most serious consequence of this process is that the thickening of the ear canal lining will result in narrowing of the ear canal, as the cartilage outer cone will not allow the ear canal to expand outwards. The final result is that the ear canal becomes much narrower than it should be and is very susceptible to secondary infection because of reduced ventilation in this narrow channel. This thickening makes the skin at the entrance to the ear canal appear similar to elephant skin in comparison to the smooth skin elsewhere on the body. Technically this is called hyperkeratosis or lichenification.

Thus, when a dog develops an ear infection, we must not only treat the pain and infection in the first instance but also try to identify how and why the infection developed. Many times the infection may have developed for no apparent reason but we should always look to see if it developed secondarily to the narrowing of the ear canal due to the inflammation caused by an allergy action. This is even more important in the case of recurring ear infections, as the long term allergic inflammation and recurrent secondary infections will result in ongoing narrowing of the ear canal throughout the dog's life and thus secondary ear infections will occur more and more often as the dog grows older. An important point to make here is that an inflamed ear canal containing abnormal matter is not necessarily an infected ear. One will get a very good idea of what secondary problem has affected the ear canal by looking at the abnormal matter accumulating in the ear canal. Pus would suggest a bacterial infection and/or fungal and yeast infections, a black tarry substance which may look like clotted blood may suggest ear mites and a dark brown waxy substance suggests just an allergy reaction without secondary infections. The accumulation of this dark brown waxy substance is often misinterpreted as an infection as it may have a foul smell, but is generally just an overproduction of ear wax. The reason this happens is best understood by comparing the allergy reaction manifesting in a dog's ear to the allergy reaction manifesting in human beings' noses called hay fever. In the case of human beings, hay fever produces inflammation in the lining of the nose, the nose does not know whether the inflammation is due to an allergic reaction or an infection starting in the nose, so it does the only thing it can to protect itself – it produces a protective layer of mucous. In the case of hay fever sufferers it effectively overdoes it and we develop a very watery, bunged up snotty nose. The ear canal, when it is inflamed, also does not know whether the inflammation is due to allergy or infection and it also does the only thing it can to protect itself which is to produce more wax to build up a defensive barrier. The wax production is however also often overdone and thus we see a dark brown waxy accumulation of 'muck' in the ear canal in cases of allergies manifesting in dogs' ear canals.

1b(ii) Itchy feet

The second most common presentation of allergies, especially atopy, in dogs is itchy feet. Most dog owners will often think that the dogs are just biting their nails as some human beings do, or that the dogs are just fastidious in that they lick their feet clean a lot of the time. This is a very easy manifestation of allergy to diagnose in dogs with white or light coloured hair as the licking stains the hair a brick red colour. Thus any dog who has feet stained a brick red colour with no other obvious problems affecting the feet are almost invariably just licking their feet because they manifest their allergy as itchy feet.

1b(iii) Itchy bottoms

The third manifestation of allergy, especially atopy, in dogs are those dogs who lick their bottoms a lot or drag their bottoms along the ground. There are three common causes of itchy bottoms in dogs. The first and most common is that the dog is an allergic individual who manifests its allergy as an itchy bottom with or without having itchy ears and feet. The second most common reason is a problem with the anal sacs which lie next to the anus. The anal sacs are scent glands on either side of the anus which may become uncomfortable to dogs when they become blocked, infected or possibly develop tumours. The clinical result of any of these three problems affecting the anal sacs is an itchy bottom which is licked a lot or dragged along the ground in what is described as 'scooting'. The third most common cause of an itchy bottom is a worm problem in the dog. The cause of the itching in these individuals is the worms being passed out of the anus and their wriggling movement causes itching. Excluding worms and anal sac problems as the cause of the problem often makes the diagnosis of allergy causing the itchy bottom a problem.

1c Hot spots

A common sequel to allergy causing itchy ears or bottom is the development of 'hot spots' or more technically acute focal exudative pyotraumatic dermatitis. These are painful, weeping sores which generally develop very suddenly in the vicinity of the ears or bottom. These lesions look like weeping scabby sores with little or no hair covering them. They quickly spread outwards and enlarge as the centre of the lesion develops a thick crust or scab which matts the surrounding fur. These lesions are self inflicted and are caused by the dogs licking, rubbing and scratching themselves until they remove the top layer of the skin and secondary infection sets in very quickly. Dog owners often describe the lesions as patches of wet eczema. I prefer the common name of 'hot spots' because I do not like the word eczema for the reasons I have discussed before. The lesions *per se* are very easy to treat. In fact they would heal of their own accord if we could rationalise with our dogs and ask them to stop licking, biting or scratching the affected area. Because we cannot ask the dogs to stop agitating the lesion the next option is to use treatments to stop the itching and this usually involves cortisone in the form of creams or tablets. Some vets will also use a short course of antibiotics to combat the secondary bacterial infection.

The big question to pose in the presence of a hot spot is not how to treat the hot spot but rather why did the dog damage the skin to the point where a hot spot developed. The areas where most hot spots develop gives us the answer to this question. Most of these lesions occur behind, below or in front of the ears or somewhere in the vicinity of the base of the tail. Thus if the lesion is in the vicinity of the ear the first thing to do is examine the ear and more often than not we will find allergic inflammation in the ear canals. This causes itching of the ears and the dogs will rub and scratch at the ear and inadvertently damage the skin adjacent to the ear and thus the hot spot is born and will expand rapidly if the rubbing and scratching is not stopped. Any other irritation in the ear, such as grass seeds in the ear, true ear infections or scabies mites in the skin of the ear flaps, can also precipitate enough itchiness for the dog to scratch and create a hot spot. In my experience allergic otitis is the most common factor of hot spots in this region. The same is true for hot spots in the vicinity of the tail base and anus. The lesions develop due to damage to the skin in his area as dogs try to lick and rub their itchy bottoms. As discussed above there are three common causes and I have found allergic inflammation in this area to be the most common one although tere are cases where no reason can be found to explain why the dog has scratched himself or herself to the point where a hot spot has developed. One should always try to find a reason because, just as in the case of ear infections, one should not only treat the obvious lesion but we should try to see the big picture. If an underlying reason, like allergy, can be identified then one can attempt to prevent or minimise further similar lesions developing in the future.

The treatment of allergies in cats and dogs should be aimed at two levels. Firstly we should try to identify and avoid the substances that cause the allergy (the allergens) and secondly we need to relieve the itching. The process of identifying the cause of the allergy may be expensive, time consuming and depending on the results, may not change the treatment options available to the affected individual. The way in which we try to identify the substances which cause the allergy (the allergen/s) is the same as in human beings. The traditional method is to inject very small amounts of all the substances the patient comes into contact with under the skin and measure the size of the wheal which forms. This sounds painful but people who have this testing done will describe it only as being uncomfortable. The test is done as follows: a small amount of sterile water is injected under the skin and small swelling will appear. This small swelling is called the control, which means that it is used to compare all the other reactions to. All the suspected allergens are then injected in the same quantity (diluted in water) in the adjacent skin and after about ten to thirty minutes later the size of every swelling is measured and compared to the size of the control. The larger the swelling the more allergic that individual is to that specific substance. In this way a list can be compiled of all the substances that individual is allergic to. An alternative way of compiling this list is to have tests done on a blood sample. Another option is to have the allergy testing done by a kinesiologist.

There is at present no perfect method of testing for allergies and any system may produce errors for a variety of reasons but at least most allergens can be identified for each individual. Once the list of allergens has been drawn up for that individual then, in some cases, one can consider trialing a hyposensitisation course. This means that the substance that that individual is allergic to is injected into that individual in slowly increasing concentrations over a period of several weeks to several months. The object of this exercise is to build up slowly the body's tolerance to that substance until it no longer produces an allergy reaction. This process of hyposensitisation produces a very variable success rate in that it produces little to no benefit in some patients and excellent results in others. The benefits may be temporary or permanent and thus the medical community is divided on whether this is a justified mode of treatment or not. My feeling is that it offers the potential for, at the very least, a temporary reduction in medication for allergy in those cases where it works.

A further complication in identifying a list of allergens for an individual is that most are allergic to several substances and most of these substances are factors beyond our control. What this means is that if the list of allergens includes a number of grasses and pollens commonly found in that environment, there is very little we can do to avoid them. Similarly if house dust and house dust mites appear on the list, we know from experience in managing human beings with these allergies, that it is impossible to completely eradicate house dust and house dust mites. Realistically the only allergens we can act against are those in food and in skin parasites (fleas). Thus if an individual is allergic to certain food types then we can avoid those foods. The most common allergy is to flea bites and that means that we can significantly help an individual with this particular allergy by using good flea control measures.

1d Flea allergies

A flea bite allergy is not the same as a flea problem on the dog. Most dogs will have a few fleas on them at various times of the year and they will scratch at the fleas for a few moments in response to the flea biting them. This scratching will usually only last for a few moments after the flea has bitten and then the dog will carry on doing what they were doing. If there are hundreds of fleas on the dog then there are many more bites taking place and thus the dog spends more time scratching. I would describe this as a flea problem *per se* and simply treating the dog for fleas will correct the problem. In the case of an individual with an allergy to flea bites the problem is entirely different. Firstly it takes only one fleabite to start the allergy reaction and even if the dog scratches and immediately kills the offending flea, the allergy reaction has already started. Consider a human being with an allergy to cats: it does not take hundreds of cats to set off their allergy. In fact if only takes one cat hair to set them off and even if they immediately removed that one cat hair it is too late because their allergy has already been set off, and they will then suffer full-blown hay fever for several hours to several days. This complete overreaction by the body to an apparently minor irritation is what differentiates the allergy sufferer from everyone else. Contrast this to someone who is not allergic to cats – if a cat hair goes up their nose they will sneeze once or twice to dislodge that hair and then the sneezing stops. This same principal applies in dogs – the dog who is not allergic to fleas will scratch once or twice when a flea bites and will stop scratching when the flea stops biting. If a flea bites a flea allergic dog just once, even if he then immediately kills that flea, he will be scratching for several hours to several days because the allergy has been set off.

The next point regarding flea bite allergy is that it is impossible to ensure that your dog is completely protected from fleas even if you are using the best products and the best treatment protocols. Statistically, sooner or later, one flea will slip through the defences and just one bite will trigger the allergy which, just like the example of the person allergic to cats, is completely out of proportion to the trigger that sets it off. Thus one must accept that we must apply much tighter flea controls to allergic dogs than to non-allergic dogs and that despite our best efforts we can never achieve one hundred per cent flea control. All the pets in the household must be treated with an appropriate flea control product and the house must also be treated with an appropriate product. This is further complicated by the fact that fleas are continuously developing resistance to these products and new ones must be developed The product which worked well last year may not be effective this year. The vet will advise on which products are currently efficient.

The symptoms of flea allergy are easy to identify and the usual one is that the dog is most severely itchy along the lower back where the back joins onto the tail. This area over the top of the tail-base is often only covered with sparse hair and may have small cuts and scratches caused by the dog scratching and rubbing the area. One will often be able to see fleas in this area and if you scratch this area it will be so pleasurable for the dog that they will often sit down or curl their backs and start scratching with one of their back legs.

Thus, even if a thorough list of allergens is obtained for an individual, we can only act against some of the substances on that list. Environmental allergens are beyond our control but by controlling the components we can, we will reduce the total number of things conspiring to trigger an allergy response in our pets and thereby reduce the total number of allergic reactions that will require treatment each year. This is the principle of maintaining the allergic individual below their 'allergic threshold'.

In those cases where our efforts at maintaining the individual below their allergic threshold fails, we should first find out why we have failed. It may be because the allergens are substances beyond our control like seasonal pollens, or it may be because we are still feeding the wrong food or using ineffective flea control products. If the allergens are environmental substances beyond our control then our efforts should be directed at controlling the symptoms of the allergy i.e. inflammation and itching. This approach is called symptomatic treatment and the principle is to treat the symptoms when we cannot treat the cause adequately. In human beings we can achieve this very easily by using antihistamines which are freely available at pharmacists. In the context of veterinary medicine, antihistamines very rarely have any effect at all. The only guaranteed way of controlling allergies in dogs is by using cortisone in either tablet form or occasionally in topical applications like ointments, creams and gels. Most people object to the use of cortisone because they are concerned about side effects that they may have heard about. There are indeed possible side effects when using cortisone but this is true for any medication. Consider our use of aspirin or paracetamol to treat pain like headaches. If we take the recommended dose, then we get all the benefits without the side effects. If we exceed the dose or the duration of treatment, then we are very likely to suffer unpleasant side effects. Cortisone may produce side effects, but if used correctly is unlikely to cause any significant problems.

The cortisone we use to control skin allergies in dogs is the same thing that millions of human beings use all over the world to control their asthma without any side effects. The most commonly used cortisones are prednisolone or prednisone tablets. This type of treatment is virtually identical to the natural steroid produced in all mammals' bodies by the adrenal glands. Thus cortisone is a natural ingredient in the body and when we take the synthetic form as tablets the effect is to temporarily increase the natural level of cortisone in the body. There are simple rules to be followed when using cortisone and if one follows the rules then significant side effects are very unlikely and if they do occur they will resolve when the treatment is stopped. The rules are simple: where possible use very short courses of less than three consecutive days' treatment. If more than three days of treatment is required then do not stop the treatment abruptly when the symptoms have disappeared, instead reduce the dose gradually over one or two weeks until it is withdrawn. Use the lowest possible dose to control the symptoms in each individual. Every dog is an individual and will require a different dose to control their itching. If the treatment is given once daily, then give it in the morning because then it mimics the body's natural levels of cortisone which is naturally highest in the morning.

The most common side effects that people report to me when their dogs are taking prednisolone is that they are slightly hungrier and sometimes drink more water and pee more. This side effect will go away when the treatment is stopped and will cause no permanent effect on the body. It is a transient side effect which is only seen in some individuals while on this treatment. The worst case scenario is potentially a dog who needs to take prednisolone regularly throughout their life. In this scenario the individual may start to develop side effects after a long term of treatment and the treatment may have to be adjusted to compensate. The first side effect is weight gain, the next more serious side effect is thinning of the skin and after a long period of time we may notice that secondary bacterial skin infections are becoming increasingly common. These side effects must be weighed up against the alternative problems encountered in the individual if no treatment is used to control their allergy. The benchmark is: which of these two options affects the overall quality of life of the individual the least? If the dog is not treated and the itching is so severe that the dog spends most of their time itching and scratching at the skin causing a succession of self inflicted wounds that require treatment of their own, then I personally feel that I would rather treat the allergy in that individual and accept that they become slightly overweight. I feel that the side effects caused by long term treatment cause less of an impact on the individual quality of life than enduring a lifetime of relentless itching. I think that the level of itching probably feels like we do when we have sunburn. The itching and discomfort caused by sunburn will never kill me but I certainly would not want to spend my entire life suffering these sensations. If I could select the alternative side effects of being slightly overweight but having no discomfort from my skin then I would certainly do so.

This 'worst case' scenario is rarely encountered in practice. My feeling at the outset of a severe case of skin allergy is to try all other treatment options before I accept that there is no alternative to a lifetime of intermittent treatment with cortisone. Some of the alternatives have been mentioned before viz. trialling different food to reduce the allergic threshold, eliminating fleas as best we can, courses of hyposensitization treatment and changing bedding. If none of these is appropriate or effective for an individual then other options can be explored. The first is the soothing effect of regular bathing in anti-inflammatory shampoos containing coal tar and/or evening primrose oils which often significantly reduce the symptoms of skin allergies. The second option is to explore the benefits of natural or homoeopathic remedies. The most common natural remedies used are evening primrose oils, either in tablet form or in shampoo form, or homoeopathic sulphur in tablet or powder form. These natural remedies are very variable in the effect with some dogs responding very well and others not responding at all. I feel that they are worth trying because even a partial response to this treatment would mean that cortisone would be required less often and at lower doses. The biggest problem with long-term evening primrose oil treatment is that the tablets are expensive. The option of using homoeopathic sulphur is much more affordable but the response to treatment is equally unpredictable. I would always recommend trialling sulphur treatment for at least six weeks because although it may never help the dog it will certainly never harm them either.

The objective of any of these treatments is to have the dog 'comfortably itchy'. What this means is to control the inflammation and itching caused by the skin allergy to the point were the impact on the individual's quality of life is negligible. This means that in the long term less medication is required, fewer possible side effects will occur, the expense to the dog's owner is less and the dog is comfortable enough to lead a full and happy life. The specific treatment and its specific dose which is required to achieve this state of being 'comfortably itchy' will differ from one individual to another. Finding the treatment and dose which will achieve this is often a matter of trial and error but is definitely worth it if one considers that without treatment the dog is living with the permanent sensation of sunburn.

The classic presentation of dogs with allergies is that of itchy feet and/or itchy ears and rears. Many dogs however simply seem itchy all over and will often scratch all over, roll on their backs and drag themselves along the ground on their bellies. Close inspection of their skins will often show that it is pinker than normal, drier than normal, has scaling/dandruff, thin hair growth, bald areas, areas with pimples or circular scaly lesions, or any combination of these. In these cases allergy may be the underlying problem but we would have to rule out three other major common categories of itching, viz. skin parasites, endocrine system problems and immune system disorders.

2 Skin infections and skin parasites

Many parasites may attack a dog's skin, some of these are opportunists and others are primary pathogens. Opportunist parasites are generally found as an additional component to the primary problem. The opportunist organism is not the cause of the problem but rather is a parasite which can only gain a foothold in the skin when the skin has already been disrupted by another condition. Consider a cut on yourself that may become infected. The bacteria, which generally cause the secondary infection in the cut, are the types of bacteria that are commonly found almost everywhere in the world. These bacteria are present all over our bodies but the body's defence system stops them from causing any problems and thus we don't even know that they are there. If the defences of the skin are breached by a cut, graze, burn inflammation etc then these opportunist bacteria can gain a foothold and multiply, thereby causing a problem. If the skin defences had not been breached then the body would have shrugged off the bacteria's attempts to infect the skin. A primary pathogen is a parasite that can inflict itself on our bodies despite the body's defence systems functioning normally. A good way to demonstrate this is to consider the flu virus which is a primary pathogen that can attack and infect a healthy person by overcoming their defence systems. The flu will sometimes develop complications like chest infections because the virus has caused enough disruption of the body's defence mechanisms to allow opportunist bacteria the opportunity to cause secondary infections. These opportunist bacteria would normally have been easily destroyed by the body's defence mechanisms if there had been no other problems present to weaken it. When skin parasites are identified on a dog's coat then we must decide whether they are primary pathogens or secondary opportunist parasites. The reason for this is that if the parasite is a primary pathogen then the treatment is directed solely at destroying the parasite. If the parasite is a secondary opportunist then we must destroy it and identify what the primary problem is that allowed the opportunist to gain a foothold. If we fail to do this then the secondary parasite will simply keep re-occurring. Let us consider primary skin parasites in sequence of increasing size of the parasites:

2a Bacterial skin infections

Bacteria are usually secondary parasites and thus when they are found to be causing lesions the primary underlying cause of their presence should be determined but there are instances where the bacteria can be the primary pathogen. The complicating factor here is that the lesions caused by primary or secondary bacterial infections appear the same. The lesions may be pimples, scaly skin, pink or red circular scaly lesions, multiple deep weeping small crater-like lesions or large areas of weeping, oozing skin. Any of these lesions caused by bacteria may or may not itch depending on the individual. The exact type of bacteria causing the problem, and the most appropriate antibiotic to eliminate the bacteria, can be determined by taking a swab from the lesion. These swabs are then sent to specialist laboratories that will run tests to determine the type of bacteria and which antibiotic will destroy it most efficiently.

Pimples are often seen in young dogs in the groin and on the belly and the condition is often referred to as impetigo. In these cases I would only treat the pimples if they were causing sufficient itching to make the young dog scratch the area and thereby aggravate the lesion. If there is no significant itching then I would leave the puppy to outgrow the problem just as adolescent humans outgrow acne. If the pimples are present in dogs older than about six months then I would suspect that the pimples are secondary to an allergic reaction and rather than treat this 'rash' or 'acne' problem, would try to identify and treat the underlying allergy problem. This can be done by determining the cause of the allergy and eliminating it or treating it. If the cause of the allergy is a food allergy, then one should change the food and if the pimples appear shortly after buying a new bed or blanket for the dog, then one might suspect that the reaction is an allergic or irritant reaction to the new bed or blanket and it should be removed. If it was the cause of the problem then the pimples will disappear without the need for any other action. An important step in assessing the pimples is to examine a smear made from one of the pimples because a third cause of pimples is a kind of skin mite called demodex canis which will be discussed in more detail later.

The most common lesion caused by bacterial infections in the skin is called pyoderma. There are two variations on this theme – superficial and deep pyoderma. The term pyoderma is in fact very non-specific. The first part of the word 'pyo' means simply that bacteria are involved and the second part of the word 'derma' means that the skin is the affected tissue. In the case of superficial pyoderma only the top layer of the skin is affected. In this instance the lesions produced are simply a scaly skin or pink to red circular scaly lesions. These circular lesions may be only a few millimetres in diameter or up to several centimetres in diameter. The lesions may or may not be itchy. These lesions may very rarely be a primary skin infection but most commonly are secondary lesions with skin allergy being the most common underlying factor. If the problem is not controlled quickly the lesions may expand very rapidly to affect large areas of skin. The treatment objective here is to stop the infection with antibiotics in severe cases and then also control the underlying problem by controlling or eliminating the allergy. If the problem is treated with only antibiotics then the lesions will disappear but when the antibiotics have finished they will reappear because the underlying, inciting problem has not been resolved. Other common underlying causes include endocrine problems like hypothyroidism and Cushing's disease which will be discussed later.

Deep pyoderma, as the name implies, is a bacterial infection penetrating deep into the skin. This has a very different appearance to superficial pyoderma. With deep skin infections the affected portion of skin is thickened and inflamed and may ooze pus. The pus can be made to appear by pressing or squeezing the skin and the affected skin may be painful to varying degrees. These cases all require antibiotics. The most commonly affected breeds are English bull terriers and Shar Peis. Any breed can be affected but breeds with short coats are affected far more commonly than breeds with long coats. The most commonly affected areas are the hocks (ankles), paws, cheeks, chins and the top of the tail base. In most of these cases no definite underlying cause can be found and we postulate that certain breeds are simply more susceptible to this condition because of their genetic make-up. The deep infections often require very long term antibiotics and are likely to be a recurrent problem. An attempt should be made however to identify an underlying cause. In the case of the paws being affected the underlying cause often includes a mite infection in the skin called demodex canis and if the mite is not eradicated at the same time as the bacteria then the bacterial infection is likely to recur.

German shepherd dogs may develop a condition loosely termed German shepherd pyoderma. This is a poorly understood condition seen almost exclusively in this breed characterised by many small, red-raw, crater like lesions which usually develop along the belly and in the groin. The entire body may be affected and varying degrees of itching and discomfort may be associated. The treatment for this condition may include antibiotics; steroid based anti-inflammatory drugs and various topical washes. The response to treatment varies a lot from one individual to another and the condition has a tendency to recur. This condition is thought to be due to a genetic problem in the breed.

The final type of bacterial skin infection most commonly seen is the inflamed, oozing patch of dermatitis common called the 'hot spot'. This has been discussed earlier in the section on allergy as it develops secondarily to dogs scratching and rubbing itchy areas. These lesions develop very quickly, sometimes virtually overnight, and can be very painful. The treatment is aimed at eliminating the infection and the cause of the itching with antibiotic and steroid based anti-inflammatory tablets and a variety of topical treatments. The exact combination of products used will depend on the severity of the symptoms.

2b Skin yeast infections
These are almost invariably secondary invaders which are seen most usually in dogs with skin allergies. The yeasts most commonly colonise the ear canals but can just as easily affect the entire

surface of the skin. The presence of the yeasts may or may not be associated with itching. They are often associated with a greasy feel to the skin or coat. The most commonly encountered yeast is called Mallassezia pachydermatitis and is diagnosed by examining samples taken from the skin with Sellotape under a microscope. The yeast is eliminated using appropriate shampoos or tablets but one must once again try to identify and treat the underlying cause of their presence which most commonly is found to be skin allergy.

2c Fungal skin infections

Fungi may infect the skin as primary invaders. The most common fungal skin infection is the inappropriately named ringworm. Two types of fungi called micosporum and trichophyton cause ringworm infections. ringworm infections are rare but one must be on the lookout for them because it can be spread to almost any animal including human beings. The classic appearance of the infection is a circular, reddish, scaly area of hair loss which may or may not itch. Sometimes only one such lesion is seen but more often many similar lesions appear at any site on the body. The infection does not always present as this classic circular lesion, it may produce almost any scaly, reddened area with or without hair loss or itching affecting any area of skin at any position on the body. The lesions caused by this infection may appear similar to any of the lesions associated with bacterial infections as discussed earlier. The diagnosis is made by testing hairs plucked painlessly from the skin. In my experience ringworm infections are very uncommon.

2d Skin mites

Skin mites are the largest microscopic skin invaders encountered in dogs. Three common types of skin mite may be found and all three are quite different. Demodex canis is a skin mite most commonly found on young dogs which causes demodectic mange (Fig. 9b). The mite burrows down into the deeper layers of the skin and is often associated with a simultaneous secondary bacterial infection which often produces pimples on the affected portion of skin. The demodex mite causes thickened areas of bald skin most commonly on the face, the flanks or tail base of young dogs. Any age dog may be affected similarly but in mature dogs the paws seem to be most commonly affected. Generally the affected skin is not very itchy but sometimes it can be if secondary bacterial invaders are present. The mite is not contagious. The diagnosis is made by microscopic examination of skin scrapings made painlessly from several sites on the skin. The mite is eradicated by using specially designed skin washes. Most of these washes are diluted in water and affected dogs are washed with the solution at weekly intervals until no mites can be found on repeated skin scrapings. Often several washes will be required. Some dogs, most commonly short-coated breeds like Staffordshire bull terriers, English bull terriers and Jack Russell terriers may be very difficult to cure. In these difficult cases the vet may often suggest using a product called Ivermectin. This is usually used for treating cattle but has been found to be affective against stubborn cases of demodex canis. The product can be used as an injectable agent or can be given orally; usually these cases will require long term treatment to achieve a cure. Some dogs affected by demodex skin mites may prove to be incurable. This is fortunately a rare occurrence and the reason for this is unknown. We currently postulate that these incurable individuals have a genetic weakness to the mites. This brings me to the next point viz. if the mite is not contagious how does it suddenly appear on a particular individual? The answer to this is not clear but we currently think that most dogs carry a few mites which are held in check by their skin's defence systems and that the mite is only able to cause full blown symptoms in individuals with a genetic weakness to the mite.

The next mite to consider is sarcoptes scabei, also known as scabies, sarcoptic mange or fox mange (Fig. 9c). This is a highly contagious skin mite which can also affect human beings. The typical lesions associated with this mite are severely itchy, reddened areas of hair loss affecting the ear edges, the elbows and the hocks. This is probably the itchiest skin condition that dogs can suffer from and affected individuals scratch and rub themselves incessantly. The lesions are not necessarily restricted to the areas mentioned above and many individuals will itch all over their bodies. The diagnosis is made by microscopic examination of skin scrapings taken from several sites. There are often not a great many mites on the body and thus mites may not be seen in the scrapings taken. The fact that no mites are seen does not necessarily confirm that there are none present. This is referred to as a false negative test result which means that although the test has shown that that individual has tested negative, the result may be false. This is because of the potential for 'sampling error'. Sampling error may occur because the sections of skin which are tested may not contain mites because often there may be very few mites spread sparsely over the body. Thus, if I find no mites in a dog which I strongly suspect has sarcoptic mange, I will often treat them for the condition anyway just to eliminate the possibility. The treatment may take the form of multiple special skin washes or spot-on liquid remedies.

The third type of skin mite is called cheyletiella which is sometimes called walking dandruff. This mite causes large flakes of dandruff over only small parts of the body or over the entire body. It may or may not be associated with itching. The diagnosis is made by microscopic examination of the dandruff and is treated with special skin washes. This mite most commonly affects puppies less than eight months old.

2e Fleas

The most common skin parasite is the flea which is easily visible to the naked eye (Fig. 9a). The fleas cause skin itching simply by the affect of biting the skin or because the bites cause an allergic reaction as discussed earlier. All dogs will suffer from fleas at some point in their lives. The flea has a four-stage life cycle consisting of the egg, the larva, the pupa and the adult stage. The stage we see on our pets is the adult stage. The adults live on blood which they suck from our pets and ourselves. The flea is black or brown in colour and is approximately two millimetres long. They move very quickly and can jump large distances. They move along the dogs' skin between the hairs over the entire body. The faeces of the fleas have the appearance of small black grains of sand in the dog's coat lying on the skin. Often we will be unable to see any live fleas on a dog but the presence of the black grains confirms the presence of fleas. The flea faeces are euphemistically called flea dirt. The flea faeces are composed primarily of undigested blood from their intestines. If one is uncertain whether the black sand-like grains in the dog's coat are flea faeces a simple test is to place them on a white piece of paper, wet them with a small drop of water and then smear them across the paper. If the grains are flea dirt/faeces they will smear red because the drop of water has softened the blood content of the grains. This confirms that fleas are present even if no live adult fleas can be seen. The best spot on the dog to check for flea dirt is at the base of the spine where it is attached

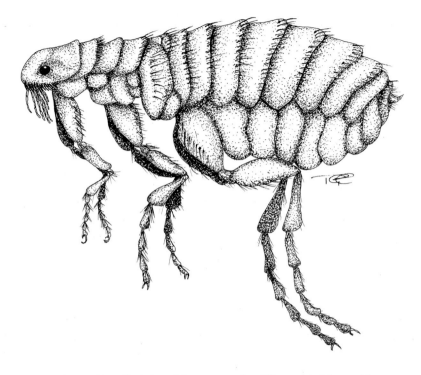

Fig 9a Magnified view of the common flea (*Ctenocephalides canis*).

Fig 9b Magnified view of a demodectic mite (*Demodex canis*).

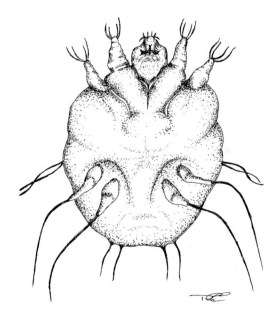

Fig 9c Magnified view of a sarcoptic mite (*Sarcoptes scabei*).

to the tail. Many flea remedies are available on the market but not all of them work equally well, this is because, over time, fleas will develop resistance to the active chemicals in these products and thus new chemicals are being produced all the time. Fortunately these new products are generally not only more efficient but they are also more environmentally friendly and safer for dogs and their owners. To successfully control fleas one must treat all the cats and dogs in the household and treat the house itself. This is because the products available generally only work on one or two of the stages in the flea's lifecycle. The products which we apply directly to dogs and cats work against the adult fleas and the products used to treat the house will work on one or more of the other stages.

3 Endocrine disorders causing skin disease

The third common category of conditions which may result in itchy skin are a variety of endocrine system problems which cause a number of abnormalities sometimes including skin disorders. These skin disorders are usually not itchy *per se* but may become so due to secondary bacterial skin invaders. The two most common conditions in this category are hypothyroidism and hyperadreno-cortisism (Cushing's disease) which will be discussed in more detail in later chapters.

3a Hypothyroidism (underactive thyroid glands)

Dogs have thyroid glands just like we do. The thyroids are glands normally situated on either side of the windpipe (trachea) just below the voice box (larynx). Normal thyroid glands in the dog are too small to feel.

To understand the symptoms in the next paragraph, we have to understand what the thyroid glands do. The thyroid glands in dogs, just like in human beings, control the basic metabolic rate of an individual. There is quite a big range in what is considered normal thyroid function and subconsciously we have all noticed this when out to dinner with friends. Some people eat mountains of food without gaining any weight and others gain weight very easily even though they may eat comparatively little. Think about these slim people who eat as much as they like and remain slim. They probably have a level of thyroid function which, although it is still in the normal range, will be at the high end of the scale. Other people we know may struggle to keep weight off despite eating very little because their thyroid function is probably at the low end of the range of normal. The thyroid hormone controls the basic rate that every cell is functioning at. Thus, every living cell in a dog with underactive thyroid function is functioning much more slowly than those of a normal dog. Thus they tend to gain weight despite a normal or decreased appetite because the cells are literally storing energy rather than burning it off. The obvious clinical effect is that these individuals are overweight.

The normal dog's heart rate in the consulting room, even when the dog is stressed by their visit to the vet, is usually between one hundred to one hundred and twenty beats per minute. Dogs with underactive thyroids (hypothyroidism) generally have heart rates below ninety beats per minute. These dogs are usually overweight despite not eating large amounts of food. They are lethargic at home and tend to do very little and sleep a lot. They will often want to spend most of their time in the warmest part of the room or house. Their skin may sometimes seem slightly 'thicker' than normal dog skin. Their hair overall may seem thinner than normal or they may have several bald patches over their body and the tail may be very bald. The skin in the bald areas may seem to be darker in colour than skin elsewhere in the body. These dogs are usually not itchy until opportunist bacteria or yeasts cause skin infections and/or nail bed infections. These bacteria and yeast are present everywhere in the environment but the normal skin's self-defence system stops them from causing any problems and thus we don't even know that they are there. If the defences of the skin are compromised by an underactive thyroid problem then these opportunist bacteria and yeast can gain a foothold and multiply, thereby causing a problem. If the thyroid function had been normal then the body would have shrugged off the bacteria's attempts to infect the skin.

The diagnosis of hypothyroidism is confirmed by performing blood tests and the treatment is usually lifelong thyroid supplementation tablets. The dose of the treatment is different in every individual and the vet will keep changing the dose until all the symptoms mentioned earlier are cured. In the first week or two of treatment the vet may also use treatments to eliminate the secondary bacterial and/or yeast infection. Thus, if a dog has an itchy skin due to secondary skin infections because of hypothyroidism, the problem will only be rectified if the dog is successfully treated for both hypothyroidism and the secondary skin infection. The treatment with thyroid tablets may take several weeks before we see an improvement in the condition of the skin and the coat. Once the treatment has started working we will notice that the dog will seem much more energetic and will start to lose the excess weight.

3b Hyperadrenocortisism (Cushing's disease/overactive adrenal glands)
Cushing's disease is discussed in chapter 4. Sufferers may develop secondary skin infections which cause them to have itchy skins in addition to all the other symptoms associated with this condition. Thus if a dog has an itchy skin due to secondary skin infections because of Cushing's disease, the problem will only be rectified if the dog is successfully treated for both Cushing's disease and the secondary skin infection.

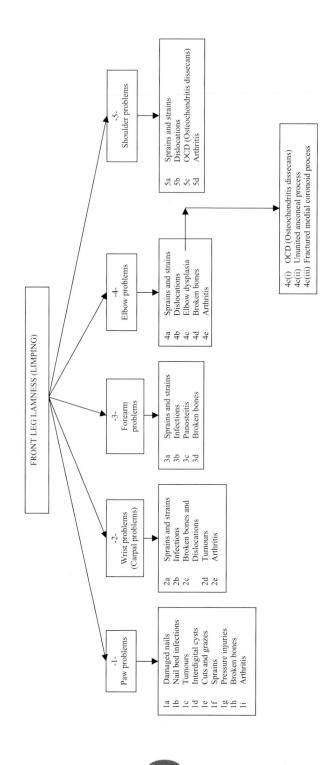

FRONT LEG LAMNESS (LIMPING)

-1-
Paw problems

1a   Damaged nails
1b   Nail bed infections
1c   Tumours
1d   Interdigital cysts
1e   Cuts and grazes
1f   Sprains
1g   Pressure injuries
1h   Broken bones
1i   Arthritis

-2-
Wrist problems
(Carpal problems)

2a   Sprains and strains
2b   Infections
2c   Broken bones and
     Dislocations
2d   Tumours
2e   Arthritis

-3-
Forearm
problems

3a   Sprains and strains
3b   Infections
3c   Panosteitis
3d   Broken bones

-4-
Elbow problems

4a   Sprains and strains
4b   Dislocations
4c   Elbow dysplasia
4d   Broken bones
4e   Arthritis

4c(i)   OCD (Osteochondritis dissecans)
4c(ii)   Ununited anconeal process
4c(iii)   Fractured medial coronoid process

-5-
Shoulder problems

5a   Sprains and strains
5b   Dislocations
5c   OCD (Osteochondritis dissecans)
5d   Arthritis

8

Front Leg Lameness (limping)

Dogs may limp on one or both of their front legs for many reasons. I examine lame dogs by examining the entire leg starting from the paw and working my way up to the top of the leg. I will discuss the problems that one might encounter as the cause of the lameness in this order. A very important part of the investigation of a lame dog is the information that you, the owner, are able to give the vet to describe the lameness. The questions the vet will ask may include the following:

- How long has the dog been lame?
- Did the lameness develop very suddenly or gradually?
- Has the lameness become more or less severe since it was first noticed or has it remained the same?
- Is the dog licking or biting at any part of the lame leg?
- Is the lameness most severe after exercise or after the dog has been resting/sleeping?
- Does the dog seem unwell in any other way besides the lameness?

These are very important questions and I ask my clients to answer them as accurately as possible and stress that if they do not know to say so because if they take a guess or tell me what they think I want to hear, it may mislead me. There is no shame in not knowing the answer to any or all of these questions. Not being able to answer the questions does not imply that you are not concerned about your dog.

Many owners will have examined their dog themselves before consulting a vet and I encourage people to do so. The anatomy of the dog's leg has the same components as our own arms and hands and one should think about them as functioning much the same as our own. The bones, joints, tendons, muscles and ligaments are virtually identical to our own. The two big differences are that dogs do not have collarbones and they walk on the tips of their toes not on the palms of their hands as we do when we are on our hands and knees. A good tip is to compare what you think may be abnormal to the same area on the other front leg.

1 Paw problems

Examine the paw by looking at the nails, the toes, the pads and the spaces between the pads. What we are looking for are areas of inflammation, bleeding, swelling and bruising. The next step is to part the fur at the base of each toenail and examine the nail beds. Each toe is then carefully felt to check for pain, swelling, heat or abnormal movement. Each toe consists of three bones (phalanges) just as our fingers do and each individual joint must be checked for normal movement. The spaces between the pads should also be carefully felt to check for the same things. The same visual and manual examination is then continued up the bones (metacarpal bones) leading to the wrist (carpus).

The most common problems encountered when examining the paws are:

1a Broken or torn nails
These are treated by removing the broken part of the nail and the vet may prescribe antibiotics, painkillers and footbaths as necessary.

1b Nail bed infections (paronychia)
The nail bed is the groove between the nail and the skin and infections may arise in this groove. The infection may be caused by bacteria, fungal infections or skin mites (most commonly demodex mites). One would suspect an infection in the nail bed if the nail feels very loose or if there is a discharge from the nail bed. The discharge which may develop has the appearance of a watery or pussy infection and may or may not have a foul odour. Once the vet has determined what kind of parasite has caused the infection they will prescribe appropriate treatment. The important question to ask in cases of nail bed infections is 'what has allowed the infection to develop?' The answer may be simply that a cut or graze in that area has become infected and the infection has moved into the nail bed. If a number of toes have the same infection we should ask ourselves why the body has not been able to fight off the infection. The explanation may be that the dog has diabetes and the high blood sugar levels has resulted in a high sugar content in the moisture in the nail bed and this has favoured the development of an infection. Other disease conditions which may compromise the body's ability to fight off infections are Cushing's disease and hypothyroidism.

1c Tumours
In larger breeds of dogs a possible underlying cause for an infection in a single nail bed may be a tumour growing in the nail bed. Several types of tumour may develop in the nail bed and most often the tumour is not easily seen initially and the first sign of a problem in the nail bed is a secondary infection. If the vet suspects that the infection is the result of a tumour they will often investigate further by taking X-rays and biopsies from the affected toe. Most nail bed tumours are not cancerous and the vet will most commonly advise eliminating the infection first and then amputating the affected toe to remove the tumour. This seems a very extreme way of treating the problem but fortunately dogs do not seem to miss the removed toe at all and function perfectly normally without it.

1d Interdigital cysts
Cysts may develop very suddenly between any two toes on any foot. These cysts usually look like rounded, red, swollen, shiny lumps between the toes. The dog will usually continuously lick the cyst

and thus the hair on the paw is constantly wet with their saliva. These cysts are often very painful and many dogs will be reluctant to let you examine the paw. Interdigital cysts may develop for a variety of reasons. The cyst may develop after the skin between the toes has been punctured by a thorn, a grass seed, a splinter etc. In these cases the cyst will progressively enlarge and eventually one or more holes will appear in the cyst and either pus or a blood-tinged clear fluid will ooze out of the cyst. The dilemma for the vet when examining these cases is deciding whether or not the object that punctured the skin is still lodged in the paw. I usually treat these cases with antibiotics for a few days and suggest that the paw is soaked in a warm salt-water solution for a few minutes twice a day. If the cyst heals then that is the end of the problem. If the cyst does not heal within a few days then one would be suspicious that the object that punctured the skin may still be lodged in the paw. In these cases the vet will suggest surgery to try to find and remove the grass seed, thorn, splinter etc. The second most common cause of interdigital cysts is reaction around the base of the hair follicles between the toes. The hairs on the skin each grow from a structure called a hair follicle. One can imagine the hair follicle as being like a vase and the hair is the flower stem in the vase. The vase holds the flower stem in position and feeds the flower in the same way that the follicle holds and feeds the hair. If the hair follicle becomes damaged for any reason then the hair root may puncture the hair follicle. If the hair follicle is punctured or if the hair shaft sticks through the hair follicle, the body will respond to the problem in the same way that it responds to puncture wounds by thorns. The body's reaction will thus cause the same type of cyst as seen in cases of puncture wounds by grass seeds and thorns. These interdigital cysts will usually resolve within a few days of treatment with antibiotics and painkillers. It is only very rarely necessary to surgically remove this type of interdigital cyst.

1e Cuts, grazes and puncture wounds from glass and thorns
These may be treated by stitching, bandaging, removing the glass or thorns and antibiotics and painkillers as necessary.

1f Swelling and bruising from sprains
These are treated with painkillers/anti-inflammatories, support bandages and rest from exercise as necessary.

1g Pressure injuries
Swelling from pressure injuries like someone stepping on the paw or objects dropped onto the paw. These are treated with painkillers and rest from exercise as necessary.

1h Broken bones
Severe painful swelling of one or more toes may suggest that one of the bones has been broken. Broken toe bones are most common in dogs older than one year old because puppies have very flexible, soft bones which tend to bend rather than break when the paw is injured. X-rays are sometimes required to confirm that a bone has been broken. If any bones are broken then the fracture is treated either with casts and bandages or through surgical repair as necessary.

1i Arthritis in the joints of the toes

Dogs with arthritis in their toes look just like people do when they have arthritis in their fingers and toes. The knuckles (the joints between the bones of the fingers or toes) are hard, enlarged and thickened and generally are not painful when gently squeezed. When the joints are moved around during the examination of the toes one may notice that they do not move as freely as the toes without joint thickening and the dogs may show some degree of pain when the joints are moved around. Often only the toes on the inside or outside edge of the paws are affected and the reason for this is that some dogs, just like people, do not walk squarely on the feet but carry more weight on either the inside or the outside of their feet. People who walk like this will often have special insoles in the shoes to correct this very subtle problem. If people do not correct they way the walk they too will develop arthritis in the inside or outside toes of their feet, in these cases we call the thickening of the toe joint a bunion. Please refer to the paragraph at the end of this chapter for a discussion on arthritis and appropriate treatment.

2 The wrist (carpus)

This is also examined with your eyes and hands. The wrist is a complicated joint composed of the arm bones at the top and the metacarpal bones at the bottom. The wrist bones consist of seven individual bones arranged in two rows between the arm bones and the metacarpal bones. All of these bones are held together by many small ligaments and joint capsules. Start by looking at the wrist and comparing it to the wrist on the other leg. Look for swelling, bruising and wounds. When feeling the wrist one should bend (flex) and straighten (extend) the wrist to check for signs of pain. The wrist should also be bent gently to the left and right.

   The most common problems encountered when examining the wrist are:

2a Sprains and strains which cause pain and swelling

These are treated with rest from exercise, support bandages and anti-inflammatories/painkillers as necessary.

2b Infection in and around the joint which also cause pain and swelling

These are treated with rest from exercise, antibiotics and anti-inflammatories/painkillers as necessary.

2c Broken bones and dislocations

Severe painful swelling of the wrist may suggest that one or more of the bones or ligaments of the joint have been broken or dislocated. Broken wrist bones and dislocation are most common in dogs older than one year old. Broken hock bones and joint dislocations are uncommon in very young puppies as they have very flexible, soft bones which tend to bend rather than break when the hock is injured. X-rays are generally required to confirm that a bone has been broken or ligaments have been ruptured. If any bones are broken then the fracture is treated either with casts and bandages or through surgical repair as necessary. If ligaments have been ruptured or parts of the wrist are dislocated then they are treated either with casts or surgical repair depending on which ligaments have been damaged and how severely they have been damaged.

2d Tumours

Severe painful swelling of the wrist may also suggest tumours developing in the bones of the wrist. X-rays and biopsies are generally required to confirm the presence of tumours. Most tumours affecting this area are highly malignant cancers and the treatment options will often involve amputation of the leg and chemotherapy. Fortunately these tumours are the least common cause of pain and lameness in this area. Middle age and old dogs are more commonly affected by tumours than young dogs.

2e Arthritis

This may cause thickening of the whole joint or part of the joint. The thickened joint is usually firm to the touch and not painful when touched. The joint will seem thicker than the same joint on the other leg. The joint may be painful when you bend or straighten the joint and it may produce a 'crunchy' sensation when it is bent and straightened. X-rays will usually be taken of the joint to confirm the diagnosis. Please refer to the paragraph at the end of this chapter for a discussion on arthritis and appropriate treatment.

3 The forearm

This is also examined with your eyes and hands. The forearm has two long bones called the radius and ulna. These bones can be felt extending from the wrist to the elbow joint. One should check for pain and swelling when applying pressure to the bones and the surrounding muscles. The most common problems encountered when examining the forearm are:

3a Sprains and strains which cause pain and swelling
These are treated with rest from exercise, and anti-inflammatories/painkillers as necessary.

3b Infection or inflammation in and around the muscles which also cause pain and swelling
These are treated with rest from exercise, antibiotics and anti-inflammatories/painkillers as necessary.

3c Panosteitis
This causes pain and inflammation in the bones. Panosteitis is one of the conditions that our grandparents vaguely referred to as 'growing pains'. The condition is most commonly found in rapidly growing young dogs and causes inflammation and pain in bones which in turn causes lameness. The condition most commonly presents as a 'shifting lameness'. This means that it causes pain and lameness in one leg for a short while then that leg recovers and another leg becomes affected and the dog is then lame on that leg for a while. This shifting lameness may keep moving from one leg to another over a period of several weeks to several months. The condition is caused by inflammation in any of the long bones in any leg. The vet would become suspicious that panosteitis is the cause of the lameness if the lameness keeps shifting from one leg to another and if the dog shows pain when firm pressure is applied to the affected bone during the examination. The only way to confirm

the diagnosis is to take an X-ray of the affected bone. Dogs will eventually outgrow the problem and it will simply go away when they have finished growing. If the pain is severe the vet may prescribe short courses of anti-inflammatories. This is the only instance when I would use simple aspirin to control the pain rather than more modern anti-inflammatories. The vet will advise you on how much aspirin to use and for how long.

3d Broken bones

Severe, painful swelling of the forearm may suggest that one or both forearms have been broken. Broken bones in the forearm are uncommon in very young puppies as they have very flexible, soft bones which tend to bend rather than break when the wrist is injured. X-rays are often required to confirm that a bone has been broken and most fractures that do occur in the long bones in young dogs are found to be 'greenstick fractures'. A 'greenstick fracture' is exactly what the name implies. If you bend a dry stick or branch it tends to snap in half but if you bend a green stick or branch it tends to splinter only on one side and the stick does not break into two pieces. The same thing happens in the bones of young growing dogs because, like a green stick/branch, they are softer and more 'bendy' than a dried stick which is more like a mature bone. If any bones are broken then the fracture is treated either with casts and bandages or through surgical repair as necessary.

4 Elbow problems

The anatomical design of the elbow joint in cats and dogs is the same as our own human elbow (Figs 10a and 10b). The basic structure of the elbow is a hinge joint. The bone of the upper arm (humerus) is at the top and the forearm bones (the radius and the ulna) are at the bottom. The joint between these bones is composed of the ends of these bones, the joint capsule and the collateral ligaments on either side.

The ends of the bones forming moving joints are covered with a layer of cartilage called articular or joint cartilage. This cartilage is very smooth and is essential for smooth movement of the joint. This joint cartilage has very few nerve cells supplying it and this relatively nerve-free layer is essential in covering the bone ends which have a good nerve supply. The best way to understand this concept is to consider the forces acting on the ends of the bones when they are bearing weight during walking or standing. When we walk or stand our entire body weight is pressing down on our joints, the reason that this does not cause pain is the layer of numb cartilage covering the ends of the bones (the articular cartilage). If we did not have this layer of articular cartilage then the ends of the bones would be pressed together by our body weight and as the bone ends have a good nerve supply this would cause severe pain. Even small areas of damage to this articular cartilage allow small areas of bone to be exposed and pressure on this exposed bone causes pain. These bone ends are held together by the joint capsule which effectively forms a sealed bag around the bone ends. The purpose of the joint capsule is not only to hold the ends of the bones forming the joint together but also to produce joint fluid, which fills the joint. The joint fluid in turn has two main purposes namely to serve as lubrication for the joint in the same way that oil lubricates a door hinge and secondly to carry nutrients to feed and maintain the articular cartilages and other structures inside the joint. This joint fluid is called synovial fluid and is produced by the synovial membrane, which is the inside layer of the joint capsule. To my knowledge there are no man-made lubricants for machinery, which are as efficient as synovial fluid in terms of lubricating moving parts.

On either side of the elbow we find ligaments called collateral ligaments. The ligament on the inner aspect of the joint is called the medial collateral ligament and the one on the outer aspect is called the lateral collateral ligament. These ligaments run from the humerus (the bone of the upper arm) to the radius and ulna (the bones of the forearm) and allow the elbow to bend in one plane only viz. the elbow can only bend (flex) or straighten (extend). Consider your own elbow, it can only bend and straighten. The reason that it cannot bend sideways so that that the outer surface of the wrist touches the outer surface of the shoulder is that the collateral ligaments do not allow this movement. The elbow functions in only one plane in much the same way as a door hinge. These collateral ligaments are found on the outside surface of the joint capsule.

The elbow is a very tightly fitting and complicated joint. The anatomy of the elbow joint in dogs is exactly the same as our own elbow joints. It is a very tightly fitting joint and thus even 'minor' problems that may cause little or no pain in a loose joint like the shoulder, are liable to cause significant pain and lameness in the elbow joint. The most common problems encountered when examining the elbow are:

4a Sprains and strains which cause pain and swelling
These are treated with rest from exercise, support bandages and anti-inflammatories/painkillers as necessary.

4b Dislocations
These are very uncommon because it is such a tightly fitting joint. If the elbow has been dislocated the dog will have to have a general anaesthetic to put the elbow back into its normal position. This is because it is very painful to relieve the dislocation but fortunately it can usually be done by manipulation only, without the need for surgery. Surgery however may be required if the elbow does not remain in position after the dislocation has been reduced. The object of this surgery will be to repair the torn ligaments which help to hold the bones in the correct position.

4c Elbow dysplasia
There are three conditions which may affect the elbow joint which are collectively grouped together and called elbow dysplasia. The word dysplasia simply means 'not properly formed or developed'. This implies that during the growing process some parts of the elbow joint have not developed normally to produce a perfect joint. This failure to grow and develop perfectly is due to genetic problems that may be passed from parents to their offspring and also because of environmental factors such as growing too quickly and putting too much force through the growing/developing joint during play and exercise. Dogs who are genetically programmed to have less than perfectly formed elbow joints may well pass this characteristic onto their puppies. The fact that part of the problem is genetic has led to schemes whereby we advise people to have dogs' elbows X-rayed prior to breeding.

The three conditions which we may encounter as the cause of a front leg lameness in a young dog are called osteochondritis dissecans, ununited anconeal processes and fractured medial coronoid processes. If any of these conditions is encountered in the elbow of a dog then the other elbow should also be examined and X-rayed even if it is not causing lameness. This is because these conditions often affect both elbows even though only one leg may be affected to the point of being lame.

4c(i) Osteochondritis dissecans

The ends of the bones which form the elbow joint are covered with a layer of joint cartilage for the reasons discussed earlier in this chapter. This layer of joint cartilage grows with the bones as the dog grows larger. If the dog grows very quickly then the cartilage will have to grow and develop very quickly to match the growth of the bones. The cartilage needs a good blood supply to grow normally and sometimes the cartilage is developing faster than the blood vessels that feed it. If this happens then there may be areas of cartilage which have an inadequate blood supply and the newly formed cartilage is starved of nutrients and oxygen. The result of this is that the undernourished piece of cartilage becomes brittle and may peel off from the rest of the cartilage layer (Fig. 10b). This is the same principle seen in dry or sunburnt skin which may start to peel off the underlying skin. If a piece of cartilage starts to peel away from the end of the bone then the nerves in the underlying bone are exposed and the dog may experience pain when walking. The loose flap of cartilage also causes pain as it exerts pressure points in the joint in the same way as a small pebble in your shoe may cause pain when walking. This flap of cartilage may even tear off the end of the bone and float around the joint causing pain like the pebble in a shoe. If this happens the free floating piece of cartilage is called a joint mouse. In severe cases more than one such tear may develop and thus more than one joint mouse may be identified when the diagnosis is made. This diagnosis should be suspected in any young, rapidly growing dog which has front leg lameness due to pain in the elbow joint. The diagnosis is confirmed by taking X-rays of the joint. The other elbow must always be X-rayed at the same time even if it seems normal because the condition often develops in both elbows even though only one may be painful at a given time. The treatment for this condition depends on the dog's age, how long the lesion has been present and how severe the lesion is.

The surgical treatment for this condition involves opening the affected joint and removing the flap of cartilage. This will leave a small crater-like lesion in the joint cartilage. The edges of this crater are scraped away until the edges bleed slightly. This is done because all the cartilage which has an inadequate blood supply must be removed as it will be unable to heal without a good blood supply. Once the edges have been scraped away leaving only healthy cartilage the joint is sutured closed and the dog must rest for a few weeks while new cartilage grows into the crater. During this period of rest the dogs should have light, controlled exercise to keep the joint mobile and supple. Some dogs will develop some degree of arthritis in the elbow despite prompt effective surgery. This arthritis may develop despite the skill of the surgeon and may also worsen as time goes by. The obvious question to ask in the face of this information is why do we bother to repair the problem if arthritis may develop anyway? The answer is that the repair is done as a damage limitation exercise. The sooner the elbow is operated on, the less severely and the less rapidly the arthritis may develop. The object of the surgery is, at best, to avoid future arthritis and at worst, to restrict the potential for arthritis to the point were it is so limited that although one can demonstrate its presence on X-rays, it will not be sufficient to cause lameness after the dog has recovered from the surgery. The arthritis may take weeks, months or years to develop and may vary from insignificant

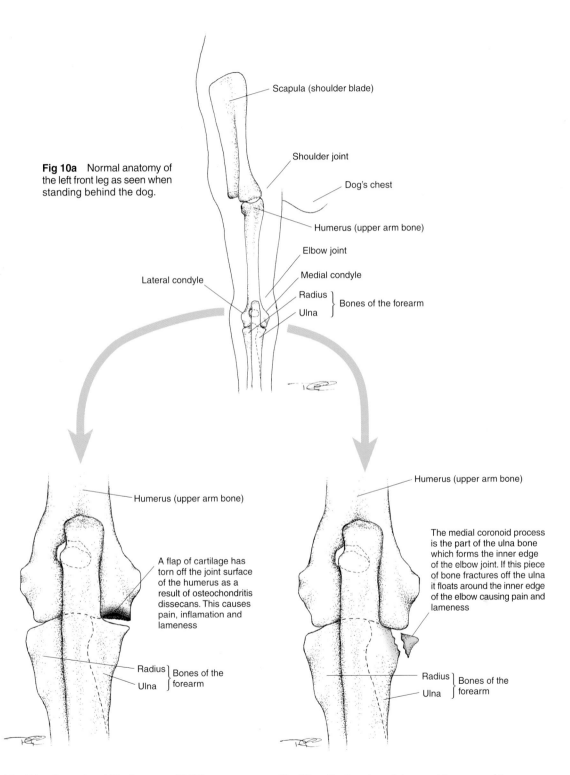

Fig 10a Normal anatomy of the left front leg as seen when standing behind the dog.

Scapula (shoulder blade)

Shoulder joint

Dog's chest

Humerus (upper arm bone)

Elbow joint

Medial condyle

Lateral condyle

Radius ⎫
Ulna ⎭ Bones of the forearm

Humerus (upper arm bone)

A flap of cartilage has torn off the joint surface of the humerus as a result of osteochondritis dissecans. This causes pain, inflamation and lameness

Radius ⎫ Bones of the
Ulna ⎭ forearm

Humerus (upper arm bone)

The medial coronoid process is the part of the ulna bone which forms the inner edge of the elbow joint. If this piece of bone fractures off the ulna it floats around the inner edge of the elbow causing pain and lameness

Radius ⎫ Bones of the
Ulna ⎭ forearm

Fig 10b Osteochondritis dissecans (OCD) of the elbow joint.

Fig 10c Fractured medial coronoid process of the elbow joint.

to severe, in which case long term painkillers and mobility supplements (glucosamine and chondroitin sulphate) will be required to ensure comfortable pain-free movement. The object of the surgery is to prevent the development of arthritis or at the very least to minimise the severity of the possible subsequent arthritis.

Surgical treatment of this condition is not necessarily appropriate for all dogs. In some cases the diagnosis is only made after arthritis has already started developing and if it is already very severe then the dog will not benefit significantly from the surgery. In cases where the cartilage flap is very small some surgeons will advise that surgery will not improve the lameness and the surgery may make it worse. In the cases where surgery is not appropriate for one reason or another the best course of action will be long term painkillers as and when the dog needs them and I would always recommend long term glucosamine and/or chondroitin sulphate therapy. These are agents which help the joint to produce synovial fluid to maintain its lubrication and to promote natural healing and continued health of the eroded articular cartilages covering the bone ends. This is an important component of the treatment as these erosions expose the nerve endings in the bone which cause a lot of the pain and if we can repair these areas the patient will obviously require a lower daily dose of painkillers/anti inflammatories.

A change in lifestyle also benefits these patients in that overweight individuals should lose weight to take the extra strain off the joints and gentle controlled exercise should be encouraged to maintain the size and strength of the muscles of the affected leg as they help to support the joints.

4c(ii) Ununited anconeal process

The anconeal process is a cone-shaped piece of bone which projects from the ulna into a groove in the humerus. Bones grow from cartilage growth plates at either end of the bone, when the bones have grown to their adult length then these growth plates turn to bone and all the parts of the bone thus fuse into a single structure. Some bones have special bony projections which serve special functions like the anconeal process which slots into a groove in the humerus to provide the elbow joint with extra strength and stability. While young dogs are still growing the anconeal process has its own growth plate which is simply a strip of cartilage which attaches it to the rest of the ulna. When the dog has finished growing this cartilage growth plate turns to bone and the anconeal process and the rest of the ulna fuse together to form a single rigid unit. The anconeal growth pale usually fuses when the dog is about twenty weeks old before most of the other growth plates of the body. In some dogs this process fails to happen and the anconeal process fails to fuse rigidly with the ulna (Fig. 11c). The only thing holding these two parts of bone together is the cartilage layer that was the growth plate. The result of this is that the anconeal process is not rigidly adhered to the rest of the bone and thus moves a fraction of a millimetre when the elbow is moved. This minute instability causes irritation in the elbow joint and this produces inflammation and ultimately arthritis will develop. This diagnosis should be suspected in any young, rapidly growing dog which has a front leg lameness due to pain in the elbow joint. The diagnosis is confirmed by taking X-rays of the joint. The other elbow must always be X-rayed at the same time even if it seems normal because the condition often develops in both elbows even though only one may be painful at a given time. The treatment for this condition depends on the dog's age, how long the lesion has been present and how severe the lesion is.

The surgical treatment is a choice between fusing the two pieces of bone with bone screws or removing the unfused anconeal process. The choice of operation is determined by the size of the anconeal process and the amount of arthritis which has already developed in the joint at the time of the diagnosis. After the surgery the dog must be rested for six weeks. During this period of rest the dog should have light, controlled exercise to keep the joint mobile and supple. Some dogs will develop a degree of arthritis in the elbow despite prompt effective surgery. This arthritis may develop despite the skill of the surgeon and may also worsen as time goes by. The obvious question to ask in the face of this information is why do we bother to repair the problem if arthritis may develop anyway? The answer is that the repair is done as a damage limitation exercise. The sooner the elbow is operated on, the less severely and the less rapidly the arthritis may develop. The object of the surgery is, at best, to avoid future arthritis and at worst, to restrict the potential for arthritis to the point were it is so limited that although one can demonstrate its presence on X-rays, it will not be sufficient to cause lameness after the dog has recovered from the surgery. The arthritis may take weeks, months or years to develop and may vary from insignificant to severe, in which case long term painkillers and mobility supplements (glucosamine and chondroitin sulphate) will be required to ensure comfortable pain-free movement. The object of the surgery is to prevent the development of arthritis or at the very least to minimise the severity of the possible subsequent arthritis.

Surgical treatment of this condition is not necessarily appropriate for all dogs. In some cases the diagnosis is only made after arthritis has already started developing and if it is already very severe then the dog will not benefit significantly from the surgery. In cases where the anconeal process instability is very minor some surgeons will advise that surgery will not improve the lameness and the surgery may make it worse. In the cases where surgery is not appropriate for one reason or another the best course of action will be long term painkillers as and when the dog needs them and I would always recommend long term glucosamine and/or chondroitin sulphate therapy. These are agents which help the joint to produce synovial fluid to maintain its lubrication and to promote natural healing and continued health of the articular cartilages covering the bone ends. This is an important component of the treatment as it means that the patient will require a lower daily dose of painkillers/anti inflammatories.

A change in lifestyle also benefits these patients in that overweight individuals should lose weight to take the extra strain off the joints and gentle controlled exercise should be encouraged to maintain the size and strength of the muscles of the affected leg as they help to support the joints.

4c(iii) Fractured medial coronoid process.

The medial coronoid process is a small piece of bone on the inside (medial) edge of the ulna which forms the inner (medial) portion of the elbow joint. This is a very small piece of bone and it may snap off the ulna when sufficient forces are exerted on it. The small chip of bone usually does not move more than one or two millimetres from the fracture site but it fails to grow back onto the ulna and remains unstable (Fig. 10c). This minute instability causes irritation in the elbow joint and this produces inflammation and ultimately arthritis will develop. This diagnosis should be suspected in any young, rapidly growing dog which has a front leg lameness due to pain in the elbow joint. The diagnosis is confirmed by taking X-rays of the joint. The other elbow must always be X-rayed at the same time even if it seems normal because the condition often develops in both elbows even though only one may be painful at a given time. The treatment for this condition depends on the dog's age, how long the lesion has been present and how severe the lesion is.

The surgical approach to this problem is to reattach the small chip of bone if it is big enough to do so and if not to remove it. After the surgery the dog must be rested for six weeks. During this period of rest the dogs should have light, controlled exercise to keep the joint mobile and supple. Some dogs will develop some degree of arthritis in the elbow despite prompt effective surgery. This arthritis may develop despite the skill of the surgeon and may also worsen as time goes by. The obvious question to ask in the face of this information is why do we bother to repair the problem if arthritis may develop anyway? The answer is that the repair is done as a damage limitation exercise. The sooner the elbow is operated on, the less severely and the less rapidly the arthritis may develop. The object of the surgery is, at best, to avoid future arthritis and at worst, to restrict the potential for arthritis to the point were it is so limited that although one can demonstrate its presence on X-rays, it will not be sufficient to cause lameness after the dog has recovered from the surgery. The arthritis may take weeks, months or years to develop and may vary from insignificant to severe, in which case long term painkillers and mobility supplements (glucosamine and chondroitin sulphate) will be required to ensure comfortable pain-free movement. The object of the surgery is to prevent the development of arthritis or at the very least to minimise the severity of the possible subsequent arthritis.

Surgical treatment of this condition is not necessarily appropriate for all dogs. In some cases the diagnosis is only made after arthritis has already started developing and if it is already very severe then the dog will not benefit significantly from the surgery. In cases where the anconeal process instability is very minor some surgeons will advise that surgery will not improve the lameness and the surgery may make it worse. In the cases where surgery is not appropriate for one reason or another the best course of action will be long term painkillers as and when the dog needs them and I would always recommend long term glucosamine and/or chondroitin sulphate therapy. These are agents which help the joint to produce synovial fluid to maintain its lubrication and to promote natural healing and continued health of the articular cartilages covering the bone ends. This is an important component of the treatment as it means that the patient will require a lower daily dose of painkillers/anti inflammatories.

A change in lifestyle also benefits these patients in that overweight individuals should lose weight to take the extra strain off the joints and gentle controlled exercise should be encouraged to maintain the size and strength of the muscles of the affected leg as they help to support the joints.

4d Broken bones

Fractures of the bones forming the elbow are fortunately not very common. Fractured elbow bones are most commonly diagnosed in spaniels as they may have genetic weaknesses regarding the normal development of the lower part of the humerus (upper arm bone). This bone forms two condyles which form the upper part of the elbow (Fig. 10a). In the young growing dog these two condyles are held together by a growth plate which is simply a strip of cartilage from which the bone grows. This growth plate turns to bone when the dog has grown to their full size and thus the two condyles are rigidly fused together. In some individuals, especially spaniels, this fusion is not as

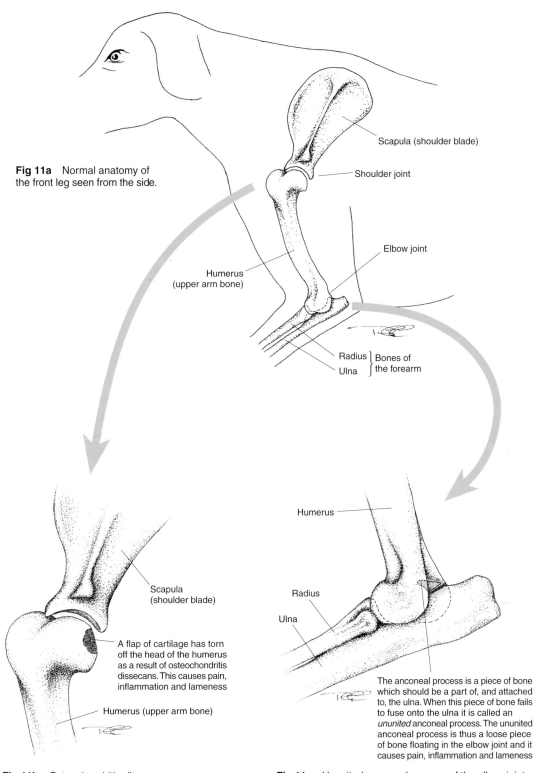

Fig 11a Normal anatomy of the front leg seen from the side.

Scapula (shoulder blade)

Shoulder joint

Elbow joint

Humerus (upper arm bone)

Radius ⎫
Ulna ⎬ Bones of the forearm

Scapula (shoulder blade)

A flap of cartilage has torn off the head of the humerus as a result of osteochondritis dissecans. This causes pain, inflammation and lameness

Humerus (upper arm bone)

Fig 11b Osteochondritis dissecans (OCD) of the shoulder joint.

Humerus

Radius

Ulna

The anconeal process is a piece of bone which should be a part of, and attached to, the ulna. When this piece of bone fails to fuse onto the ulna it is called an *ununited* anconeal process. The ununited anconeal process is thus a loose piece of bone floating in the elbow joint and it causes pain, inflammation and lameness

Fig 11c Ununited anconeal process of the elbow joint.

strong as it should be and a fracture may occur at this point. This fracture should be repaired as soon as possible and as accurately as possible to ensure a smooth joint surface. The repair may involve bone screws, pins and bone plates. After the surgery the dog must be rested for six weeks. During this period of rest the dogs should have light, controlled exercise to keep the joint mobile and supple.

4e Arthritis

Arthritis may cause thickening of the whole joint or part of the joint. The thickened joint is usually firm to the touch and not painful when touched. The joint will seem thicker than the same joint on the other leg. The joint may be painful when you bend or straighten the joint and it may produce a 'crunchy' sensation when it is bent and straightened. X-rays will usually be taken of the joint to confirm the diagnosis. Please refer to the paragraph at the end of this chapter for a discussion on arthritis and appropriate treatment.

5 Shoulder problems

5a Sprains and strains which cause pain and swelling

These are treated with rest from exercise and anti-inflammatories/painkillers as necessary.

5b Dislocations of the shoulder

These are very uncommon. If the shoulder has been dislocated the dog will have to have a general anaesthetic to put the shoulder back into its normal position. This is because it is very painful to relive the dislocation but fortunately it can usually be done by manipulation only, without the need for surgery. Surgery however may be required if the shoulder does not remain in position after the dislocation has been reduced. The object of this surgery will be to repair the torn ligaments which help to hold the bones in the correct position.

5c OCD

The shoulder joint may develop osteochondritis dissecans (OCD) as discussed in the section on the elbow. If osteochondritis dissecans is diagnosed in the shoulder, the principles and treatment are exactly the same as described in the elbow with the difference that subsequent arthritis is very unlikely (Fig. 11b).

5d Arthritis

Arthritis may cause thickening of the whole joint or part of the joint. The thickened joint is usually firm to the touch and not painful when touched. The joint will seem thicker than the same joint on the other leg. The joint may be painful when you bend or straighten the joint and it may produce a 'crunchy' sensation when it is bent and straightened. X-rays will usually be taken of the joint to confirm the diagnosis.

Arthritis

The word arthritis means inflammation of a joint. The arthritis may be acute (developed very suddenly) or chronic (developed over a long period of time). Factors that cause acute arthritis may develop into chronic arthritis. Arthritis may develop after a joint has been injured or infected. The types of injuries which may cause acute or chronic arthritis are sprains, fractures, dislocations etc. Injuries to joints should thus be treated as quickly and efficiently as possible to try to prevent long term permanent arthritis from developing in that joint. We are all familiar with the concept of someone injuring a joint and then either having permanent low grade discomfort in that joint, or the injury may have seemed to heal well but as we get older the joint may cause us discomfort due to the delayed onset of arthritis. Arthritis may also develop in a joint which is not anatomically perfectly formed i.e. it is dysplastic. Dysplasia is the technical description for a joint which is not perfectly formed. Most people are familiar with the term hip dysplasia which means that the hips are not properly formed but any joint may suffer from dysplasia. If a joint is dysplastic then it will wear out faster than a normally formed joint. This process of wearing out causes arthritis. Arthritis may also develop simply due to normal 'wear and tear' in a normal joint due to old age.

Chronic arthritis is most commonly encountered in older dogs or dogs who have suffered from an injury or infection affecting one or more joints. The process of chronic arthritis is often referred to as degenerative joint disease (DJD). Chronic arthritis causes thickening of the tissues around the joint. This thickening is caused by 'scar tissue' forming around the joint. The bones forming the joint will develop irregular thickenings called osteophytes. The lining of the joint will be permanently inflamed and thickened. These three changes represent the body's attempt to heal and strengthen the affected joint and often make the arthritis worse as they will continue permanently and lead to the pain of the arthritis becoming progressively worse. The second effect of these three processes is that the joint will lose its full range of movement. This happens because the 'scar tissue' laid down around the joint will make it less flexible, and thus the joint is less able to perform its full range of movements.

Once the three processes of chronic arthritis have been present for a few months or years the affected joint will feel thicker than the same joint on the other leg. When a joint with chronic arthritis is flexed and extended one will notice that it may not be able to bend or straighten as much as a healthy joint does. During bending and straightening one may also notice a 'crunchy' sound or feeling in the joint. This 'crunchy' sensation is called crepitus. Once the process of chronic arthritis has started, the changes in the joint are irreversible. The changes in fact will become more severe as time goes on. This process of arthritis is identical to the process of arthritis in human beings.

When the vet is faced with an arthritic joint the treatment they apply will have three objectives i.e.:

- Relieve the pain and inflammation in the joint.
- Slow down the ongoing changes which worsen the arthritis over time.
- Improve the range of movement of the joint.

The vet will achieve this by using painkillers and anti-inflammatories to make the joint more comfortable. They may also recommend the use of medications called 'mobility supplements' and may recommend a physiotherapy programme to maintain a good range of joint movement and to slow down the rate of worsening arthritis.

The first step is to find a suitable long-term anti-inflammatory drug that will alleviate the pain in the joint. Most anti-inflammatory medications are synthetic (man-made) and the three most common examples are Metacam, Rimadyl and Zubrin. There is one natural anti-inflammatory which I find consistently works very well to alleviate the pain of long term arthritis which is green lipped mussel extract. Optimal results are achieved when green lipped mussel extract is used concurrently with one of the synthetic anti-inflammatory drugs. The second treatment I use is the category of agents called mobility supplements (chondroitin sulphate and/or glucosamine). These are agents that help the joint to produce synovial fluid to maintain its lubrication and to promote natural healing of the eroded articular cartilages covering the bone ends. This is an important component of the treatment as these erosions expose the nerve endings in the bone which cause a lot of the pain and if we can repair these areas the patient will obviously require a lower daily dose of anti-inflammatories.

A change in lifestyle also benefits these patients in that overweight individuals should lose weight to take the extra strain off the joints and gentle controlled exercise should be encouraged to maintain the size and strength of the muscles of the affected leg as they help to support the joints. The gentle exercise may include swimming if facilities are available. This programme of sustained, controlled exercise is effectively the same as a physiotherapy programme for human beings and the objective is to keep the joints as flexible as possible as this will make movement easier and less uncomfortable for the dog.

The individuals who show very little or no pain can often be successfully treated using only natural remedies like green lipped mussel extract or glucosamine and chondroitin sulphate or natural oils like cod liver oil and evening primrose oil or homoeopathic remedies like sulphur, arnica and rhus tox. These remedies work by relieving the pain and, in the case of glucosamine and chondroitin sulphate, also help the joint to lubricate itself and repair the damage to the joint cartilage caused by the grinding action of the unstable bone ends. If these products are not sufficient to alleviate the pain then they should be combined with long term anti-inflammatory and painkilling medications. Many anti-inflammatory/painkilling treatments are available for dogs and are safe for long term and permanent use. If one particular medication does not seem to help much then another should be tried and thus different medicines should be used until one is found that works for your individual dog. This trial and error period in which different medicines in different combinations are tried should be controlled and monitored by your vet, as there are many medicines that should not be used in combination with other medicines.

Most dogs who have developed arthritis for whatever reason should be able to enjoy an active and happy life when the appropriate treatments are used. The process of developing arthritis is, just as in human beings, something one should expect in old age but one does not have to accept the pain or discomfort which may accompany the arthritis. Modern treatment and management of arthritis means that we, and our dogs, should be able to live comfortably in our golden years.

9

HIND LEG LAMENESS (LIMPING)

D
ogs may limp on one or both of their back legs for many reasons. I examine lame dogs by examining the entire leg starting from the paw and working my way up to the top of the leg. I will discuss the problems that one might encounter as the cause of the lameness in this order. A very important part of the investigation of a lame dog is the information that you, the owner, are able to give the vet to describe the lameness. The questions the vet will ask may include the following:

- How long has the dog been lame?
- Did the lameness develop very suddenly or gradually?
- Has the lameness become more or less severe since it was first noticed or has it remained the same?
- Is the dog licking or biting at any part of the lame leg?
- Is the lameness most severe after exercise or after the dog has been resting/sleeping?
- Does the dog seem unwell in any other way besides the lameness?

These are very important questions and I ask my clients to answer them as accurately as possible and as I have said before, if they do not know the answer to any or all the questions to say so because if they are uncertain and merely take a guess or tell me what they think I want to hear, it may mislead me.

Many dog owners will have examined their dog themselves before consulting a vet and I encourage people to do so. The anatomy of the dog's hind leg has the same components as our own feet and legs and one should think about them as functioning much the same as our own. The bones, joints, tendons, muscles and ligaments are virtually identical to our own. The big difference is that dogs walk on their toes not on the palms of their hands as we do when we are on our hands and knees. A good tip is to compare what you think may be abnormal to the same area on the other leg.

1 Paw

Examine the paw by looking at the nails, the toes, the pads and the spaces between the pads. What we are looking for are areas of inflammation, bleeding, swelling, thickening and bruising. The first

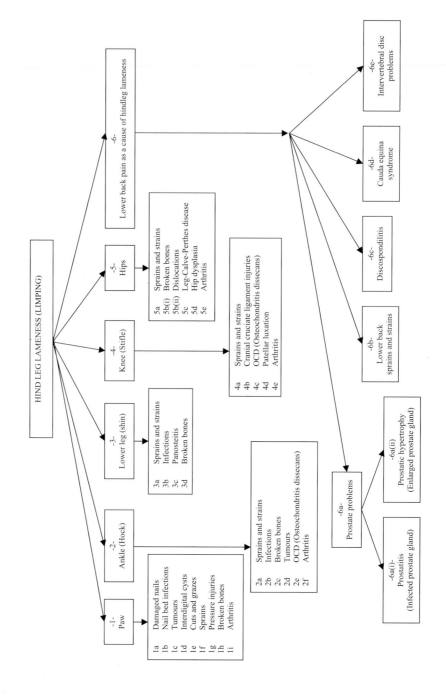

HIND LEG LAMENESS (LIMPING)

-1-
Paw

1a Damaged nails
1b Nail bed infections
1c Tumours
1d Interdigital cysts
1e Cuts and grazes
1f Sprains
1g Pressure injuries
1h Broken bones
1i Arthritis

-2-
Ankle (Hock)

2a Sprains and strains
2b Infections
2c Broken bones
2d Tumours
2e OCD (Osteochondritis dissecans)
2f Arthritis

-3-
Lower leg (shin)

3a Sprains and strains
3b Infections
3c Panosteitis
3d Broken bones

-4-
Knee (Stifle)

4a Sprains and strains
4b Cranial cruciate ligament injuries
4c OCD (Osteochondritis dissecans)
4d Patellar luxation
4e Arthritis

-5-
Hips

5a Sprains and strains
5b(i) Broken bones
5b(ii) Dislocations
5c Leg-Calve-Perthes disease
5d Hip dysplasia
5e Arthritis

-6-
Lower back pain as a cause of hindleg lameness

-6a-
Prostate problems

-6a(i)-
Prostatitis
(Infected prostate gland)

-6a(ii)-
Prostatic hypertrophy
(Enlarged prostate gland)

-6b-
Lower back
sprains and strains

-6c-
Discospondilitis

-6d-
Cauda equina
syndrome

-6e-
Intervertebral disc
problems

step is to part the fur at the base of each toenail and examine the nail beds. Each toe is then carefully felt to check for pain, swelling, thickening, heat or abnormal movement. Each toe consists of three bones (phalanges) just as our toes do and each individual joint must be checked for normal movement. The spaces between the pads should also be carefully felt to check for the same things. The same visual and manual examination is then continued up the bones (metatarsal bones) leading to the ankle (hock). The most common problems encountered when examining the paws are:

1a Broken or torn nails
These are treated by removing the broken part of the nail and the vet may prescribe antibiotics, painkillers and footbaths as necessary.

1b Nail bed infections (paronychia)
The nail bed is the groove between the nail and the skin and infections may arise in this groove. The infection may be caused by bacteria, fungal infections or skin mites (most commonly demodex mites). One would suspect an infection in the nail bed if the nail feels very loose or if there is a discharge from the nail bed. The discharge which may develop has the appearance of a watery or pussy infection and may or may not have a foul odour. Once the vet has determined what kind of parasite has caused the infection they will prescribe appropriate treatment. The important question to ask in cases of nail bed infections is 'what has allowed the infection to develop?' The answer may be simply that a cut or graze in that area has become infected and the infection has moved into the nail bed. If a number of toes have the same infection we should ask ourselves why the body has not been able to fight off the infection. The explanation may be that the dog has diabetes and the high blood sugar levels has resulted in a high sugar content in the moisture in the nail bed and this has favoured the development of an infection. Other disease conditions which may compromise the body's ability to fight off infections are Cushing's disease and hypothyroidism.

1c Tumours
In larger breeds of dogs a possible underlying cause for an infection in a single nail bed may be a tumour growing in the nail bed. Several types of tumours may develop in the nail bed and most often the tumour is not easily seen initially and the first sign of a problem in the nail bed is a secondary infection. If the vet suspects that the infection is the result of a tumour they will often investigate further by taking X-rays and biopsies from the affected toe. Most nail bed tumours are not cancerous and the vet will most commonly advise eliminating the infection first and then amputating the affected toe to remove the tumour. This seems a very extreme way of treating the problem but fortunately dogs do not seem to miss the removed toe at all and function perfectly normally without it.

1d Interdigital cysts
Cysts may develop very suddenly between any two toes on any foot. These cysts usually look like rounded, red, swollen, shiny lumps between the toes. The dog will usually continuously lick the cyst and thus the hair on the paw is constantly wet with their saliva. These cysts are often very painful and many dogs will be reluctant to let you examine the paw. Interdigital cysts may develop for a

variety of reasons. The cyst may develop after the skin between the toes has been punctured by a thorn, a grass seed, a splinter etc. In these cases the cyst will progressively enlarge and eventually one or more holes will appear in the cyst and either pus or a blood-tinged clear fluid will ooze out of the cyst. The dilemma for the vet when examining these cases is deciding whether or not the object that punctured the skin is still lodged in the paw. I usually treat these cases with antibiotics for a few days and suggest that the paw is soaked in a warm salt-water solution for a few minutes twice a day. If the cysts heals then that is the end of the problem. If the cyst does not heal within a few days then one would be suspicious that the object that punctured the skin may still be lodged in the paw. In these cases the vet will suggest surgery to try to find and remove the grass seed, thorn, splinter etc. The second most common cause of interdigital cysts are reactions around the base of the hair follicles between the toes. The hairs on the skin each grow from a structure called a hair follicle. One can imagine the hair follicle as being like a vase and the hair is like a flower stem in the vase. The vase holds the flower stem in position and feeds the flower in the same way that the follicle holds and feeds the hair. If the hair follicle becomes damaged for any reason then the hair root may puncture the hair follicle. If the hair follicle is punctured or if the hair shaft sticks through the hair follicle, the body will respond to the problem in the same way that it responds to puncture wounds by thorns. The body's reaction will thus cause the same type of cyst as seen in cases of puncture wounds by grass seeds and thorns. These interdigital cysts will usually resolve within a few days of treatment with antibiotics and painkillers. It is only very rarely necessary to surgically remove this type of interdigital cyst.

1e Cuts, grazes and puncture wounds from glass and thorns
These may be treated by stitching, bandaging, removing the glass or thorns and antibiotics and painkillers as necessary.

1f Swelling and bruising from sprains
These are treated with painkillers/anti-inflammatories, support bandages and rest from exercise as necessary.

1g Pressure injuries
Swelling from pressure injuries like someone stepping on the paw or objects dropped onto the paw. These are treated with painkillers and rest from exercise as necessary.

1h Broken bones
Severe painful swelling of one or more toes may suggest that one of the bones have been broken. Broken toe bones are most common in dogs older than one year old. Broken bones and joint dislocations are uncommon in very young puppies as they have very flexible, soft bones which tend to bend rather than break when the paw is injured. X-rays are sometimes required to confirm that a bone has been broken. If any bones are broken then the fracture is treated either with casts and bandages or through surgical repair as necessary.

1i Arthritis in the joints of the toes

Dogs with arthritis in their toes look just like people do when they have arthritis in their fingers and toes. The knuckles (the joints between the bones of the fingers or toes) are hard, enlarged and thickened and generally are not painful when gently squeezed. When the joints are moved around during the examination of the toes one may notice that they do not move as freely as the toes without joint thickening and the dogs may show some degree of pain when the joints are moved around. Often only the toes on the inside or outside edge of the paws are affected and the reason for this is that some dogs, just like people, do not walk squarely on the feet but carry more weight on either the inside or the outside of their feet. People who walk like this will often have special insoles in the shoes to correct this very subtle problem. If people do not correct the way they walk they too will develop arthritis in the inside or outside toes of their feet, in human cases we call the thickening of the toe joint a bunion. Please refer to the paragraph at the end of this chapter for a discussion on arthritis and appropriate treatment.

2 The ankle (hock)

This is also examined with your eyes and hands. The hock is a complicated joint composed of the shinbones at the top and the metatarsal bones at the bottom. The hock bones consist of seven individual bones arranged in two rows between the shinbones and the metatarsal bones. All of these bones are held together by many small ligaments and joint capsules. Start by looking at the hock and comparing it to the hock on the other leg. Look for swelling, bruising and wounds. When feeling the hock one should bend (flex) and straighten (extend) the wrist to check for signs of pain. The hock should also be bent gently to the left and right. The most common problems encountered when examining the hock are:

2a Sprains and strains which cause pain and swelling

These are treated with rest from exercise, support bandages and anti-inflammatories/painkillers as necessary.

2b Infection in and around the joint which also cause pain and swelling

These are treated with rest from exercise, antibiotics and anti-inflammatories/painkillers as necessary.

2c Broken bones

Severe painful swelling of the hock may suggest that one or more of the bones or ligaments of the joint have been broken or dislocated. Broken hock bones and dislocations are most common in dogs older than one year old. Broken hock bones and joint dislocations are uncommon in very young puppies as they have very flexible, soft bones which tend to bend rather than break when the hock is injured. X-rays are generally required to confirm that a bone has been broken or ligaments have been ruptured. If any bones are broken then the fracture is treated either with casts and bandages or through surgical repair as necessary. If ligaments have been ruptured or parts of the hock are dislocated then they are treated either with casts or surgical repair depending on which ligaments have been damaged and how severely they have been damaged.

2d Tumours

Severe painful swelling of the hock may also suggest tumours developing in the bones of the hock. X-rays and biopsies are generally required to confirm the presence of tumours. Most tumours affecting this area are highly malignant cancers and the treatment options will often involve amputation of the leg and chemotherapy. Fortunately these tumours are the least common cause of pain and lameness in this area. Middle age and old dogs are more commonly affected by tumours than young dogs.

2e Osteochondritis dissecans

This is a condition which may develop in young growing dogs. This condition and its treatment will be discussed in the section on conditions affecting the knee joint, as it is the same condition which may affect either joint.

2f Arthritis

This may cause thickening of the whole joint or part of the joint. The thickened joint is usually firm to the touch and not painful when touched. The joint will seem thicker than the same joint on the other leg. The joint may be painful when you bend or straighten the joint and it may produce a 'crunchy' sensation when it is bent and straightened. X-rays will usually be taken of the joint to confirm the diagnosis. Please refer to the paragraph at the end of this chapter for a discussion on arthritis and appropriate treatment.

3 The lower leg (shin)

Again examined with your eyes and hands. The lower leg has two long bones called the tibia and fibula. These bones can be felt extending from the hock to the knee joint. One should check for pain and swelling when applying pressure to the bones and the surrounding muscles. The most common problems encountered when examining the lower leg are:

3a Sprains and strains which cause pain and swelling

These are treated with rest from exercise, and anti-inflammatories/painkillers as necessary.

3b Infections

Infection or inflammation in and around the muscles which also cause pain and swelling. These are treated with rest from exercise, antibiotics and anti-inflammatories/painkillers as necessary.

3c Panosteitis

This causes pain and inflammation in the bones. Panosteitis is one of the conditions that our grandparents vaguely referred to as 'growing pains'. The condition is most commonly found in rapidly growing young dogs and causes inflammation and pain in bones which in turn causes lameness. The condition most commonly presents as a 'shifting lameness'. This means that it causes pain and lameness in one leg for a short while then that leg recovers and another leg becomes affected and the dog is then lame on that leg for a while. This shifting lameness may keep moving from one leg to another over a period of several weeks to several months. The condition is caused by inflammation in any of the long bones in any leg. The vet would become suspicious that panosteitis is the cause of the lameness if the lameness keeps shifting from one leg to another and if the dog shows pain when firm pressure is applied to the affected bone during the examination. The only way to confirm the diagnosis is to take a X-ray of the affected bone. Dogs will eventually outgrow the problem and it will simply go away when they have finished growing. If the pain is severe then the vet may prescribe short courses of anti-inflammatories. This is the only instance when I would use simple aspirin to control the pain rather than more modern anti-inflammatories. The vet will advise you on how much aspirin to use and for how long.

3d Broken bones

Severe painful swelling of the lower leg may suggest that one or more of the bones have been broken. Broken bones in the lower leg are uncommon in very young puppies as they have very flexible, soft bones which tend to bend rather than break when the wrist is injured. X-rays are often required to confirm that a bone has been broken. Most fractures that do occur in the long bones in young dogs are found to be 'greenstick fractures' when X-rays have been taken. A 'greenstick fracture' is exactly what the name implies. If you bend a dry stick or branch it tends to snap in half but if you bend a green stick or branch it tends to splinter only on one side and the stick does not break into two pieces. The same thing happens in the bones of young growing dogs because, like a green stick/branch, they are softer and more 'bendy' than a dried stick which is more like a mature bone. If any bones are broken then the fracture is treated either with casts and bandages or through surgical repair as necessary.

4 The knee joint (the stifle)

The anatomical design of the knee joint in cats and dogs is the same as our own human knee (Fig. 12a). The veterinary term for the knee is the stifle. The basic structure of the stifle is a hinge joint. The thigh bone (femur) is at the top and the shin bones (tibia and fibula) are at the bottom. The joint between these bones is composed of the joint capsule, the kneecap (patella) and its tendon, the collateral ligaments on either side, the two internal cruciate ligaments and two internal cartilage cushions called the menisci.

The ends of the bones forming any joint are covered with a layer of cartilage called articular or joint cartilage. This cartilage is very smooth and is essential for smooth movement of the joint. This joint cartilage has very few nerve cells supplying it and this relatively nerve-free layer is essential in covering the bone ends which have a good nerve supply. The best way to understand this concept is to consider the forces on the ends of the bones when they are bearing weight during walking or standing. When we walk or stand our entire body weight is pressing down on our joints, the reason that this does not cause pain is the layer of numb cartilage covering the ends of the bones (the articular cartilage). If we did not have this layer of articular cartilage then the ends of the bones would be pressed together by our body weight and as the bone ends have a good nerve supply this would cause severe pain. Even small areas of damage to this articular cartilage allow small areas of bone to be exposed and pressure on this exposed bone causes pain. These bone ends are held together by the joint capsule which effectively forms a sealed bag around the bone ends. The purpose of the joint capsule is not only to hold the ends of the bones forming the joint together but also to produce joint fluid, which fills the joint. The joint fluid in turn serves two main purposes namely to serve as lubrication for the joint in the same way that oil lubricates a door hinge and secondly to carry nutrients to feed and maintain the articular cartilages and other structures inside the joint. This joint fluid is called synovial fluid and is produced by the synovial membrane, which is the inside layer of the joint capsule. To my knowledge there are no man-made lubricants for machinery, which are as efficient as synovial fluid in terms of lubricating moving parts.

On either side of the stifle we find ligaments called collateral ligaments. The ligament on the inner aspect of the joint is called the medial collateral ligament and the one on the outer aspect is called the lateral collateral ligament. These ligaments run from the thigh bone to the shin bones and allow the knee to bend in one plane only viz. the knee can only bend (flex) or straighten (extend). Consider your own knee, it can only bend and straighten. The reason that it cannot bend sideways so that that the ankle joint touches the hip joint is that the collateral ligaments do not allow this movement. The knee functions in only one plane in much the same way as a door hinge. These collateral ligaments are found on the outside surface of the joint capsule.

The knee cap or patella is a small bone in the tendon of the large thigh muscle on the front of the thighbone called the quadriceps femoris muscle. This muscle starts at the top of the thigh bone and attaches to the top of the shin bone at a point called the tibial crest. The tibial crest is the bulge of bone at the front edge of the top of the shinbone just below the knee joint. This is a very long muscle and the bottom edge of the muscle crosses the knee joint before attaching to the shin bone. The reason the knee cap is there is to serve as a guide to make sure the bottom part of this very long muscle does not slide off the side of the knee. The knee cap slides up and down in a groove at the bottom of the thigh bone called the trochlear groove. The reason for this is that the knee can only bend and straighten so the muscle which straightens the knee should only work from a position across the front of the knee. If the muscle were to slip off to the side, the effect of contacting the thigh muscle would be to try to bend the knee sideways, which would not be allowed by the collateral ligaments. Thus, by developing a small guide bone in the bottom part of such a long muscle, and having a groove along the front end of the thigh bone for this bone to slide in, the body ensures that the muscle stays in a straight line and thus can only move the knee joint in one direction. The tendon which then runs from the knee cap to the shin bone is the one doctors tap with a small rubber hammer to check our knee reflexes. This tendon together with the collateral ligaments and the joint capsule helps to keep the knee joint tight and stable.

Inside the knee joint are two more ligaments called the cruciate ligaments. The word cruciate comes from the Latin word meaning, 'crossed'. The cruciate ligaments are indeed two independent short ligaments inside the knee joint, which run across each other to look like the letter 'x'. The function of these two ligaments is to keep the ends of the bones forming the joint together. The cranial cruciate ligament stops the shin bone sliding forwards and the caudal cruciate ligament stops the shin bone sliding backwards.

The bones forming the knee joint do not fit together very well. Compare the knee joint to the hip joint which functions like a ball and socket joint, which fits together very well. To overcome this relatively poor fit the knee joint has two strips of cartilage wedged between the ends of the bones, one on the left side and the other on the right. This cartilage is called a meniscus; the plural of meniscus is menisci. These menisci function like two small lumps of putty in that they are compressed between the bones and conform themselves to the bone surfaces. Imagine clenching your fists and compressing a lump of putty between your fists, the putty will compress in the centre and squelch out at the edges thereby conforming itself to your fists and the space between them. The menisci function in exactly the same way and this gives the bones of the knee joint a much better fit. The most common problems encountered when examining the knee (stifle) are:

4a Sprains and strains which cause pain and swelling
These are treated with rest from exercise, and anti-inflammatories/painkillers as necessary.

4b Cranial cruciate ligament injuries
Dogs with injuries to the cranial cruciate ligament present in one of two ways. The more common presentation is a sudden, total lameness of one of the hind legs. The leg is held in a bent position with the foot well clear of the ground. The other presentation is a dog that has a long-term (several week or months) lameness affecting one or both hind legs. These dogs will walk on the affected leg but do so with an obvious limp and are reluctant to go for long walks. The diagnosis in these long-term cases is suggested by the presence of a thickening of the joint capsule and adjacent tissues over the inside (medial) surface of the knee (stifle). There may also be a crunching sensation felt inside the knee when it is flexed and extended. Occasionally, in these cases of long standing injury, the examining vet will also be able to demonstrate what is called the anterior drawer sign. In the case of dogs who have suffered a recent acute injury to the cranial cruciate ligament, the presence of the anterior drawer sign is what confirms the diagnosis. The anterior drawer sign is the test that isolates the cause of the lameness to the cranial cruciate ligament. The test involves grasping the thigh bone and shin bones above and below the knee and sliding the shin bone forwards while holding the thigh bone very still. The ability to demonstrate this forward sliding movement is called the anterior drawer sign (Fig. 12b). One will only be able to elicit this movement if the cranial cruciate is stretched or ruptured. The major obstacle to demonstrating the anterior drawer sign is that it may be painful to the patient and they will often flex all the muscles of the leg in response to the pain of the injury and the examination. The result is that the dog's tensed muscles will not allow the test to be carried out. The demonstration of the anterior drawer sign is vital to make the diagnosis. Thus if there is a sufficiently strong suspicion of a cranial cruciate ligament injury many dogs will need to be anaesthetised to relax the muscles so that the anterior drawer test may be done on a completely relaxed leg.

In the case of a longstanding (chronic) injury to the cranial cruciate ligament one may not be able to demonstrate the anterior drawer sign even if the dog has been anaesthetised. This is because the thickening over the inside (medial) aspect of the knee is composed of scar tissue which has contracted and holds the shin bone too tightly to allow it to slide forwards. In these cases the diagnosis is based largely on the presence of this band of thickened tissue which can be felt and seen on X-rays of the knee. Other associated changes on X-rays will further support the diagnosis. These changes include displacement of the sesamoid bones associated with the knee joint and signs of arthritis affecting the knee.

Human beings, typically skiers and football players, occasionally suffer damage to their cruciate ligaments just as dogs do. The injury in humans usually results as a consequence of twisting or hyperextending the knee. Human beings suffer the injury through sheer misfortune in that there is generally no underlying or predisposing factor which ultimately will result in injury to the cruciate ligament. The situation in dogs is far more complex and is not entirely understood. We currently postulate that cranial cruciate ligament injury in dogs is the end result of long term strain being placed on the ligament because of very subtle malformation of the knee joint. Two current theories are used to explain why this subtle malformation ultimately results in injury to this ligament. The first theory is that the low-grade malformation of the knee causes long-term low-grade inflammation (arthritis) in the knee joint. Although this low-grade arthritis *per se* is not severe enough to cause obvious pain or lameness, the result is to weaken the cranial cruciate ligament to the point where it ultimately ruptures and causes sudden onset lameness in the affected leg. The second theory is that the top surface of the shin bone which forms the joint surface that bears the body weight is not level (parallel) to the ground but is in fact tilted slightly downwards toward the back of the knee. The result of this is that the weight-bearing surface is not parallel to the ground but is in fact a slight decline extending to the back of the joint. The result of this is that the thigh bone, which rests on this surface, tends to try to slide down this decline off the back of the joint. The primary structure which prevents the thighbone from sliding back and down is the cranial cruciate ligament. Thus the long-term effect of this force acting on the ligament weakens it to the point where it eventually ruptures. This is the same effect and force that we experience as pain in our knees when we walk down a steep hill. When walking down a steep incline we are creating a joint position where the thigh bone is angled to slide off the back of the joint, i.e. the knee is being hyperextended.

The weight-bearing surface in the human knee is parallel to the ground thus the ligament ruptures purely as misadventure due to extreme, abnormal forces through the ligament often during sport. The modern approach to cranial cruciate rupture in human beings is turning toward non-surgical treatment. This is possible because although the ligament has ruptured, the weight-bearing surface of the shin bone is parallel to the ground. Thus under normal walking conditions there is no tendency for the thigh bone to slide backwards as the weight of the body presses it firmly downwards onto a flat surface. This has resulted in a shift from surgical repair to physiotherapy to strengthen the muscles around the knee to help keep the bones aligned. This new approach in human treatment is generally inappropriate in veterinary patients for two reasons. The physiotherapy is virtually impossible to apply to non compliant animal patients and the declined weight-bearing surface will still tend to cause the thigh bone to slide off the back of the joint and even more so once the cruciate ligament has ruptured. Thus, animal patients who do not have the joint surgically stabilised will develop severe arthritis as a result of the thigh bone sliding over the shin bone. This sliding motion leads to a grinding effect, which damages the joint surfaces producing pain and inflammation, and as a consequence arthritis develops very rapidly.

There are a number of additional factors which make the diagnosis and treatment of cranial cruciate ligament injury even more difficult in dogs. The first is that the ligament may not rupture entirely. This is because it consists of two components which act to support the knee under different stress situations in different knee positions. If only one portion of the ligament has ruptured then the patient will present with all the signs of cranial cruciate ligament injury but the vet will be unable to demonstrate an anterior drawer sign as the remaining, intact portion of the ligament will prevent the shin bone from being slid forward during the examination. The second factor is that the ligament may not have ruptured and the lameness which is seen is due to the ligament having only been stretched. If the ligament has been severely stretched an anterior drawer sign will be present and the diagnosis and treatment are the same as for a ruptured ligament. The difficult diagnosis to make is when the ligament has not stretched enough to result in an anterior drawer sign but has stretched enough to cause microinstability of the joint. In these cases the shin and thigh bone are sliding across each other sufficiently to cause pain but not sufficiently to be appreciated on examination of the knee. These cases usually present as long standing cases of hind leg lameness with the thickening over the medial (inside) aspect of the knee. This thickening represents the body's attempt to stabilise the knee to eliminate the microinstability. This attempt by the body however is largely ineffective and arthritis will worsen rapidly in the affected knee. The third factor is that the effect of the bones sliding across each other after the ligament has ruptured may crush, pinch or tear the meniscal cartilages inside the knee. The presence of damaged cartilages as a component of the lameness in the knee is alluded to by a crunching sensation which may be heard or felt when the knee is flexed and extended. These three complicating factors will often need to confirmed by examining the inside of the knee via arthroscopic examination (placing a small camera inside the knee joint) or more commonly by surgically opening the joint and direct visualisation of all the structures within the joint.

A further complicating factor is that many different techniques are used to repair the damaged joint and this implies that there is not one particular technique which is superior to the others. Research has shown that all the modern techniques deliver approximately the same success rate. This is a concern to me because the same research has also shown that all dogs will have some degree of permanent arthritis in the affected knee within six months of the injury. This arthritis will develop despite the skill of the surgeon and the type of repair technique used. The arthritis will also worsen as time goes by. The obvious question to ask in the face of this research is why do we bother to repair the injury if arthritis will develop anyway? The answer is that the repair is done as a damage limitation exercise. The sooner the knee is operated on, the less severely and the less rapidly the arthritis will develop. The object of the surgery is to restrict the inevitable arthritis to the point were it is so limited that although one can demonstrate its presence on X-rays it will not be sufficient to cause lameness after the dog has recovered from the surgery.

Many factors will affect the success of the surgery. The first is the length of time that has elapsed from the moment of injury to the moment of repair. The sooner the knee is operated on the better the long-term prospects for the knee. As a general rule I would want to operate on the knee within three weeks of the injury occurring. The second factor is the presence of any other structures being injured in addition to the cranial cruciate ligament. The most common associated injury is damage to the menisci (cartilages) inside the joint. One or both menisci may be damaged as a result of the joint instability. The medial (inner aspect) meniscus is more commonly damaged. The damage to the meniscus varies from mild to severe and the extent of the damage correlates directly with the severity of the arthritis which will develop. If the meniscal damage is minor and can be repaired then the long-term prognosis is good. If the damage to the meniscus is more severe then the damaged portion must be removed. The amount of meniscus that must be removed correlates with the degree of arthritis which will ensue. The greater the amount of meniscus which must be removed results in progressively more severe, inevitable arthritis because effectively a greater amount of cushion between the bone ends has been removed. If one were not to remove the damaged meniscus the outcome would be even worse. Another structure which may be found to be damaged at the same time is the lateral collateral ligament. If this is the case this must be repaired at the same time and should be regarded as a significant injury in its own right and should be repaired individually. The third factor is the personality of the patient. The more boisterous the dog, the less likely they are to rest the operated leg and consequently the greater the risk of them damaging the repair before the knee has healed.

The best course of action with all cruciate injuries is swift diagnosis and swift treatment. Current wisdom is that all dogs with stretched or ruptured cranial cruciate ligaments should be repaired surgically and the meniscal cartilages must be examined and treated as required at the same time. Up until very recently the advice was that dogs which weigh less than 15kg are very likely to heal sufficiently well if rested for six to eight weeks after the injury. The reason for this is that they are light and agile enough to carry the leg off the ground to allow the leg to produce enough scar tissue around the knee to stabilise it. The second reason is that their small size ensures that there are less extreme forces acting through the joint than in large dogs and thus the amount of arthritis which will result from instability of the joint is often insignificant. The current wisdom offered by specialists is that all dogs should have this injury repaired. In my experience the small breeds do very well without surgery and my criteria for natural healing through enforced rest is a patient with no other injuries to the other components of the knee joint, a calm disposition, weighs less than 10kg and has a slight build. I would very often rest these patients for six to twelve weeks and only operate on those who did not show a full return to function. The same philosophy applies to cats who have suffered this injury.

The approach to patients with a long-standing injury is far more subjective. Many of these patients have developed a significant thickening of the tissues on the medial (inside) aspect of the knee as discussed earlier and have significant arthritis already established in the joint. I tend to assess these patients under anaesthetic to assess the anterior drawer sign. If there is no appreciable instability in the joint, no indication of meniscal damage and evidence of advanced arthritic changes on X-rays of the joint then I feel there is no benefit from surgery as the object of surgery is to achieve stability of the joint and to preserve the menisci. In these cases these two objectives will have been achieved by natural healing but at the cost of severe arthritis and thus I concentrate my efforts at treating the arthritis with long-term arthritis remedies. If, however, there is instability and/or suspicion of meniscal damage then the patient would benefit from surgery.

When one commits to treating these patients with long-standing injuries which are not surgical candidates for the reasons described above, two treatments should be used. The first is a suitable long-term anti-inflammatory drug which will alleviate the pain in the joint. The second treatment I use is the category of agents called mobility supplements (chondroitin sulphate and/or glucosamine). These are agents which help the joint to produce synovial fluid to maintain its lubrication and to promote natural healing of the eroded articular cartilages covering the bone ends. This is an important component of the treatment as these erosions expose the nerve endings in the bone which cause a lot of the pain and if we can repair these areas the patient will obviously require a lower daily dose of anti-inflammatories.

A change in lifestyle also benefits these patients in that overweight individuals should lose weight to take the extra strain off the joints and gentle controlled exercise should be encouraged to maintain the size and strength of the muscles of the affected leg as they help to support the joints.

The goals of surgical repair of injured cranial cruciate ligaments are very simple. The primary goal is to stabilise the joint to eliminate the anterior drawer sign. The other essential component of the repair is to examine the inside of the joint and treat additional injuries including damage to the menisci. There are currently three more common techniques used by surgeons depending on their personal preference.

The first technique is called the 'over the top' technique. This technique uses a graft obtained from the muscle sheath over the outer aspect of the thigh. The graft is then pulled through the joint to run along approximately the same route that the original cranial cruciate followed prior to rupture. The free end of the graft is then sutured in position once it has been pulled tight enough to eliminate the anterior drawer movement. The most common problem with this technique is that the graft may snap before it has had enough time to grow in this position.

The second technique is often called the 'modified de angelis' technique (Fig. 12c). This technique places a nylon or wire band on the outside of the joint running in the same direction as the original cranial cruciate ligament. The problems encountered here are that the nylon or wire implant may rupture before the knee has healed in this supported position. The problem here is not that the implant snapped but that it did so prematurely. The object, when placing this type of implant, is to pull it tight enough to eliminate the anterior drawer sign and thus restore stability to the joint by holding the bones in the correct alignment. The knee capsule will then thicken slightly around the joint and this, together with strong scar tissue which forms around the implant, will keep the knee stable in the future. All artificial implants will eventually snap through repeated use, as the artificial material will fatigue with repeated movement. Compare this to repeatedly bending a piece of wire at the same point until it snaps. This happens because the wire develops metal fatigue. The wire or nylon implant used will eventually snap approximately six to eight weeks after the surgery. This poses no problems because the implant has held the knee in the correct position while the joint capsule has grown thicker and stronger and a strong band of scar tissue has developed along the implant. Thus when the implant snaps the healing process has been guided to hold the knee in the correct position. The ruptured ends of the implant rarely cause problems and thus are generally not removed. The problem which can arise with this technique is premature rupture of the implant before the necessary guided healing has taken place. The implant *per se* may have ruptured or it may have torn out of the tissue it has been stitched into which acts as an anchor. Either event will result in instability of the joint just as it was when the cranial cruciate ruptured initially. If this happens the usual best course of action is to replace the implants. The decision to perform repeat surgery depends on the stability of the joint at the time of implant rupture.

The third technique is a recent development and involves cutting the top of the tibia (shin bone) and plating it in a different position. The object of this technique is to tilt the weight-bearing surface of the tibia sufficiently to make it parallel to the ground as in the case of human knees. This new technique shows great promise but no long-term studies have been done.

The recovery from this surgery, in terms of regaining full use of the leg, varies a lot from one individual to another. After the surgery all dogs will hold the leg up with the foot well clear of the ground for one to several weeks before starting to use it again. Some textbooks state that the average time taken to start walking on the leg again is four months. I find that most dogs are walking on the leg long before that. The surgery is very painful and I feel very strongly that all these patients should receive painkillers until they no longer require them. This varies from one individual to another and may be as long as several months. I generally advise strict house rest on non slip surfaces for six weeks then a gradual return to full exercise.

The disappointing aspect of treating cranial cruciate injuries in dogs, and to a lesser extent in cats, is that the knee will develop some degree of arthritis at some point after the injury. The object of the surgery is to delay the onset of arthritis for as long as possible and restrict it to as minor as possible. This may be achieved with only a single episode of surgery but unfortunately a significant percentage of dog and human patients will require further surgery on the knee for one reason or another to restrict the development of arthritis. Dogs who present for repeat surgery usually do so for one of two reasons. The first is premature rupture of the implant used to stabilise the joint. The second is damage to the meniscal cartilage which needs to addressed, as failure to do so will result in accelerated arthritis. The meniscal injuries are usually treated, as discussed earlier, by suturing or removing tears which cause pain in the joint. The traditional approach has been to surgically open the knee up again to gain access to these tears but more and more vets are doing this arthroscopically via a small camera placed into the joint via a very small hole. This is much more desirable as there is significantly less pain involved and the recovery is a few days as opposed to a few weeks or months.

The long-term prospects for dogs who suffer this injury are not as good as in human beings but all these dogs can be expected to live out their lives comfortably and with sufficient pain-free mobility to do whatever they wish. There are many long term, safe, effective arthritis treatments available today to control the arthritis which will ensue at some time in the dog's life. The objective which I strive for with my patients is to have a happy, pain-free, mobile dog who will live comfortably for their full natural life span.

4c Osteochondritis dissecans

The ends of the bones which form the knee joint are covered with a layer of joint cartilage for the reasons discussed earlier in this chapter. This layer of joint cartilage grows with the bones as the dog grows larger. If the dog grows very quickly then the cartilage will have to grow and develop very quickly to match the growth of the bones. The cartilage needs a good blood supply to grow normally and sometimes the cartilage is developing faster than the blood vessels that feed it. If this happens then there may be areas of cartilage which have an inadequate blood supply and the newly formed cartilage is starved of nutrients and oxygen. The result of this is that the undernourished piece of cartilage becomes brittle and may peel off from the rest of the cartilage layer. This is the same principle seen in dry or sunburnt skin which may start to peel off the underlying skin. If a piece of cartilage starts to peel away from the end of the bone then the nerves in the underlying bone are

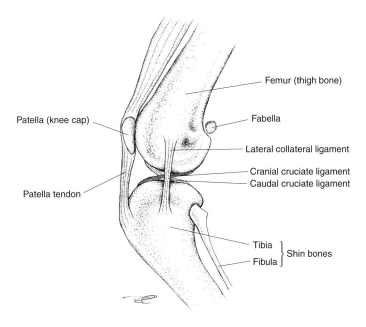

Fig 12a The normal knee joint (stifle) seen from the side.

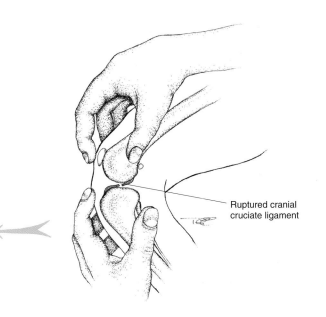

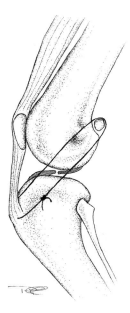

Fig 12b The condition of the cranial cruciate ligament can be assessed by checking the knee for an "anterior drawer sign" as illustrated above. The "anterior drawer sign" means that the shin bones can be moved forwards using your hands as illustrated. The shin bones can only be moved forwards if the cranial cruciate ligament has been stretched or ruptured. This test confirms a suspicion of injury to the cranial cruciate ligament. To perform this test accurately the dog's leg must be relaxed.

Fig 12c This is currently the most commonly used technique to repair a ruptured cranial cruciate ligament. The surgeon will implant a nylon or wire band as illustrated. This implant runs in the same direction as the cranial cruciate ligament and is tied tightly enough to have the same effect as the intact ligament i.e. it stops the shin bones from sliding forwards.

exposed and the dog may experience pain when walking. The loose flap of cartilage also causes pain as it exerts pressure points in the joint in the same way as a small pebble in your shoe may cause pain when walking. This flap of cartilage may even tear off the end of the bone and float around the joint causing. If this happens the free floating piece of cartilage is called a joint mouse. In severe cases more than one such tear may develop and thus more than one joint mouse may be identified when the diagnosis is made. This diagnosis should be suspected in any young, rapidly growing dog which has hind leg lameness due to pain in the knee joint. The diagnosis is confirmed by taking X-rays of the joint. The other knee must always be X-rayed at the same time even if it seems normal because the condition often develops in both knees even though only one may be painful at a given time.

The treatment for this condition depends on the dog's age, how long the lesion has been present and how severe the lesion is.

The surgical treatment for this condition involves opening the affected joint and removing the flap of cartilage. This will leave a small crater-like lesion in the joint cartilage. The edges of this crater are scraped away until the edges bleed slightly. This is done because all the cartilage which has an inadequate blood supply must be removed as it will be unable to heal without a good blood supply. Once the edges have been scraped away leaving only healthy cartilage the joint is sutured closed and the dog must rest for a few weeks while new cartilage grows into the crater. During this period of rest the dogs should have light, controlled exercise to keep the joint mobile and supple. Some dogs will develop some degree of arthritis in the elbow despite prompt effective surgery. This arthritis may develop despite the skill of the surgeon and may also worsen as time goes by. The obvious question to ask in the face of this information is why do we bother to repair the problem if arthritis may develop anyway? The answer is that the repair is done as a damage limitation exercise. The sooner the knee is operated on, the less severely and the less rapidly the arthritis may develop. The object of the surgery is, at best, to avoid future arthritis and at worst, to restrict the potential for arthritis to the point were it is so limited that although one can demonstrate its presence on X-rays, it will not be sufficient to cause lameness after the dog has recovered from the surgery. The arthritis may take weeks, months or years to develop and may vary from insignificant to severe, in which case long term painkillers and mobility supplements (glucosamine and chondroitin sulphate) will be required to ensure comfortable pain free movement. The object of the surgery is to prevent the development of arthritis or at the very least to minimise the severity of the possible subsequent arthritis.

Surgical treatment of this condition is not necessarily appropriate for all dogs. In some cases the diagnosis is only made after arthritis has already started developing and if it is already very severe then the dog will not benefit significantly from the surgery. In cases where the cartilage flap is very small some surgeons will advise that surgery will not improve the lameness and the surgery may make it worse. In the cases where surgery is not appropriate for one reason or another the best course of action will be long term painkillers as and when the dog needs them and I would always recommend long term glucosamine and/or chondroitin sulphate therapy. These are agents which help the joint to produce synovial fluid to maintain its lubrication and to promote natural healing and continued health of the eroded articular cartilages covering the bone ends. This is an important component of the treatment as these erosions expose the nerve endings in the bone which cause a lot of the pain and if we can repair these areas the patient will obviously require a lower daily dose of painkillers/anti inflammatories.

A change in lifestyle also benefits these patients in that overweight individuals should lose weight to take the extra strain off the joints and gentle controlled exercise should be encouraged to maintain the size and strength of the muscles of the affected leg as they help to support the joints.

4d Patellar luxation (unstable kneecaps)

The kneecap or patella is a small bone in the tendon of the large thigh muscle on the front of the thigh bone called the quadriceps femoris muscle. This muscle starts at the top of the thigh bone and attaches to the top of the shin bone at a point called the tibial crest. The tibial crest is the bulge of bone at the front edge of the top of the shin bone just below the knee joint. This is a very long muscle and the bottom edge of the muscle crosses the knee joint before attaching to the shin bone. The reason the kneecap is there is to serve as a guide to make sure the bottom part of this very long muscle does not slide off the side of the knee. The kneecap slides up and down in a groove at the bottom of the thigh bone called the trochlear groove. The reason for this is that the knee can only bend and straighten so the muscle which straightens the knee should only work from a position across the front of the knee. If the muscle were to slip off to the side, the effect of contacting the thigh muscle would be to try to bend the knee sideways, which would not be allowed by the collateral ligaments. Thus, by developing a small guide bone in the bottom part of such a long muscle, and having a groove along the front end of the thigh bone for this bone to slide in, the body ensures that the muscle stays in a straight line and thus can only move the knee joint in one direction. The tendon which then runs from the knee cap to the shin bone is the one doctors tap with a small rubber hammer to check our knee reflexes. This tendon together with the collateral ligaments and the joint capsule helps to keep the knee joint tight and stable.

Patellar luxation (unstable kneecaps) implies that the kneecap has slipped out of its normal position in the trochlear groove in the thighbone. Most case of patellar luxation are the result of the kneecap slipping out of the trochlear groove towards the inside edge of the knee (medially).

Some dogs, most commonly small bow-legged breeds, have unstable knee caps which may slip out of the trochlear groove and thus the long thigh muscle cannot function properly and the leg will appear lame. This lameness is generally not painful but is rather the result of the impaired function of the thigh muscle when the kneecap is out of position. This is something that we have all commonly seen when watching small dogs running while out on a walk. What we commonly see is a small dog running quite normally then suddenly running on only three legs with one of the hind legs held off the ground for a few yards then they continue running quite normally again on all four legs. What is happening in this situation is that the knee cap has painlessly slipped out of its groove and the dog then carries the leg off the ground for a few steps until it is able to click the kneecap back into position and then it uses the leg as normal. These dogs usually have had unstable kneecaps since birth and the have learnt how to click the knee back into position when it slips out of its groove. These cases are called congenital patellar instability and this means that the dogs were born with the problem. Congenital patellar instability may be the result of several 'deformities' of the knee joint. The most common 'deformity' is that the trochlear groove is simply too shallow to keep the kneecap in position. In other cases the groove may be deep enough but the tibial crest may be in the wrong position. In these cases the tibial crest has been formed slightly to the inside of its normal position. When the thigh muscle tenses up during walking or running the thigh muscle will follow the shortest line between its beginning (at the top of the thigh bone) and its end (on the tibial crest). This is the same effect that we will see when we tighten a piece of string attached to two points. If we imagine that the thigh muscle is the piece of string we will see that it follows the shortest route between the two points when it is pulled tight. If you imagine that the middle of the string is the kneecap and the trochlear groove is not directly between the two points one will appreciate that the kneecap will be pulled out of the trochlear groove when the string is pulled tight.

In cases of congenital patellar instability both knees are usually affected with one being worse than the other. Acquired cases of patellar luxation (unstable kneecaps) are the result of trauma to one knee which forces the kneecap out of its groove. In these cases the knees are normally formed at birth but at some point in the dog's life an overexertion of one of the knees has forced the kneecap out of its groove. This forceful injury usually results in damage to the edge of the groove at the point that the kneecap has been forced out of the groove. In these cases the knee is painful and the dog will be lame after the injury even if they have been able to click the kneecap back into its groove. These cases are called acquired patellar instability because they have not been present since birth and have been acquired at some point in the dog's life. The pain is the result of the kneecap slipping out of its groove and grazing the edge of the groove in the process.

Congenital patellar instability is graded on a scale of one to four. Grade one instability implies that the kneecap only slips out of its groove occasionally and easily slips back into the groove. Grade two instability means that the kneecap slips out of position more often but is still in the groove most of the time. In grade three cases the kneecap is out of position most of the time but is easily put back into its normal position. Grade four cases mean that the kneecap is out of position all of the time and will slip out of its groove even when it is placed in its normal position.

The treatment for this problem is to surgically correct the 'deformity' causing the problem. This involves making the trochlear groove deeper and/or moving the tibial crest to its proper position. As a general rule I feel that one should only repair the problem if it is bothering the dog i.e. if it is causing pain or if it is affecting the function of the leg all or most of the time. In practical terms this means that grade three and four cases should be repaired and grade one or two cases generally do not require surgery. Acquired patellar luxation is the result of a single episode of trauma and many cases will heal naturally to resume normal function. I would only recommend surgery in these cases if the knee were not able to repair itself within a few weeks of the injury.

4e Arthritis

This may cause thickening of the whole joint or part of the joint. The thickened joint is usually firm to the touch and not painful when touched. The joint will seem thicker than the same joint on the other leg. The joint may be painful when you bend or straighten the joint and it may produce a 'crunchy' sensation when it is bent and straightened. X-rays will usually be taken of the joint to confirm the diagnosis. Please refer to the paragraph at the end of this chapter for a discussion on arthritis and appropriate treatment.

5 The hip joints

The anatomy of the pelvis and the hip joints in dogs is exactly the same as our own (Fig. 13a). The hip joint is a ball and socket joint held together by a ligament inside the joint and a joint capsule around the outside of the joint. The joint capsule produces joint fluid which feeds and lubricates the joint. The muscles positioned around the outside of the joint also help to support the joint and keep the ball in position in the socket. The ball part of the joint is the rounded head of the thigh bone (the femur) and the socket (the acetabulum) is a cave-like depression in the pelvic bone. This ball and socket joint is a tightly fitting joint which allows movement in almost any direction because of its spherical design. The ends of the bones forming the joint are covered with a layer of cartilage called articular or joint cartilage. This cartilage is very smooth and is essential for smooth movement of the joint. This joint cartilage has very few nerve cells supplying it and this relatively nerve-free layer is essential in covering the bone ends which have a good nerve supply. The best way to understand this concept is to consider the forces on the ends of the bones when they are bearing weight during walking or standing. When we walk or stand our entire body weight is pressing down on our joints, the reason that this does not cause pain is the layer of numb cartilage covering the ends of the bones (the articular cartilage). If we did not have this layer of articular cartilage then the ends of the bones wound be pressed together by our body weight and as the bone ends have a good nerve supply this would cause severe pain. Even small areas of damage to this articular cartilage allow small areas of bone to be exposed and pressure on this exposed bone causes pain. These bone ends are held together by the joint capsule which effectively forms a sealed bag around the bone ends. The purpose of the joint capsule is not only to hold the ends of the bones forming the joint together but also to produce joint fluid, which fills the joint. The joint fluid in turn has two main purposes namely to serve as lubrication for the joint in the same way that oil lubricates a door hinge and secondly to carry nutrients to feed and maintain the articular cartilages and other structures inside the joint. This joint fluid is called synovial fluid and is produced by the synovial membrane, which is the inside layer of the joint capsule. To my knowledge there are no man-made lubricants for machinery, which are as efficient as synovial fluid in terms of lubricating moving parts.

The examination of the hip joints involves moving the thighbone forwards, backwards, inwards and outwards. If any of these movements cause pain the one should suspect that the hip is the cause of the lameness in the hind leg. If pain is identified in a hip joint then one should always examine the other hip joint, as the conditions which cause pain in the hip joint are often present in both hip joints with one being more severely affected than the other is. The most common problems affecting the hip joints are:

5a Sprains and strains which cause pain and swelling
These are treated with rest from exercise and anti-inflammatories/painkillers as necessary.

5b Fractures and dislocations
Severe painful swelling of the hip may suggest that one or more of the bones or ligaments of the joint have been broken or hip joint has been dislocated. X-rays are generally required to confirm

that a bone has been broken or ligaments have been ruptured. If any bones are broken then the fracture is usually treated through surgical repair as necessary.

If the hip is dislocated the vet will have to administer a general anaesthetic to try to put the hip back into position. Most cases of hip dislocation can be treated in this way and after the hip is put back into position the vet may put the leg into a special type of sling called a velpeau bandage. The object of this sling is to keep the hip joint in position for anything from a few days to weeks to ensure that it does not dislocate again before it has had a chance to heal. In some cases the vet will be unable to put the hip back into position or it may keep dislocating. The reason for this is that a large blood clot may have formed in the socket part of the joint (the acetabulum) and this prevents the ball part of the joint moving back into the socket. In these cases the vet will have to operate to remove the blood clot and then put the hip joint back into position. In some severe cases the hip joint will keep dislocating and the vet may have to perform further surgery to keep the joint in position.

5c Legge-Calve-Perthes disease (aseptic femoral head necrosis)

Some small breeds of dog may develop a condition called Legge-Calve-Perthes disease. This is a little understood condition in which the blood supply to the ball part of the hip joint (the head of the thigh bone) is suddenly stopped for no apparent reason. The result of this is that this part of the hip joint starts to wither away and gradually shrinks in size. The end result of this process is that the ball part of the hip joint slowly dies off and becomes small, misshapen and as soft as putty. Once this has happened the hip joint can no longer work normally and becomes unstable and painful. There is no treatment to restore the blood supply and the only option for these dogs is to remove this piece of dying bone. The aim of the surgery is thus to remove the ball part of the ball and socket hip joint and thus the joint is no longer a joint. The reason that this surgery must be performed is that, as the hip joint becomes more and unstable, the two bones forming the joint start to grate against each other and this causes severe pain. Once the ball part of the joint has been removed the thigh bone and the pelvic bone no longer rub and grate against each other and thus the pain stops. The amazing next step is that as time goes by the body will make a new false hip joint between the muscles overlying the hip and the top of the thighbone (the femur). This process is usually so efficient that within a few weeks these dogs will be able to walk and run normally and without pain. This condition often affects both hips and even if both hips are operated on most of these dogs will be able to live full, pain-free lives.

5d Hip dysplasia

The word dysplasia means 'not properly formed' thus hip dysplasia means that the hip joint has not formed properly. The hip joint is a ball and socket joint held together by a ligament inside the joint and a joint capsule around the outside of the joint. The joint capsule produces joint fluid which feeds and lubricates the joint. The muscles positioned around the outside of the joint also help to support the joint and keep the ball in position in the socket. The ball part of the joint is the rounded head of the thigh bone (the femur) and the socket (the acetabulum) is a cave-like depression in the pelvic bone. This ball and socket joint is a tightly fitting joint which allows movement in almost any direction because of its spherical design. Hip dysplasia means that the ball part or the socket part of the joint has not formed properly (Figs 13b to 13d). The problem may be that the ball part of the joint has not formed as a spherical ball but rather as a shortened, stumpy, square-shaped structure that does not fit neatly and tightly into the socket in the pelvic bone. The problem may also be that the socket part of the joint is too shallow and thus the ball part of the joint is not held firmly in position. The most common cases of hip dysplasia involve malformation of the ball and the socket. Hip dysplasia causes pain because the poor fitting ball and socket joint results in an unstable joint and this leads to instability of the bone ends forming that joint. The instability of the joint means that the ball part of the joint grinds against the socket and this grinding action of the bones causes arthritis to develop in the hip and this results in pain.

The extent to which the components of the joint are malformed varies and thus dogs are 'hip scored' to determine the severity of hip dysplasia in each individual. Different hip scoring systems exist in different parts of the world but the principle remains the same. X-rays are taken of the hips and are examined by a panel of experts. The panel will then ascribe penalty points to the hips according to how severely various parts of the hips are malformed and how severely arthritis may have developed in the hip. All the penalty points are then added together and a total score is allocated to the hips of that individual. The lower the score is, the better the hips are. Each breed of dog has an average hip score and this varies a lot from one breed to another. Thus if you have your dog's hips scored you should compare their score to the average score for that breed to determine whether they are better or worse than the average. The object of hip-scoring is to breed only from dogs with good hips because if they have bad hips their puppies will very likely have bad hips too. This is an important moral issue from two points of view. The first point is that we need to do everything we can to avoid bringing new puppies into this world who may then suffer a lifetime of hip pain. The second point is that it is heartbreaking to discover that your dog has hip dysplasia a few months or years after they have become a loved member of your family. The family then has the stress and expense of alleviating the pain and suffering that can be caused by this condition. The object of the hip-scoring scheme is thus to try to avoid breeding dogs who may suffer from the pain of this condition in later life.

Hip dysplasia is more common in certain breeds than others. Although any breed may be affected the condition is most commonly seen in the larger dog breeds i.e. breeds that are heavier than twenty kilograms. The more commonly affected breeds are German shepherd dogs, Labradors and golden retrievers.

The most important point to make is that the severity of the hip dysplasia as seen on the X-rays often does not correlate with the amount of pain that the individual experiences. I have frequently seen dogs with severe hip dysplasia, as seen on their X-rays, who show no signs of any pain or discomfort and conversely I have seen dogs who have a great deal of hip pain but only very mild hip dysplasia is evident on their hip X-rays. This is a common finding and the advice I give to people is to 'treat the dog not the X-ray'. Thus if a dog has little or no hip pain, despite a significant degree of hip dysplasia as seen on their X-rays, they will require little or no treatment until the hips start to bother them. This is because it is not the hip dysplasia *per se* that causes the pain. The hip dysplasia may cause arthritis to develop in the hip joint and it is the arthritis that causes the pain. Thus if no arthritis has developed then there will be no pain and thus no need for treatment. I would only consider applying the various treatment options to affected individuals when signs of pain appear. One might argue that we should be treating before the pain develops in an attempt to avoid arthritis developing but this would mean that many dogs who would have lived quite comfortably with their dysplastic hips would receive unnecessary medical and/or surgical treatments. If and when the signs of pain do appear, then it is true that the sooner treatment is applied the better the long-term results may be.

The treatment for hip dysplasia involves medications and /or surgery. The amount and type of treatment is determined primarily by the amount of pain or joint restriction the individual dog is experiencing and the age of the individual dog. The X-rays of the hips will also help to decide on the most appropriate treatment but remember to 'treat the dog not the X-ray'. When one commits to treating these patients with medication only, two treatments should be used. The first is a suitable long-term anti-inflammatory drug that will alleviate the pain in the joint. The second treatment I use is the category of agents called mobility supplements (chondroitin sulphate and/or glucosamine). These are agents that help the joint to produce synovial fluid to maintain its lubrication and to promote natural healing of the eroded articular cartilages covering the bone ends. This is an important component of the treatment as these erosions expose the nerve endings in the bone which cause a lot of the pain and if we can repair these areas the patient will obviously require a lower daily dose of anti-inflammatories.

A change in lifestyle also benefits these patients in that overweight individuals should lose weight to take the extra strain off the joints and gentle controlled exercise should be encouraged to maintain the size and strength of the muscles of the affected leg as they help to support the joints. The individuals who show very little or no pain can often be successfully treated using only natural remedies like glucosamine and chondroitin sulphate or natural oils like cod liver oil and evening primrose oil or homoeopathic remedies like sulphur, arnica and rhus tox. These remedies work by relieving the pain and, in the case of glucosamine and chondroitin sulphate, also help the joint to lubricate itself and repair the damage to the joint cartilage caused by the grinding action of the unstable bone ends. If these products are not sufficient to alleviate the pain then they should be combined with long term anti-inflammatory and painkilling medications. Many anti-inflammatory/painkilling treatments are available for dogs and are safe for long term and permanent use. If one particular medication does not seem to help much then another should be tried and thus different medicines should be used until one is found that works for your individual dog. This trial and error period in which different medicines in different combinations are tried should be controlled and monitored by your vet, as there are many medicines that should not be used in combination with other medicines.

The surgical options available to help in cases of hip dysplasia include relatively minor procedures such as minor muscle transection (pectineal myectomy) or more major surgery such as total hip replacement (the same operation that many people have done) or reconstruction of the hip joint (triple pelvic osteotomy). In very severe or very advanced cases the only option may be removal of the ball part of the joint in an operation called an excision arthroplasty. Not all dogs would be suitable candidates for these various operations and each individual case should be assessed for suitability on their own merits, your vet will advise you whether surgery is appropriate or not and which particular operation would be the most appropriate for your dog.

The objective which I strive for with my patients is to have a happy, pain-free, mobile dog who will live comfortably for their full natural life span.

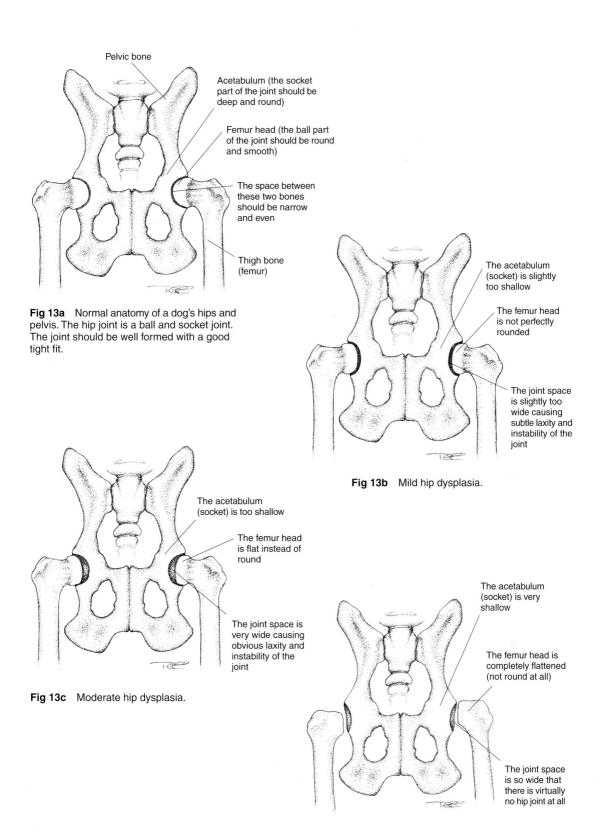

Pelvic bone

Acetabulum (the socket part of the joint should be deep and round)

Femur head (the ball part of the joint should be round and smooth)

The space between these two bones should be narrow and even

Thigh bone (femur)

Fig 13a Normal anatomy of a dog's hips and pelvis. The hip joint is a ball and socket joint. The joint should be well formed with a good tight fit.

The acetabulum (socket) is slightly too shallow

The femur head is not perfectly rounded

The joint space is slightly too wide causing subtle laxity and instability of the joint

Fig 13b Mild hip dysplasia.

The acetabulum (socket) is too shallow

The femur head is flat instead of round

The joint space is very wide causing obvious laxity and instability of the joint

Fig 13c Moderate hip dysplasia.

The acetabulum (socket) is very shallow

The femur head is completely flattened (not round at all)

The joint space is so wide that there is virtually no hip joint at all

Fig 13d Severe hip dysplasia.

5e Arthritis

This may cause thickening of the whole joint or part of the joint. The thickened joint is usually firm to the touch and not painful when touched. The joint will seem thicker than the same joint on the other leg. The joint may be painful when you bend or straighten and it may produce a 'crunchy' sensation when it is bent and straightened. X-rays will usually be taken of the joint to confirm the diagnosis. Please refer to the paragraph at the end of this chapter for a discussion on arthritis and appropriate treatment.

6 Lower back pain as a cause of hind leg lameness

Lameness in one or both back legs may be due to lower back pain rather than a problem directly affecting the back legs. Many of these cases may look like hip problems in that these dogs will walk with an arched lower back and walk with stiff back legs and take only short strides with the back legs. A further similarity to hip problems is that these cases will also be reluctant to go up stairs or climb into cars or onto the beds and furniture at home. They will however seem to be more comfortable going down stairs or climbing down from furniture or out of the car. This is because when they are moving upwards most of the body weight is being transferred to the lower back and the back legs but when they move downwards most of the weight is transferred to the front legs.

Five common conditions may cause lower back pain viz. prostate problems, lower back sprains and strains, discospondilitis, cauda-equina syndrome and intervertebral disc disease.

6a Prostate gland problems

The prostate gland is only found in male dogs. The gland is situated at the point where the bladder leads into the urethra (this is the tube which runs inside the penis which is used to urinate through.) The prostate gland is a spherically-shaped gland which lies around the first part of the urethra at the point where it is connected to the bladder (Fig. 8a). The gland is not truly spherical in that it is composed of a left and a right lobe. The function of the prostate gland is to produce the fluid which carries and feeds sperm during ejaculation when dogs mate.

Two common conditions may arise in the prostate gland which may cause a variable amount of pain which causes affected individuals to walk with an arched back and stiff back legs taking shorter than normal steps during walking. The most painful condition is infection and inflammation in the prostate gland which is called prostatitis. The second condition is much less painful and is called prostatic hypertrophy. In the case of prostatic hypertrophy the prostate gland is swollen and enlarged because of the affect of hormones acting on the gland and is not due to infection. The swelling of the prostate gland associated with both of these conditions may also cause the urethra to be compressed at the point where it runs through the prostate gland. The result of this swelling and compression is that affected dogs may find it difficult and painful to urinate through the compressed urethra. These dogs will strain more than normal when trying to pass urine and the urine is often passed in short intermittent spurts. The urine which is passed in this way is often blood-tinged.

6a(i) Prostatitis

Prostatitis means infection and inflammation in the prostate gland. This condition is only found in uncastrated male dogs i.e. dogs who have not had their testicles removed by a vet. The reason why the gland becomes infected is not known. The symptoms of prostatitis include walking with an arched back, stiff back legs taking shorter than normal steps during walking and lethargy and poor appetite due to the pain and fever associated with this condition. The diagnosis is made by noticing these symptoms and documenting a fever when the temperature is taken with a thermometer. The final step in making this diagnosis is feeling the prostate gland. The vet does this by inserting a finger into the anus and feeling an enlarged and painful prostate gland (Fig. 8b). The treatment for this condition may include antibiotics, anti-inflammatories and hormone injections. If the condition reoccurs often the vet may advise castration as this causes the prostate to shrink and infections in castrated male dogs are very rare. A complication of this condition is that the infection may spread into the back bones which are positioned directly above the prostate gland. This condition is called discospondilitis. The presence of discospondilitis is suspected when there is a great deal of pain and inflammation in the lower back at the level of the lumbo-sacral joint. The lumbo-sacral joint is the joint made by the lowest of the lumbar back bones and the sacrum (the bone forming the roof of the pelvis). If the vet suspects that the dog also has lumbo-sacral discospondilitis the diagnosis can be confirmed by taking X-rays of these bones. The treatment for discospondilitis is very often the same antibiotics and anti-inflammatories that are used to treat the prostatitis.

6a(ii) Prostatic hypertrophy

The prostate gland may become swollen and painful without being infected. This swelling is caused by sex hormones acting on the prostate gland causing it to swell (Fig. 8b). Two hormones may cause the problem. The first hormone which may cause this problem is testosterone which is the male sex hormone produced in the testicles. This hormone may overstimulate the prostate gland and thus cause it to swell and possibly become painful. The other hormone that may cause swelling of the prostate is the female hormone oestrogen. All male animals normally have very small amounts of female hormone in their body but when there is too much of the hormone it may affect the prostate gland. The effect of too much female hormone is that it causes swelling of the prostate and it can change the structure of the cells in the prostate gland by a process called squamous meta-plasia. If this condition develops one should try to determine why there is an increased level of female hormone in that dog's body. The most common source of excess female hormone is from a type of tumour called a sertoli cell tumour that may develop in one of the dog's testicles. The presence of a sertoli cell tumour in a testicle is that the affected testicle is often hard and lumpy and larger than the other testicle which tends to shrink because of the high levels of female hormone produced by the tumour in the other testicle.

The symptoms of walking with an arched back and stiff back legs, taking shorter than normal steps during walking are far less severe than in cases of prostatitis. The affected dog will generally not be lethargic or lose their appetite, as they do not develop a fever with this condition. Thus when the temperature is taken it will be normal and when the prostate gland is touched during the rectal examination by the vet, the prostate will be found to be enlarged and swollen but there is little or no pain when it is touched. The treatment for this condition depends on which hormone is causing the prostate gland to swell. If too much testosterone (male hormone) is the problem the dogs may be treated with injections to lower the levels of this hormone. If these injections do not solve the problem or if the problems keeps recurring then castrating the dog will solve the problem because this remove the factory which produces the male hormone. If the cause of the problem is too much oestrogen (female hormone) the solution to the problem is also to castrate the dog because this will remove the tumour in the testicle which is producing the female hormone. In cases where one cannot determine which hormone is causing the problem the vet may advise tests to investigate the problem. These tests may include blood tests, ultrasound scans of the prostate and testicles and possibly also biopsies from the prostate gland.

6b Lower back sprains and strains

Dogs may sprain or strain their lower back just as we human beings do. There may not always be an explanation for when they may have strained their back but the pain will cause the symptoms of walking with an arched back and stiff back legs, taking shorter than normal steps during walking. These dogs will also be reluctant to go up stairs or climb into cars or onto the beds and furniture at home. They will however seem to be more comfortable going down stairs or climbing down from furniture or out of the car. This is because when they are moving upwards most of the body weight is being transferred to the lower back and the back legs but when they move downwards most of the weight is transferred to the front legs.

The vet will be able to feel heat, pain and swelling over the lower back and the treatment for this condition involves the use of anti-inflammatories and rest for one to several weeks just as in the case of human beings with the same condition. Manipulation of the bones in the back by a trained osteopath will often help to relieve the pain and speed up the recovery time.

6c Discospondilitis

Dogs may develop infections in the back bones which are positioned directly above the prostate gland. This condition is called discospondilitis. The presence of discospondilitis is suspected when there is a great deal of pain and inflammation in the lower back at the level of the lumbo-sacral joint. The lumbo-sacral joint is the joint made by the lowest of the lumbar back bones and the sacrum which is the bone forming the roof of the pelvis. The cause of the infection is often not determined but it may be the result of a spread of infection from other organs like the prostate gland, the bladder or the kidneys. If the vet suspects that the dog has lumbo-sacral discospondilitis the diagnosis can be confirmed by taking X-rays of these bones. The treatment for discospondilitis is very often the same antibiotics and anti-inflammatories that are used to treat infections in the bladder, kidneys or prostate gland.

6d Cauda – equina syndrome

The lumbo-sacral joint is the joint made by the lowest of the lumbar back bones and the sacrum (the bone forming the roof of the pelvis). This is a very important part of the back bone (vertebral column) as it acts as a pivot point or 'hinge' in the back during many of the dog's movements such as jumping, climbing stairs, standing up and squatting to urinate and defecate. The spinal cord is positioned in a canal which runs through the centre of all of the bones of the back, which together form the vertebral column. The vertebral column thus serves several functions which include protecting the spinal cord, providing stability for the body and providing the attachment points for many bones (e.g. ribs and hipbones) and muscles.

Cauda-equina syndrome is the collective name used to describe several problems which may affect the function of the lumbo-sacral joint. There are two more commonly encountered problems in cauda-equina syndrome. The first is that the two bones that form the lumbo-sacral joint do not form a stable joint. Thus, as the bones move around during normal body movements, they may pinch or bruise the spinal cord which runs in the bony canal inside these bones. The result of this bruising or pinching is severe pain in the area and affected dogs will often try to bite the vet when they touch the affected area. The second possible problem is that the bony canal which contains and protects the spinal cord is simply too narrow at the lumbo-sacral joint and although the joint may be perfectly stable, normal body movements may cause the spinal cord to be pinched at this point by the narrow bone canal.

The vet will often suspect cauda-equina syndrome simply on the basis that there is severe pain in the lower back area. The vet will then often advise X-rays and often also specialised X-rays called myelograms to investigate the problem. This syndrome may be effectively controlled by the use of anti-inflammatories but many of these cases will require various types of major surgery to repair the problem. Not all dogs would be suitable candidates for these various operations and each individual case should be assessed for suitability on their own merits, your vet will advise you whether surgery is appropriate or not and which particular operation would be the most appropriate for your dog.

6e Intervertebral disc disease

The backbone or vertebral column is comprised of many individual 'back bones' placed end to end called vertebrae. The individual vertebrae each have a hollow central canal running through the centre of each bone. The spinal cord is found in this canal which is called the vertebral canal. Each individual vertebra has a disc of cartilage at either end which separates it from the vertebra attached at its front and back end. This disc of cartilage is called the intervertebral disc. The function of these discs is to act as a shock absorber between the vertebrae and also to prevent the ends of the vertebrae rubbing against each other. These discs are held in position by ligaments attached to the vertebrae.

The ligaments holding the intervertebral discs and the discs themselves may weaken with time and the disc may then move out of its normal position. This is called a disc prolapse. If the disc moves upwards it may bump into and press against the spinal cord. This may be a slow and gradual process and the primary symptom will be back pain which progressively becomes worse. This slow process of prolapse is called a Hansen type two prolapse. If the disc is suddenly and forcefully prolapsed it may severely damage the spinal cord causing partial or total paralysis and often severe pain. This severe and forceful type of prolapse is called a Hansen type one prolapse. Both types of disc prolapse may occur at any point along the vertebral column but generally type one prolapses are seen in the neck area and type two prolapses occur in the middle and lower back.

Hansen type two prolapse of the intervertebral disc in the lower back causes a slowly increasing amount of pressure to be exerted on the spinal cord. This process causes a progressively worsening back pain. Many of these cases may look like hip problems in that these dogs will walk with an arched lower back and walk with stiff back legs and take only short strides with the back legs. A further similarity to hip problems is that these cases will also be reluctant to go up stairs or climb into cars or onto the beds and furniture at home. They will however seem to be more comfortable going down stairs or climbing down from furniture or out of the car. This is because when they are moving upwards most of the body weight is being transferred to the lower back and the back legs but when they move downwards most of the weight is transferred to the front legs.

If the vet suspects that the cause of the problem is a prolapsed disc they will usually suggest that X-rays be taken of the back. Routine and specialised X-rays called myelograms are often needed to diagnose the problem. Myelograms are like normal X-rays except that special types of dye are first injected into the vertebral canal in much the same way that epidural anaesthetic injections are given to women while giving birth. This special dye is injected because often the disc has only moved very slightly and this cannot be seen on normal X-rays. The myelogram dye in the vertebral canal will however help to show up even very minor disc prolapse.

Once the diagnosis of disc prolapse has been confirmed and the vet knows which disc has moved and sometimes also how many discs have moved, they will be able to discuss the various types of treatment that are available. In minor cases of disc prolapse the problem can often be solved with short to medium term courses of anti-inflammatories. In more severe cases or in cases where anti-inflammatory treatment has not solved the problem the only treatment option may be spinal surgery. Not all dogs would be suitable candidates for these operations and each individual case should be assessed for suitability on their own merits, your vet will advise you whether surgery is appropriate or not and which particular operation would be the most appropriate for your dog.

Arthritis

The word arthritis means inflammation of a joint. The arthritis may be acute (developed very suddenly) or chronic (developed over a long period of time). Factors that cause acute arthritis may develop into chronic arthritis. Arthritis may develop after a joint has been injured or infected. The types of injuries which may cause acute or chronic arthritis are sprains, fractures, dislocations etc. Injuries to joints should thus be treated as quickly and efficiently as possible to try to prevent long term permanent arthritis from developing in that joint. We are all familiar with the concept of someone injuring a joint and then either having permanent low grade discomfort in that joint, or the injury may have seemed to heal well but as we get older the joint may cause us discomfort due to the delayed onset of arthritis. Arthritis may also develop in a joint which is not anatomically perfectly formed i.e. it is dysplastic. Dysplasia is the technical description for a joint which is not perfectly formed. Most people are most familiar with the term hip dysplasia which means that the hips are not properly formed but any joint may suffer from dysplasia. If a joint is dysplastic then it will wear out faster than a normally formed joint. This process of wearing out causes arthritis. Arthritis may also develop simply due to normal 'wear and tear' in a normal joint due to old age.

Chronic arthritis is most commonly encountered in older dogs or dogs who have suffered from an injury or infection affecting one or more joints. The process of chronic arthritis is often referred to as degenerative joint disease (DJD). Chronic arthritis causes thickening of the tissues around the joint. This thickening is caused by 'scar tissue' forming around the joint. The bones forming the joint will develop irregular thickenings called osteophytes. The lining of the joint will be permanently inflamed and thickened. These three changes represent the body's attempt to heal and strengthen the affected joint. These changes often make the arthritis worse as they will continue permanently and lead to the pain of the arthritis becoming progressively worse. The second effect of these three processes is that the joint will lose its full range of movement. This happens because the 'scar tissue' laid down around the joint will make it less flexible, and thus the joint is less able to perform its full range of movements.

Once the three processes of chronic arthritis have been present for a few months or years the affected joint will feel thicker than the same joint on the other leg will. When a joint with chronic arthritis is flexed and extended one will notice that it may not be able to bend or straighten as much as a healthy joint does. During bending and straightening one may also notice a 'crunchy' sound or feeling in the joint. This 'crunchy' sensation is called crepitus. Once the process of chronic arthritis has started, the changes in the joint are irreversible. The changes in fact will become more severe as time goes on. This process of arthritis is identical to the process of arthritis in human beings.

When the vet is faced with an arthritic joint the treatment they apply will have three objectives i.e.:

- Relieve the pain and inflammation in the joint.
- Slow down the ongoing changes which worsen the arthritis over time.
- Improve the range of movement of the joint.

The vet will achieve this by using painkillers and anti-inflammatories to make the joint more comfortable. They may also recommend the use of medications called 'mobility supplements' and may recommend a physiotherapy programme to maintain a good range of joint movement and to slow down the rate of worsening arthritis.

The first step is to find a suitable long-term anti-inflammatory drug that will alleviate the pain in the joint. Most anti-inflammatory medications are synthetic (man-made) and the three most common examples are Metacam, Rimadyl and Zubrin. There is one natural anti-inflammatory which I find consistently works very well to alleviate the pain of long term arthritis which is green lipped mussel extract. Optimal results are achieved when green lipped mussel extract is used concurrently with one of the synthetic anti-inflammatory drugs. The second treatment I use is the category of agents called mobility supplements (chondroitin sulphate and/or glucosamine). These are agents that help the joint to produce synovial fluid to maintain its lubrication and to promote natural healing of the eroded articular cartilages covering the bone ends. This is an important component of the treatment as these erosions expose the nerve endings in the bone which cause a lot of the pain and if we can repair these areas the patient will obviously require a lower daily dose of anti-inflammatories. A change in lifestyle also benefits these patients in that overweight individuals should lose weight to take the extra strain off the joints and gentle controlled exercise should be encouraged to maintain the size and strength of the muscles of the affected leg as they help to support the joints. The gentle exercise may include swimming if facilities are available. This programme of sustained, controlled exercise is effectively the same as a physiotherapy programme for human beings. The objective of this programme of activity (physiotherapy) is to keep the joints as flexible as possible as this will make movement easier and less uncomfortable for the dog.

The individuals who show very little or no pain can often be successfully treated using only natural remedies like green lipped mussel extract or glucosamine and chondroitin sulphate or natural oils like cod liver oil and evening primrose oil or homoeopathic remedies like sulphur, arnica and rhus tox. These remedies work by relieving the pain and, in the case of glucosamine and chondroitin sulphate, also help the joint to lubricate itself and repair the damage to the joint cartilage caused by the grinding action of the unstable bone ends. If these products are not sufficient to alleviate the pain then they should be combined with long term anti-inflammatory and painkilling medications. Many anti-inflammatory/painkilling treatments are available for dogs and are safe for long term and permanent use. If one particular medication does not seem to help much then another should be tried and thus different medicines should be used until one is found that works for your individual dog. This trial and error period in which different medicines in different combinations are tried should be controlled and monitored by your vet, as there are many medicines that should not be used in combination with other medicines.

Most dogs who have developed arthritis for whatever reason should be able to enjoy an active and happy life when the appropriate treatments are used. The process of developing arthritis is, just as in human beings, something one should expect in old age but one does not have to accept the pain or discomfort which may accompany the arthritis. Modern treatment and management of arthritis means that we, and our dogs, should be able to live comfortably in our golden years.

10

EAR PROBLEMS

The ears of different breeds of dog may look very different but the anatomical components are always the same. The components of the dog's ear are the same as human ears. The 'ear flap' is technically called the pinna and when we refer to more than one pinna the plural of the word is pinnae. In some breeds e.g. German shepherd dogs the pinna is upright and rigid and in other breeds e.g. spaniels the pinna hangs down along the side of the head. The pinna is simply a flat piece of cartilage covered with skin (Fig. 14a). The base of the pinna is attached to several muscles that can move the pinna in a variety of directions. The ear canal is the hollow tube that leads from the eardrum in the skull to the outside world. The ear canal is a funnel for collecting sounds and leading them to the eardrum and is simply a cone of cartilage that is lined by hairless skin. This ear canal can be divided into two parts. The first part which we can see and look down is called the vertical ear canal because it literally runs vertically downwards from the base of the earflap (pinna). The vertical ear canal then takes a sharp turn inward towards the skull to form the horizontal ear canal which is attached to the eardrum. The eardrum is simply a thin membrane, much like the membrane of a drum. On the inside of the eardrum are the middle ear and inner ear. The middle ear is a hollow chamber in the skull bone which acts like the body of a drum and the inner ear is a separate structure which is composed of rings full of fluid which act as our balance centre and have nothing to do with the process of hearing.

The first sign that may alert us to a problem affecting the ear of a dog is that they may twitch the ears more than normal. In more severe cases the dog may shake their head and scratch at one or both ears either by rubbing the head along the ground or by scratching the ear with their paws. In more advanced cases one may also notice an unusual or foul smell coming from the ear canals. When one notices that one or both ears are bothering the dog one should examine the ear flap, the ear canal and the skin around the ear.

The ear can be divided into three parts when one considers diseases and conditions that affect the ears. I will discuss conditions that affect the ear flap (pinna), the ear canal and the skin around the ear.

1 The ear flap (pinna)

The most common abnormality that one may notice when examining the pinna is that a portion of the ear flap or even the entire ear flap may seem very thick and swollen. This swelling feels firm and sometimes warm when touched but usually is not painful. Many people think that the dog has developed an abscess in the ear flap but the most common explanation for this swelling is a condition called an othaematoma.

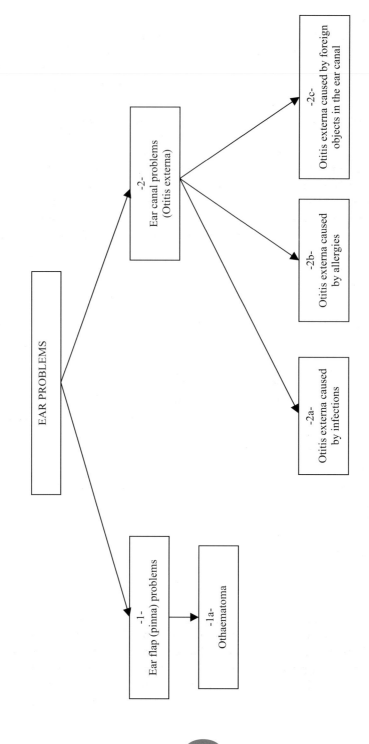

1a Othaematoma

An othaematoma is effectively a large 'blood blister' under the skin of the ear flap (Fig. 14c). Most of us have heard of rugby players and boxers developing 'cauliflower ears'. The reason that these sportsmen may develop a cauliflower ear is that when the pinna has been damaged by a punch or a hard knock, small blood vessels may be damaged and bleeding can occur under the skin, remember that the pinna is simply a flat piece of cartilage covered by skin. Thus if bleeding occurs inside the pinna the blood will accumulate in a pocket under the skin between the skin and the layer of cartilage. This pocket of blood will lift the skin layer off the cartilage layer. The amount of bleeding that occurs will determine the size of the 'blood blister'. This pocket of blood will eventually contract just like scabs do on external wounds on the skin. The effect of the blood in the othaematoma clotting is that the edges of the blood clot will stick to the skin and the cartilage layer. The next step in the natural healing process is that the blood clot, just like a scab on the skin, will start to contract and shrink. As this contraction process continues a lump of scar tissue will form and the cartilage layer and the overlying skin will be stuck together by the scar tissue. This process of natural healing often results in the ear healing in a lumpy and ultimately misformed way and the final appearance is called a 'cauliflower ear'.

Othaematomas may develop in dogs' ears in the same way that they develop in the case of sportsmen. The dogs will often start with an infection or irritation in the ear canal which causes them to shake their heads. If dogs shake their heads very violently the ear flaps may slap against the skull bones hard enough to damage blood vessels in the pinna and thus bleeding between the cartilage layer and the skin layer causes a 'blood blister' or othaematoma to develop. If one examines a dog's ear and finds an othaematoma, the first thing to do is to determine why the dog might have been shaking their head violently enough to cause this damage. The most common cause is pain, infection or irritation in the ear canal which will be discussed more fully in the section on problems of the ear canals. If one finds that there is a problem in the ear canal then it is important to treat the ear canal problem as well as the othaematoma. There are however often cases where there is no evidence of any problems in the ear canal and no signs of the dog shaking their head. These cases present simply as an othaematoma that may developed very suddenly in the ear flap. We do not fully understand why some othaematomas develop for no apparent reason but we suspect that it may be the result of an auto-immune disorder. An auto-immune disorder is a condition caused when the body's own immune system starts attacking and damaging specific tissues in the body. There is often no explanation why this happens but this process may sometimes cause bleeding in the pinna and thus an othaematoma may develop.

There are a variety of ways of treating an othaematoma. The most common way is to drain the blood out of the othaematoma using a needle and syringe and once it has been completely drained a small amount of cortizone is injected through the same needle into the remaining empty pocket between the ear skin and cartilage. This process will normally stimulate the ear to heal but sometimes the othaematoma will reform within a few days and the vet will have to redrain the blood from the ear several times. The old method of treating this condition was to make an incision in the ear flap to drain the blood away and then many large stitches were placed through the ear flap to hold the cartilage and skin layers together so that they could once again be attached to each other. This procedure can be very painful and I would only use this technique if repeatedly draining the ear and instilling cortizone into the ear flap failed to solve the problem.

An important point to make at this stage is that any problems that may be present in the ear canal must be treated at the same time. The reason for this is that if the problem in the ear canal is not treated then the dog will continue shaking their head and thus the damage to the pinna continues and the othaematoma cannot heal.

Many people ask me what would happen if we did not treat the othaematoma. The answer to this is that it will eventually heal by itself by clotting and contracting as discussed earlier. The reason for treating the ear is that if we leave it to heal naturally then the dog will end up with a cauliflower ear that will be permanently thickened and misshapen.

2 Problems/conditions affecting the ear canals

The most common symptoms one will encounter when examining the ear canal is that it may be inflamed, swollen, and painful and may have a discharge. The medical term for these symptoms is otitis externa. The most common explanations for these findings are that there may be an infection in the ear canal, there may be an allergic reaction in the ear canal or there may be a foreign body such as a piece of grass or a grass seed in the ear canal. I will discuss each of these three possibilities individually.

2a Infections in the ear canal (otitis externa due to infection)

Bacteria, yeasts, fungi and ear mites may cause infections in the ear canal. Many people refer to ear canal infections as canker. I do not like to use this word as I feel that it is too vague to mean anything. If there is an infection in the ear canal the type of discharge may often give the vet an idea of what type of infection it is. If the ear canal contains a thick, black crusty discharge then ear mites are the most likely cause of the problem. Ear mites are most commonly encountered in puppies and young dogs and are easily dealt with by using appropriate eardrops. If the ear canal contains pus then bacteria are the most likely cause of the infection. The pus may have a foul smell and the infection may be very painful. The treatment would involve the use of painkilling anti-inflammatory treatment and antibiotic drops and tablets. In more severe cases the vet may also suggest that the ear canal be flushed and cleaned under sedation or general anaesthesia. Yeast and fungal infections are often secondary infections that take advantage of an ear canal that is already inflamed or infected. Most modern eardrops contain multiple ingredients to treat all possible infections and vets will often only use tests like bacterial cultures if the problem does not resolve quickly and easily.

2b Allergic inflammation in the ear canal (allergic otitis externa)

I have used the word allergy very loosely thus far and at this point it is worth discussing in more depth. Dogs develop allergies just as people do. The allergies that they develop are often due to the same things that we develop allergies to. The most common causes of allergies in dogs and people seem to be house dust and house dust mites, grasses and pollens, and various types of food. The way that we manifest our allergies is to develop hay fever, asthma or skin eczema. Dogs only rarely develop asthma or hay fever; most dogs with allergies will develop itchy skin. The thing that causes the allergy is called the allergen. The route by which the allergen is taken into the body does not

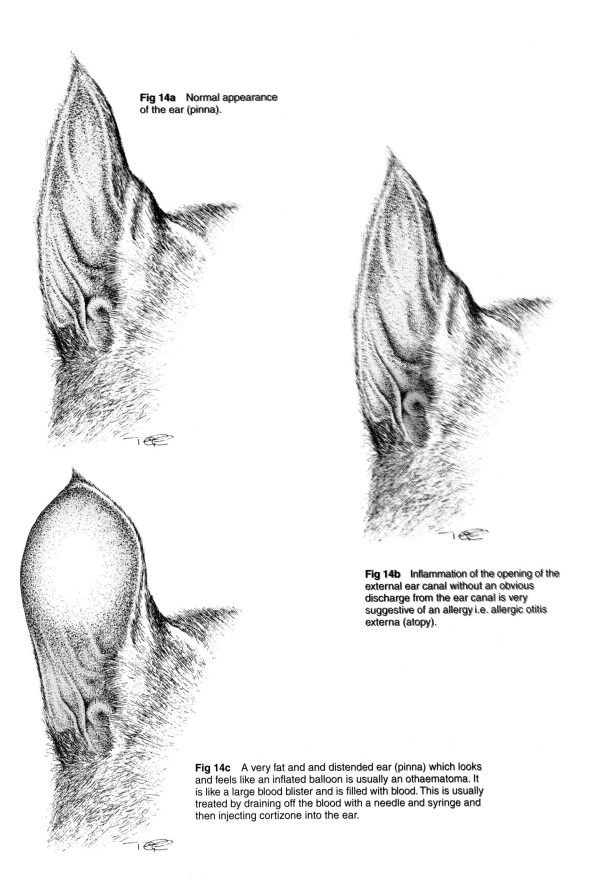

Fig 14a Normal appearance of the ear (pinna).

Fig 14b Inflammation of the opening of the external ear canal without an obvious discharge from the ear canal is very suggestive of an allergy i.e. allergic otitis externa (atopy).

Fig 14c A very fat and and distended ear (pinna) which looks and feels like an inflated balloon is usually an othaematoma. It is like a large blood blister and is filled with blood. This is usually treated by draining off the blood with a needle and syringe and then injecting cortizone into the ear.

necessarily affect where in the body the allergy effect will be produced. Consider people with an allergy to nuts or bee stings, if they are exposed to the nuts in their food or a sting in their skin they will often develop severe swelling in their airways which may cause suffocation. This demonstrates that the site of the allergy reaction does not necessarily have to be the same as the route of exposure to the allergen. The same concept applies to dogs in that they generally manifest their allergies as inflammation and itching in the skin. This applies to food allergies; inhaled allergies like pollens and house dust mites and injected allergies like fleabites. The most severe sites of itching in response to allergy reactions are the ears, paws and the anal region as mentioned before.

Dogs suffering from allergies very commonly present with itchy, inflamed ears or even infected ears. The cases where the dog's allergies have caused the inflammation and itching in the ears are called allergic otitis externa. The lining of the ear canal down to the level of the eardrum is the same type of skin that covers the rest of the body; thus inflammation due to allergic reactions extends all the way down the ear canals. The ear canal is basically a tube of cartilage lined with skin. When the skin layer becomes inflamed, the cartilage will not allow the skin layer to swell outwards, as cartilage is not pliable enough. The result is that the swelling of the skin lining is inwards. The effect of this is that the ear canal becomes narrowed when it is inflamed. The result of this is that the air movement in the ear canal is reduced and the ear canal becomes a warm, dark, moist place. Bacteria, yeast and fungi love warm, dark, moist places and thus one will often see a secondary infection in an ear canal that is inflamed due to allergies.

The inflammation that develops in one or both ear canals can be demonstrated by comparing the colour of the skin in the ear canal with a piece of skin elsewhere on the body. The skin at the opening of the ear canal is generally pinker than the skin elsewhere (Fig. 14b). The result of long-term low-grade inflammation in skin is that the skin thickens. To make sense of this consider people who work with their hands a lot. These people, like manual labourers or gardeners, will develop calluses on their hands as time goes by. This is because the long-term abrasion and irritation causes long term inflammation in the skin of the hand. The body attempts to protect the hand by thickening the skin, and in the places where it is most thickened we identify calluses. The ear canal responds in much the same way in that long term, low-grade inflammation will result in thickening of the skin lining the ear canals. The most serious consequence of this process is that the thickening of the ear canal lining will result in narrowing of the ear canal, as the cartilage outer cone will not allow the ear canal to expand outwards. The final result is that the ear canal becomes much narrower than it should be and is very susceptible to secondary infection because of reduced ventilation in this narrow channel. This thickening makes the skin at the entrance to the ear canal appear similar to elephant skin in comparison to the smooth skin elsewhere on the body. Technically this is called hyperkeratosis or lichenification.

Thus, when a dog develops an ear infection, we must not only treat the pain and infection in the first instance but also try to identify how and why the infection developed. Many times the infection may have developed for no apparent reason but we should always look to see if it developed secondarily to the narrowing of the ear canal due to the inflammation caused by an allergy action. This is even more important in the case of recurring ear infections, as the long term allergic inflammation and recurrent secondary infections will result in ongoing narrowing of the ear canal throughout the dog's life and thus secondary ear infections will occur more and more often as the dog grows older. An important point to make here is that an inflamed ear canal containing abnormal matter is not necessarily an infected ear. One will get a very good idea of what secondary problem has affected the ear canal by looking at the abnormal matter accumulating in the ear canal. Pus would suggest a bacterial infection and/or fungal and yeast infections, a black tarry substance which may look like clotted blood may suggest ear mites and a dark brown waxy substance suggests just an allergy reaction without secondary infections. The accumulation of this dark brown waxy substance is often misinterpreted as an infection as it may have a foul smell, but is generally just an overproduction of earwax. The reason this happens is best understood by comparing the allergy reaction manifesting in dogs' ears to the allergy reaction manifesting in human beings' noses called hay fever. In the case of human beings, hay fever produces inflammation in the lining of the nose, the nose does not know whether the inflammation is due to an allergic reaction or an infection starting in the nose, so it does the only thing it can to protect itself – it produces a protective layer of mucous. In the case of hay fever sufferers it effectively overdoes it and we develop a very watery, bunged up snotty nose. The ear canal, when it is inflamed, also does not know whether the inflammation is due to allergy or infection and it also does the only thing it can to protect itself which is to produce more wax to build up a defensive barrier. The wax production is however also often overdone and thus we see a dark brown waxy accumulation of 'muck' in the ear canal in cases of allergies manifesting in dogs' ear canals.

The treatment for allergic otitis externa may involve the use of eardrops, antihistamines or cortizone and antibiotics if secondary infections have developed. The long-term treatment and management of allergies is very important to avoid frequent recurrence of the problem. I have discussed the long-term treatment for allergic otitis externa in the allergy section in the chapter on itchy dogs.

2c Foreign bodies in the ear canal

Occasionally objects like pieces of grass or grass seeds/awns may fall into the ear canal. The signs that this may have happened is that the dog will suddenly start to shake their head quite violently and the ear will be very painful when one tries to examine it. These symptoms usually develop shortly after a walk during the time of year that wild grasses are producing seeds. The dogs usually will show sudden pain and discomfort in the ear and if they allow us to look into the ear there is often nothing unusual to see. This is because the grass seed often only causes pain when it has moved into the horizontal ear canal leading to the eardrum that is out of view. The vet will examine this part of the ear canal using and instrument called an otoscope. If the vet sees a foreign object in the ear canal they may be able to remove it immediately but in many cases the ear is so painful that they can only remove the object by anaesthetising the dog.

11

MY DOG IS SNEEZING AND/OR HAS A DISCHARGE FROM ONE OR BOTH NOSTRILS

The dog's 'nose' can be regarded as consisting of three parts just like a human 'nose'. The three parts are the nostrils, the nasal chamber and the nasal sinuses.

The nasal chamber is the space leading from the nostrils to the back of the throat. The floor of the nasal chamber is the hard and soft palate that also acts as the roof of the mouth. The back of the nasal chamber opens into the back of the throat where the air that is breathed in moves into the opening of the voice box (trachea). The nasal chamber is divided into two parts i.e. the left and right chamber leading back from the left and right nostril respectively. There is a thin plate of bone called the vomer bone that forms the wall between the left and right nasal chamber. Inside each nasal chamber there are three turbinate bones. Each turbinate bone is like a rolled up piece of paper that is positioned lengthways along the nasal chamber. The front opening of this rolled up wafer thin bone is just inside the nostril and the back opening of each turbinate bone leads to the back of the throat. The three turbinate bones in each nasal chamber are positioned one on top of the other. Thus each nasal chamber contains a top, middle and a bottom turbinate bone. The turbinate bones are wafer thin and are covered by a mucous membrane. The purpose of having these turbinate bones is to warm up air before it is passed to the lungs and also to filter out particles in the air like dust particles. The ethmoid bone is a sponge-like bone at the back end of the nasal chambers that is used for smell. The ethmoid bone has the same structure as a sponge and it is covered by a special type of mucous membrane that acts as our sense of smell. This mucous membrane lines all the small nooks, crannies and small tubes inside this sponge-like bone. The reason that the ethmoid bone has the same structure as a sponge is that this provides more surface area to be covered by the mucous membrane that we use for smell. This means that if we collected all the mucous membrane covering all the inside and outside surfaces of this sponge-like structure we would have a much larger flat layer of mucous membrane than if the mucous membrane simply covered a solid piece of bone of the same size as the ethmoid bone. If we collected all the mucous membrane from the human ethmoid bone and laid it flat, it would cover an area about the size of a handkerchief. If we did the same thing in an average size dog we would probably cover an area about the size of a double bed sheet. This helps to explain why a dog's sense of smell is so much better than a human being's sense of smell.

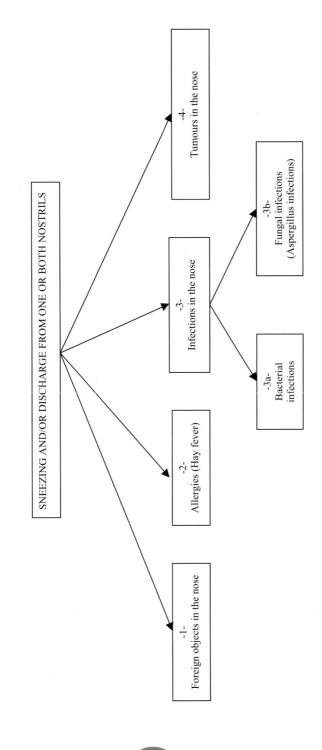

The nasal sinuses are hollow 'air pockets' in the skull bones. The most important of these are called the frontal sinuses and they are found in the bone forming the forehead called the frontal bone. These 'air pockets' are hollow chambers in the skull bones that are lined with a mucous membrane and are connected to the nasal chambers. People who suffer from hay fever and sinusitis will be well aware of the frontal sinuses as allergic inflammation in these sinuses causes the feeling of congestion, headaches and the 'bunged up' feeling associated with hay fever.

The symptoms of sneezing and/or discharge from the nostrils tell us that there is inflammation and irritation in the nasal chambers and their turbinate bones. This irritation and inflammation can be caused by allergic inflammation (hay fever), infections, tumours or particles such as dust, pieces of grass etc which have become stuck in the mucous membranes in the nasal chamber or turbinate bones. Inflammation in the nose is called rhinitis.

When a vet examines a dog which is sneezing and/or has a discharge from the nostrils, the vet's questions will help them to explain the cause of the problem. The problem that the vet will face during the consultation is that very often the final diagnosis can only be made after various tests have been performed because many different causes of sneezing and nasal discharge will often produce exactly the same symptoms. The vet's thoughts and questions will proceed along the following lines.

- Is the dog just sneezing or is there also a discharge from one or both of the nostrils?
- If there is a discharge from the nostrils is it coming from one or both of the nostrils?
- What does the discharge look like?
- How long have the symptoms been present?
- Did the symptoms appear very suddenly or did the symptoms gradually develop over a longer period of time?
- Apart from the sneezing and/or discharge does the dog seem fit and well or do they appear ill?
- Are the nostrils or the muzzle of the dog painful when touched?

The vet's thoughts will go something like this: if the dog is just sneezing and there is no nasal discharge and the symptoms developed gradually over a period of a few days or weeks then the irritation in the nose may be due to allergic inflammation (hay fever) or mild infection. If the dog suddenly started sneezing very often and very forcefully and there is no nasal discharge then the possibility that a foreign body, like a piece of grass, has recently lodged in the nasal chamber is quite likely. If sneezing started very suddenly after the dog was exploring in the garden or while out on a walk then it is also quite likely that a foreign body has lodged in the nasal chamber. If the dog has a nasal discharge then one must try to determine if it is coming from one or both nostrils and one must try to determine what the discharge looks like. If the discharge is mostly pus and coming from only one nostril then one might expect that it is due to an infection in the nasal chamber. This infection may be due to a foreign body being lodged in the nasal cavity for more than several days or it may be due to a tooth abscess or it may be a primary infection. Primary infections are cases where there is no apparent explanation for the cause of the infection. Primary infections may cause a pus-like discharge from one or both nostrils and the amount of sneezing may vary from a lot of sneezing to no sneezing at all. If there is a clear watery discharge from one or both nostrils then one might suspect allergic inflammation (hay fever). If the discharge is a clear fluid, which contains blood and is coming from only one nostril and has developed over a period of several days to several weeks, then one might consider that there might be a tumour in the nasal chamber. If the dog appears very ill or if the nostrils or the muzzle are painful then one would consider severe infection or possibly a tumour to be the cause of the problem.

The above thoughts will show that initially there may be no way that the vet will be able to say exactly what the cause of the problem is and thus they may suggest performing tests to help them make a diagnosis. The standard way of testing a dog with sneezing and/or a nasal discharge consists of several steps. The tests will need to be done with the dog sleeping under a general anaesthetic and will be done in the following order. The first step is to take X-rays and if possible an MRI scan of the nasal chambers, the nasal sinuses and the bones of the skull. The second step is to take a swab from the inside of the nasal chambers to send to a laboratory which will check for different types of bacterial and fungal infection and they will also be able to determine the best treatment for treating the infection. The third step is to look inside the nasal chambers between the turbinate bones with an endoscope. The fourth step is to take a biopsy from the nasal turbinate bones for analysis by a specialist laboratory and the final step is to take a blood sample that a laboratory may use to diagnose certain types of fungal infection.

Once the results of the tests are known the vet should be able to make an accurate diagnosis. The most common frustration in these cases of sneezing and/or nasal discharge is that, in twenty per cent of cases, the tests will not give the vet the diagnosis. This means that despite performing all the tests that we have discussed earlier, one in five of these cases will not be able to be explained. These causes are then often treated with symptomatic treatment that usually involves antibiotics and anti-inflammatory treatments. If the symptoms do not resolve within a few weeks then all the tests should be re-run to try again to establish a definite diagnosis. The reasons that the tests may not yield the diagnosis may include the following problems: endoscopes cannot reach and examine every part of the nasal chamber, very early tumours may not be detected on X-rays and MRI scans, biopsies may not contain representative tissue samples and the blood tests may unknowingly give incorrect results. The majority of cases will however yield a specific diagnosis after the appropriate tests have been performed.

The variety of possible explanations for the symptoms will be discussed individually.

1 Nasal foreign bodies

Grass seeds (grass awns) or small pieces of grass, leaves or twigs may be found lodged in the nasal cavity. These foreign bodies are removed with specially designed forceps and this will cure the problem. If the foreign body has caused an infection the vet will usually prescribe a course of antibiotics.

2 Allergic rhinitis (hay fever)

This condition is usually diagnosed from the biopsy from the nasal turbinate bones and the vet will prescribe treatment for the allergy. For a full discussion on the treatment options for allergy please refer to the allergy section in chapter 7. Although the type of allergy is different from a skin allergy the concepts for treating allergies is the same.

3 Nasal infections (infectious rhinitis)

The infection may be due to a foreign body being lodged in the nasal cavity for more than several days or it may be due to a tooth abscess or an oro-nasal fistula or it may be a primary infection. Primary infections are cases where there is no apparent explanation for the cause of the infection. Primary infections may cause a pus-like discharge from one or both nostrils and the amount of sneezing may vary from a lot of sneezing to no sneezing at all.

If the infection is due to a foreign body in the nasal chamber then removing the offending object and using a short course of antibiotics will solve the problem. If the infection is due to a tooth root abscess then treating the abscess by using antibiotics or removing the infected tooth and using a course of antibiotics will solve the problem. The infection may be caused by an oro-nasal fistula. An oro-nasal fistula is a hole in the hard palate that connects the inside of the mouth to the inside of the nasal chamber. This hole normally develops as a result of a tooth root abscess which causes the affected tooth to fall out and the bone of the hard palate in that area is dissolved by the infection. This problem is solved by suturing the hole closed and clearing the infection in the bone of the hard palate with a course of antibiotics. Oro-nasal fistulas are most commonly seen in small dogs.

3a and 3b Bacterial and fungal infections
Primary infections in the nasal chamber are caused by bacteria or fungi. These infections usually develop over a period of several weeks and often cause a pus-like nasal discharge with a variable amount of sneezing. If the infection is due to bacteria then antibiotics should cure the problem. The most common fungal infection in the nasal chambers is caused by a fungus called Aspergillus fumigatus. This infection is most easily diagnosed by the blood test mentioned earlier. The fungal infection is often accompanied by a bacterial infection at the same time. This fungal infection is very difficult to cure and treatment may involve more than just a course of tablets. The treatment for this condition may include drilling holes in the forehead into the nasal sinuses to place tubes into the nasal sinuses. These tubes are stitched into position for a few weeks and are used to squirt anti-fungal liquid treatments into the nasal sinuses twice daily for up to several weeks. This liquid then drains through the nasal sinuses and into the nasal chambers. This is an extreme form of treatment but it is sometimes the only option when treating this condition. This infection may however not respond to any form of treatment and often the best we can hope for is to try to keep the affected individual as comfortable as possible for as long as possible. Many dogs with this fungal infection will however suffer severe distress and discomfort with little or no improvement when treatment is applied and thus many people will have to consider putting these dogs to sleep if they fail to respond to all attempts at treatment.

4 Nasal tumours

Two types of tumours may develop in the nasal chamber viz. benign tumours and malignant tumours (cancer). Benign tumours in the nasal chambers are often called nasal polyps. These are growths that are not cancerous i.e. they do not spread to the rest of the body and they do not cause massive damage in the site in which they grow. They are thus not life threatening but may cause discomfort and secondary infections in the nasal chamber because as they grow, they obstruct the nasal chamber and may damage adjacent turbinate bones or the vomer bone. These tumours are often easily removed using an endoscope and if they do not regrow this will solve the problem. The most common tumours in the nasal chambers are however malignant cancers. The most common cancer in the nasal chamber is called a nasal carcinoma. This type of cancer causes massive damage to the bones of the nose and face and may spread to the rest of the body. If these tumours are diagnosed early enough, before they have spread or caused a lot of damage, the vet may discuss the option of radical surgery followed by a course of radiation therapy. This is called radical surgery because large sections of the nose and face may need to be removed and this may cause significant disfigurement of the dog's face. The surgery may be painful and dangerous as large amounts of blood may be lost during the surgery and the dog may require one or more blood transfusions. Many dogs have survived nasal cancer because of early diagnosis and prompt effective treatment and, after recovery, are unaffected by any disfigurement the treatment may have caused. The surgery and the radiation therapy may, however, not cure the problem and thus each individual case of nasal cancer should be fully discussed as promptly as possible with a cancer specialist.

Many people feel strongly about cancer in respect of the 'futility' of any treatment and feel that they would want the option of humane euthanasia for themselves in the event of a diagnosis of terminal cancer. They feel that it is not humane to ask their pets to accept the discomfort, pain or suffering that may be caused by some types of cancer and want to treat only the symptoms of the cancer; most importantly any pain or discomfort. Many people will request euthanasia when the treatment is no longer able to eliminate pain and discomfort or when they feel that the quality of life has deteriorated despite symptomatic treatment. I would not deny the request for euthanasia of a cancer patient because we are not all able to cope with the emotional strain of caring for a pet with a terminal condition. There is never a good time to say goodbye to a pet but sometimes, if they are on a downhill slide, it is better to let them go before they hit rock bottom.

12

My Dog is Licking and Rubbing Their Bum or Dragging Their Bum on the Ground

The bottom, or anus, may become uncomfortable and 'itchy' for a variety of reasons and most dogs will respond to this discomfort by licking and rubbing the anus or dragging the anus along the ground. This process of dragging the bottom along the ground is called 'scooting' and dogs do this by sitting on their bums with their back legs stretched forwards and pulling themselves along the ground with their front legs while remaining in a seated position. The three common reasons for anal discomfort are allergies, anal sac problems and worms. Most people think that worms are the most common cause of an itchy anus but in my experience this is the least common cause of the problem. I will discuss each of the possible causes of this problem individually.

1 Allergy as a cause of anal itching

As we have already seen, dogs develop allergies just as people do. The allergies that they develop are often due to the same things that we develop allergies to. The most common causes of allergies in dogs and people seem to be house dust and house dust mites, grasses and pollens, insect bites and various types of food. The thing that causes the allergy is called the allergen. The route by which the allergen is taken into the body does not necessarily affect where in the body the allergy effect will be produced. Consider people with an allergy to nuts or bee stings, if they are exposed to the nuts in their food or a sting in their skin they will often develop severe swelling in their airways which may cause suffocation. This demonstrates that the site of the allergy reaction does not necessarily have to be the same as the route of exposure to the allergen. The same concept applies to dogs in that they generally manifest their allergies as inflammation and itching in the skin. This applies to food allergies; inhaled allergies like pollens and house dust mites and injected allergies like fleabites. Inhaled allergies are called atopy. Human beings and animals with atopy are called atopic individuals. Atopy and allergy to fleabites are the most common types of allergy diagnosed in dogs. The most severe sites of itching in response to allergy reactions are the ears, paws and the anal region as mentioned before. Some dogs may have only itchy ears or only itchy bums or only

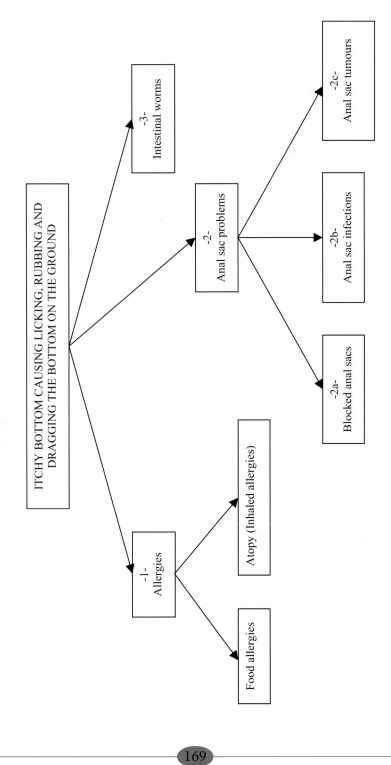

itchy feet or any combination of these three. The classic form of allergy in dogs are dogs with itchy 'ears and rears'.

Dogs with atopy may experience most of their 'itchiness' in the area of the anus. The vet will examine the anus and if they find that the anal sacs are normal and that the dog is unlikely to be suffering from intestinal worms then they will suspect that the dog has atopy. This means that the anus is itchy because the dog is breathing in pollen, house dust etc which causes atopy. The vet will then also check the rest of the skin especially the ears and feet for additional signs of atopy (inhaled allergy). Many atopic dogs have itchy bums and no itching elsewhere.

A full discussion on the cause, effect and treatment of allergies is presented in the section on itchy dogs.

2 Anal sac problems as a cause of anal itching

The anal sacs are scent glands on either side of the anus which may become uncomfortable to dogs when they become blocked, infected or possibly develop tumours (Fig. 15). Most people and vets call the anal sacs the anal glands. This is not strictly speaking correct, as the true anal glands are minute glands located all the way around the opening of the anus. The anal sacs are two sack-like structures located on either side of the anus. If one views the anus like a clock face, one anal sac is situated at the four o' clock position and the other one is situated at the eight o' clock position. The anal sacs, when full, are about the size of a marble. Each anal sac leads into a small tube that opens in the skin at the edge of the anus at the four and eight o' clock position. The anal sacs produce a foul smelling liquid which dogs use to mark their territory. Most people are familiar with the way male dogs urinate on objects to mark out their territory just as many wild animals do. The faeces produced by animals also mark out their territory. This is because the fluid produced and stored in the anal sacs is squirted out in small quantities when dogs defecate. This fluid the gives the faeces a very personal smell and thus the faeces, like the urine, marks out the dog's territory.

2a Blocked anal sacs
The anal sacs may become blocked and painful for no apparent reason. When this happens the fluid produced in the anal sac cannot be squirted out when the dog defecates. The fluid thus accumulates in the anal sac and as more and more fluid is produced the anal sac becomes severely distended and painful. This is a similar process to the formation of pimples in human beings where skin pores become blocked and as more natural skin oils are produced and accumulate in the skin pore, a pimple or blackhead may develop. The fluid that accumulates in a blocked anal sac may become very thick and ultimately may develop the consistency of toothpaste. Once this has happened the dog will not be able to squirt this material out of the very small opening in the tube of the anal sac. When the anal sac becomes blocked, the swelling causes pain and discomfort and thus dogs will try to squeeze out the contents of the anal sac by licking the anus or by dragging the anus along the ground. This is sometimes successful and thus the problem will be resolved. The blocked anal sacs can be felt as painful swellings on either side of the anus in the position of the anal sacs. When the dog is unable to squeeze out the contents of the anal sac for themselves then the vet will express the contents of the anal sac by squeezing it like a big pimple. Sometimes this can be done by

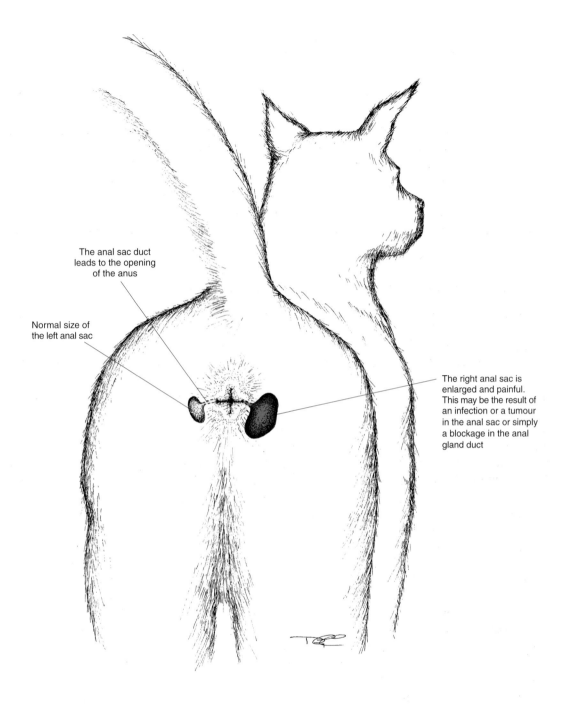

The anal sac duct
leads to the opening
of the anus

Normal size of
the left anal sac

The right anal sac is
enlarged and painful.
This may be the result of
an infection or a tumour
in the anal sac or simply
a blockage in the anal
gland duct

Fig 15   The position of the anal sacs relative to the anus.

squeezing the anal sacs from outside the anus but in some cases the vet may need to squeeze the sacs by inserting a gloved finger in the anus and squeezing the sac from the inside and the outside at the same time. Either method is uncomfortable or even painful for the dog and thus most vets will ask you to help by holding and comforting your dog while they express the blocked anal sac.

2b Anal sac infections

The anal sacs may become infected and when the vet empties the gland they will notice blood and pus coming out of the sac. When this happens the vet may need to treat the problem with antibiotics that are either administered as tablets or sometimes an antibiotic cream or ointment may be squirted directly into the anal sac. The vet will probably also prescribe a short course of painkillers/anti-inflammatories if the condition is very painful.

2c Anal sac tumours

The anal sacs may also develop tumours which cause the same symptoms of licking at the anus and dragging the anus along the ground. The vet will suspect that a tumour is present if the swelling in the anal sac area is very hard or if it has a bumpy surface. They will often examine the lump by feeling it with a gloved finger inserted in the anus. The most common anal sac tumour is an apocrine cell carcinoma which is potentially a very malignant and very infiltrative cancer. This means that it grows very deeply into the tissue surrounding the anal sac and anus and can be very difficult to remove and may spread to other parts of the body. The only appropriate form of treatment for an anal sac tumour is to remove the tumour as soon as possible. The tumour should be sent to a histopathology laboratory to be identified and the dog should have a chest X-ray at the time of tumour removal to check for signs of tumour spread to the lungs.

Some dogs may suffer from anal sacs that become blocked or infected very frequently. In these cases the vet may suggest removal of one or both of the anal sacs. Once the anal sac has been removed it will never bother the dog again. Surgical removal of the anal sacs is usually only recommended in severe cases as the surgery to remove the anal sac may cause temporary or permanent faecal incontinence. If the surgery is done carefully and delicately this should not cause faecal incontinence but the possibility of this complication should be discussed with your vet before surgery is performed.

3 Intestinal worms as a cause of anal itching

The third most common cause of an itchy anus is a worm problem in the dog. The cause of the itching in these individuals is the worms being passed out of the anus and their wriggling movement causes itching. Some types of worms can easily be seen in the dog's faeces as they are about the size of strands of spaghetti, these worms belong to the Toxocara worm family and are often called roundworms. Tapeworms look like small, flat pieces of rice in the faeces and around the bum and can often be seen wriggling. Ancylostoma worms are often called threadworms and are so small that they can be difficult to see as they are only slightly thicker than hair and only five to ten millimetres long. Worm problems are easily resolved by treating the dog with appropriate deworming treatments.

13

RED, INFLAMED EYES WITH OR WITHOUT DISCOMFORT

Dogs' eyes may become red and inflamed for long or short periods of time. When one or both eyes seem inflamed and red one might also notice that there is a discharge from one or both eyes. The eyes may also seem itchy causing the dog to rub their eyes with their paws or they may rub the eyes along furniture or the floor. The eye or eyes may be so uncomfortable that the dog holds the eyelids closed. Inflammation that affects the surface of the eye is called conjunctivitis or keratitis. When you look at your own eye or your dog's eye, they have exactly the same structure. The structures that we can see are the whites of the eyes and the coloured part of the eye with the pupil in the centre. The white part of the eye is called the sclera. The sclera is covered on its outer surface by a very thin transparent membrane called the conjunctival membrane (Fig. 16a). The word conjunctivitis simply means that this membrane is inflamed. The coloured part of the eye is called the iris and is actually situated inside the eyeball. The membrane between the iris and the outside world is also a transparent membrane and is called the cornea. The word keratitis means that the cornea is inflamed. So when one notices that one or both eyes are red and inflamed one can examine the eye to decide whether the conjunctival membrane is inflamed (conjunctivitis) or the cornea is inflamed (keratitis) or if both membranes are inflamed the condition is called keratoconjunctivitis.

Most dogs with red and inflamed eyes have conjunctivitis. The name conjunctivitis simply means that the conjunctival membrane is inflamed but it does not tell us why it is inflamed. Most people think that conjunctivitis means infection in the eye because the most common form of conjunctivitis in people, especially schoolchildren, is conjunctivitis caused by a bacterial infection which is usually contagious and often may spread from one person to another. In schools this type of conjunctivitis is often called 'pink eye'. I feel that a diagnosis of just 'conjunctivitis' is not good enough because it simply means that the membrane is inflamed and does not explain why it is inflamed. The most common causes of conjunctivitis are infection in the eye (infectious conjunctivitis), damage or irritation to the eye (traumatic conjunctivitis), allergic reactions like hay fever (allergic conjunctivitis), insufficient production of tears in the eye causing a 'dry eye' (keratoconjunctivitis sicca) and corneal ulcers. These different types of conjunctivitis may occur together, for example, if a dog scratches their eye while playing in the garden this will cause a traumatic conjunctivitis initially because the damage causes the conjunctival membrane to become inflamed. If the dog then keeps rubbing the eye bacteria may then enter the damaged membrane and then bacterial conjunctivitis may develop at the same time. Thus by the time that the eye is examined

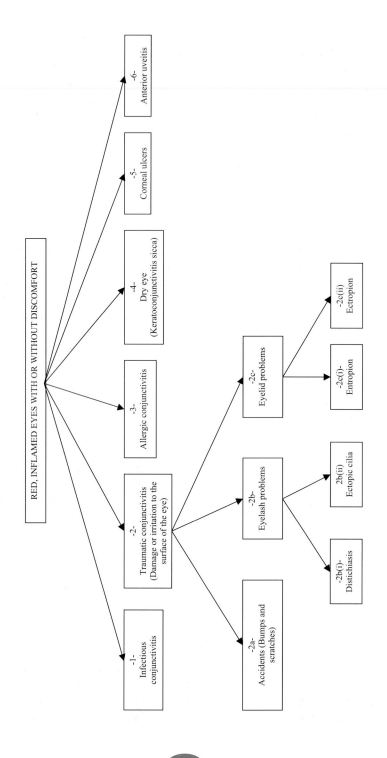

RED, INFLAMED EYES WITH OR WITHOUT DISCOMFORT

-1-
Infectious conjunctivitis

-2-
Traumatic conjunctivitis
(Damage or irritation to the surface of the eye)

-3-
Allergic conjunctivitis

-4-
Dry eye
(Keratoconjunctivitis sicca)

-5-
Corneal ulcers

-6-
Anterior uveitis

-2a-
Accidents (Bumps and scratches)

-2b-
Eyelash problems

-2c-
Eyelid problems

-2b(i)-
Distichiasis

2b(ii)
Ectopic cilia

-2c(i)-
Entropion

-2c(ii)
Ectropion

the inflammation (conjunctivitis) will be caused partly by the scratch and partly by the infection.

Conjunctivitis and keratitis may occur as separate conditions or together at the same time in the same eye. One or both eyes may be affected. The causes of conjunctivitis and keratitis are usually the same and the only difference is in which part of the surface of the eye becomes inflamed. I find that although the causes of keratitis and conjunctivitis are usually the same, it is more common to see conjunctivitis. Thus, when reading the next section, please bear in mind that the discussion of the types of conjunctivitis and their causes are equally applicable to keratitis and kerato-conjunctivitis.

I will briefly discuss the different types of conjunctivitis:

1 Infectious conjunctivitis

Infectious conjunctivitis is inflammation in one or both eyes caused by an infection in the conjunctival membrane. The infection is most commonly caused by bacteria. There are many different types of bacteria which may cause conjunctivitis and some of these may cause a pussy discharge to develop in the eyes. This pussy discharge is usually green or yellow and the dry puss on the eyelids may appear crusty. The infection may cause so much pain or discomfort in the eye that the dog may hold the eyelids closed over the eyeball, this is called blepharospasm. The treatment in these cases is simply a matter of using antibiotic eye drops in the eyes every day for five to seven days. If this does not cure the problem the vet may suggest taking a swab from the eye and sending it away for testing. The testing that is done on this swab is to determine exactly what bacteria have caused the infection and also to determine the best antibiotic eyedrops to use to clear the infection. It is very important that the vet tries to determine why the infection has occurred as the infection may be primary or secondary. A primary infection in the conjunctival membrane means that the infection has developed for no apparent reason in the same way that we may develop a cold or flu for no apparent reason. In these cases the infection will be cured by using the correct antibiotic eye drops. A secondary infection means that the infection has developed because of a pre-existing problem in the eye like a scratch or a piece of grass lodged behind the eyelids. If there is a pre-existing problem then the infection will not be cured by antibiotic drops until the pre-existing problem is cured, as for example, finding and removing the piece of grass.

2 Traumatic conjunctivitis

Traumatic conjunctivitis means that the inflammation in one or both eyes has been caused by damage to the conjunctival membrane.

2a Conjunctival bump and scratches

This damage may be due to a scratch in the membrane, something flying into the eye like a toy or a piece of grass or dirt, abnormal eyelashes rubbing the conjunctival membrane or abnormal eyelids rolling into the eye. Once the conjunctival membrane has been damaged it tends to become red, inflamed and painful. The pain is often severe enough to make the dog hold the eyelids tightly shut over the eyeball. The damaged membrane is also susceptible to secondary infections and thus the damaged membrane may quickly also become infected. The eye must thus be carefully examined to determine the cause of the damage. Most cases of traumatic conjunctivitis caused by bumps or scratches are quickly cured using eyedrops that contain anti-inflammatories and antibiotics. These cases will quickly heal by themselves and the treatment simply alleviates the discomfort and pain while the healing process progresses. If something, like a piece of grass or seed, is stuck in the eye or behind the eyelids then it must be found and removed otherwise the conjunctivitis will not go away. If the dog has abnormal eyelashes or eyelids, the eyelashes or hairs on the eyelids may constantly rub and irritate the conjunctival membrane and thus anti-inflammatory eyedrops will only temporarily and partially resolve the conjunctivitis.

2b Eyelash problems
There are two conditions associated with abnormal eyelashes.

2b(i) Distichiasis
The first condition is called distichiasis and means that the upper or lower eyelid has two rows of eyelashes instead of just one. The second row of eyelashes is just behind the outer row of normal eyelashes. This second row of eyelashes tends to grow towards the eyeball instead of away from the eyeball and thus they tend to rub the surface of the eyeball and irritate the conjunctival membrane and/or cornea. This irritation causes inflammation and discomfort and the only cure is to surgically remove the second row of eyelashes.

2b(ii) Ectopic cilia
In this condition one or several abnormal eyelashes may grow from abnormal positions in the eyelid and if they grow towards the eyeball they will rub and irritate the outer membranes of the eye and cause inflammation and pain. This condition is similar to distichiasis but the difference is that only a few abnormal eyelashes develop in the case of ectopic cilia and in the case of distichiasis an entire row of abnormal eyelashes are present. The long-term irritation caused by abnormal eyelashes means that dogs with these conditions would often have long-term secondary infections caused by bacteria taking advantage of the fact that the eye membranes are damaged. Eyedrops will only partially and temporarily relieve the conjunctivitis in these cases and the condition will only be cured when the eyelashes are removed. The abnormal eyelashes are best removed by electrolysis in much the same way that unwanted facial hair is removed from ladies.

2c Eyelid problems
There are two common conditions associated with abnormal eyelids.

2c(i) Entropion
The first condition is called entropion and means that the eyelid is folded or rolled into the eye and thus the normal hairs on the outer eyelid rub the surface of the eyeball and irritate the conjunctival membrane and/or cornea (Fig. 16b). This causes inflammation and pain and often secondary in-fections will develop. Eyedrops will only partially and temporarily relieve the conjunctivitis in these cases. The only way to cure these cases is to operate on the abnormal eyelid to prevent it from

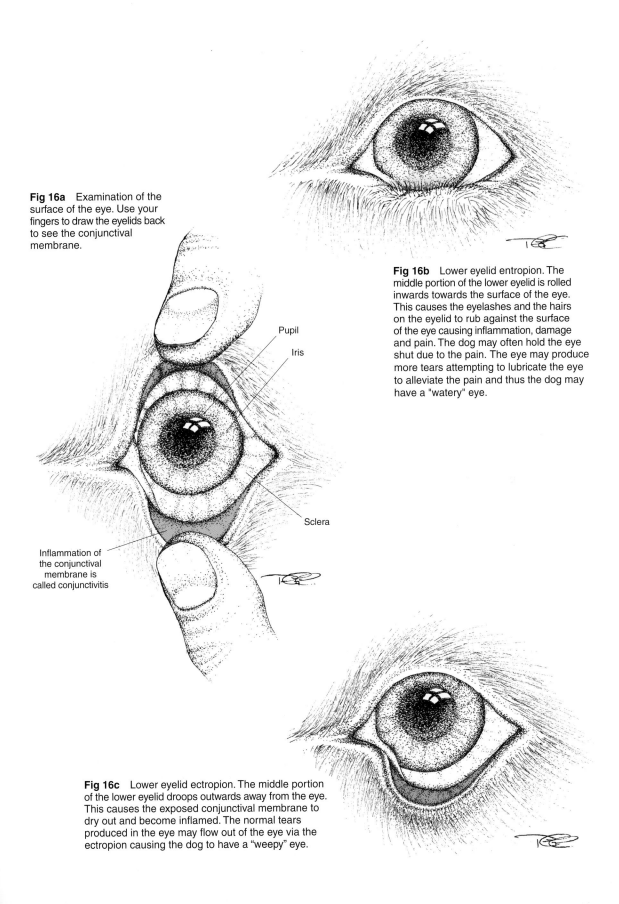

Fig 16a Examination of the surface of the eye. Use your fingers to draw the eyelids back to see the conjunctival membrane.

Pupil

Iris

Sclera

Inflammation of the conjunctival membrane is called conjunctivitis

Fig 16b Lower eyelid entropion. The middle portion of the lower eyelid is rolled inwards towards the surface of the eye. This causes the eyelashes and the hairs on the eyelid to rub against the surface of the eye causing inflammation, damage and pain. The dog may often hold the eye shut due to the pain. The eye may produce more tears attempting to lubricate the eye to alleviate the pain and thus the dog may have a "watery" eye.

Fig 16c Lower eyelid ectropion. The middle portion of the lower eyelid droops outwards away from the eye. This causes the exposed conjunctival membrane to dry out and become inflamed. The normal tears produced in the eye may flow out of the eye via the ectropion causing the dog to have a "weepy" eye.

rolling into the eye. This is done by removing a thin wedge of skin from the eyelid. This condition may affect any one or even all of the eyelids.

2c(ii) Ectropion

This means that the lower eyelids sag down too much and form a pouch (Fig. 16c). This means that the eyelids do not cover the eyeball properly and thus more of the eyeball is exposed to the air than is normal and the exposed part of the conjunctival membrane tends to dry out and this causes inflammation in the affected part of the membrane. This condition is cured by operating on the eyelids to tighten them up to ensure that they cover the eyeball normally.

Many people are reluctant to consider surgery to cure the problem of conjunctivitis caused by abnormal eyelashes or abnormal eyelids but I feel strongly that we must do the surgery because the condition is very uncomfortable. Consider how uncomfortable your own eye feels when a speck of dirt or an eyelash is rubbing the surface of the eye, the level of discomfort is ten times worse for dogs with these conditions and it never stops until we perform the surgery. It must be terrible to have permanent pain in the eye and this is why I would always recommend surgery to cure these patients.

3 Allergic conjunctivitis

People who suffer from hay fever will often also suffer from allergic conjunctivitis. This means that the allergy causes inflammation in the conjunctival membrane on the surface of the eye. This inflammation causes the eyes to appear red and inflamed and often the eyes feel itchy. Dogs may develop exactly the same allergy reaction in their eyes. These dogs can be easily treated using 'anti-allergy' eyedrops and homoeopathic treatment with euphrasia is often also effective. The treatment only alleviates the symptoms and thus to cure the problem we must determine what is causing the allergy and determine if we can take steps to avoid the substance that is causing the allergy. This is not always possible, for example if the allergy is caused by pollen then the dog will always suffer from allergic conjunctivitis during the pollen season and the best advice I can offer is to treat the condition during the problem times of the year. If the allergy is caused by other factors, for example food, the condition can be cured by changing the type of food that the dog eats. Please refer to the allergy section in chapter 7 for a more detailed discussion on allergies in dogs.

4 Keratoconjunctivitis sicca (dry eye)

The surface of the eye is a very delicate structure and it must be kept moist at all times. The body keeps the eye surface moist by constantly producing small amounts of tears that wash over the surface of the eye and drain away through small openings in the inner corner of the eyelids. This means that new tears need to be constantly produced and drained away every minute of the day. There are many glands that produce the tears to keep the eye moist. The most important tear-producing gland is the lacrimal gland which is situated above and behind the eye. The lacrimal gland produces most of the tears needed by the eye and the gland drains the tears into the eye through a small tube called a duct. The second most important gland which produces tears for the eye is called the harderian gland. This gland is situated in the inner corner of the eye tucked away under the third eyelid which is tucked under the eyelids in the inner corner of the eye. The lesser important tear producing glands are minute glands dotted along the edge of the eyelids between the eyelashes. The tears that are produced by all these glands help to keep the surface of the eye clean and moist. The tears rinse the surface of the eye and then drain away from the eye through small openings in the inner edges of the eyelids.

If the tear producing glands do not produce enough tears to keep the surface of the eye clean and moist then the membranes over the surface of the eye start to dry out. When the conjunctival membrane and the cornea are too dry they become inflamed and may become painful. The surface of the eye no longer appears clean and shiny and instead one will notice that the surface of the eye appears dull and sticky fluid sticks to the surface of the eye. This sticky fluid may be white, grey, green or yellow. If this 'dry eye' is not treated then the inflammation on the surface of the eye will become more and more severe and eventually that eye may go blind. The technical name for this condition is keratoconjunctivitis sicca which simply means that the dog has conjunctivitis (inflammation in the conjunctival membrane) and keratitis (inflammation in the cornea) because the eye surface is too dry (sicca means dry). This is not an uncommon diagnosis but once again it does not tell us why the tear producing glands have stopped working. Research suggests that the main cause of this condition is a problem with the body's own immune system. This is called an autoimmune disorder and it means that the body's own immune system is attacking its own cells for no apparent reason. It seems that the immune system simply fails to recognise that some tissues, for example the lacrimal gland, is normal tissue and it attacks it as if it were an invading bacteria. As the attack on the cells continues the cells become damaged and unable to work efficiently and eventually the cells being attacked may die.

The diagnosis of a dry eye is made when the surface of the eye is seen to be dry, dull, inflamed and has a sticky substance adhered to it. The vet will confirm this diagnosis by testing the amount of tear production in the eye. This is called the Schirmer tear test and it is quick and easy to do. The vet will place a special type of 'blotting paper' against the inside surface of the lower eyelid and measure how much fluid is absorbed by this strip of 'blotting paper'. This test reveals whether the eye surface has enough tear production or not. It will also give an indication of how severe the problem is if there is insufficient tear production for the surface of the eye. The vet will test both eyes even if only one seems to be affected because this condition often affects both eyes at different speeds.

The treatment for 'dry eye' (keratoconjunctivitis sicca) is aimed at controlling the pain and inflammation with anti-inflammatory eye drops and using artificial tears to keep the eye moist. An additional type of eye drop containing cyclosporin has proved to be very effective at controlling and treating this condition either on its own or in combination with other types of eye drops. I feel that it is important to treat this condition aggressively and keep treating it permanently as it is very uncomfortable and human beings with this condition confirm that without treatment they are in constant pain.

5 Corneal ulcers

The cornea is a thin, transparent membrane which is in front of the coloured part of the eye. The cornea is transparent so that when we look at an eye we look straight through the cornea and see the iris behind it. People who wear contact lenses will know that the contact lens is placed on the cornea and will thus also know that the cornea is very sensitive to pain and may become inflamed if it is rubbed or irritated. The cornea is very thin; it is about twenty cell layers thick and has a very poor blood supply which is why we cannot see blood vessels in it. Ulcers may develop in the cornea and they may be very shallow or very deep. A corneal ulcer is literally an ulcer in the cornea and thus it looks like an ulcer with jagged edges. The ulcer may develop on any part of the cornea and sometimes it cannot be seen by the naked eye.

If the vet suspects that there may be an ulcer on the cornea they may put a drop of green dye in the eye. This dye will stick to the ulcer but not to the rest of the cornea which is normal. Thus if a green area appears on the cornea after the dye is put in the eye then the green area is the ulcer. If, after the dye is put in the eye, parts of the cornea do not turn green then there is no ulcer. The dye is called fluorescein and is completely harmless to the eye and the green spot will disappear a few hours later. Once fluorescein dye has been placed in the eye one will often notice a green discharge from the nostril on the same side of the face. This is because the fluorescein dye mixes with the normal tears in the eye and drains away from the dye through the naso-lacrimal duct which drains tears from the eye to the nose. The tears rinse the surface of the eye and then drain away from the eye through small openings in the inner edges of the eyelids. There is one opening in the inner edge of the upper eyelid and another in the inner edge of the lower eyelid. These openings lead to small tubes called ducts. The duct from the upper and lower eyelid join together to make one single duct called the naso-lacrimal duct which leads from the eye and drains into the nose. This is why our noses run when we cry. Normally, when we are not crying, the amount of tears being drained into the nose is so small that we do not notice it.

Once an ulcer has developed in the eye it becomes very painful and often the surface of the eyeball becomes inflamed because of conjunctivitis and keratitis and the dog will hold the eyelids shut over the painful eye. Once a corneal ulcer has been diagnosed one should try to determine why an ulcer has developed. The ulcer may develop from a superficial cut or scrape on the surface of the cornea but most often no reason for the ulcer can be found. If the ulcer has developed from a cut or scrape to the cornea the vet should check to see that there is nothing lodged in the eye or behind the eyelids which may be causing the damage. Things that may be lodged in the eye include grass seeds, pieces of grass or twigs etc. If an object is found it must be removed otherwise the damage will continue and the ulcer will not heal. If no object is found the vet should examine to eyelids to make sure that the ulcer has not been caused by distichiasis, ectopic cilia, entropion or keratoconjunctivitis sicca. These conditions are explained in more detail on pages 176 to 179 in the section on conjunctivitis. If any of these conditions are identified then they must be corrected otherwise the damage to the cornea will continue and the ulcer will not heal. Thus once an ulcer has been identified one must try to find an explanation why the ulcer has developed. If an explanation is found then the underlying condition must be treated at the same time as treating the ulcer. If no underlying cause for the ulcer can be found the ulcer is treated as an unexplained corneal ulcer.

The treatment for a corneal ulcer should be started as soon as possible for two reasons – to prevent the ulcer from becoming larger and deeper and also to alleviate the pain caused by the ulcer. The way that the vet will treat the ulcer will depend on how deep the ulcer is. If it is very superficial then appropriate antibiotic eye ointment should be instilled in the eye at least three times daily. The vet will use eye ointment rather than eye drops because the ointment forms a protective and soothing layer over the surface of the eye whereas eye drops drain from the eye via the naso-lacrimal duct too quickly. The ulcer should heal very quickly over a period of one or two weeks. If the ulcer does not heal or if the ulcer is very deep and there is a risk that it may cause the eyeball to burst then the vet may recommend an operation to fix the ulcer. The simplest form of operation for a corneal ulcer is called a third eyelid flap. The third eyelid is something that most animals have but human beings don't have. The third eyelid is literally a third eyelid which is hairless, covered by the conjunctival membrane and tucked away out of site in the inner corner of the eye under the upper and lower eyelid. The operation involves pulling the third eyelid across the surface of the eye and temporarily stitching it to the upper eyelid so that it stays in position covering the eye. This is a simple and quick procedure and causes little or no discomfort to the dog. The effect of stitching the eyelid in this position is that it acts as a temporary bandage over the surface of the eye to allow the ulcer to heal because a bandage creates the best conditions for the body's tissues to heal. The stitches are removed after one or two weeks and the ulcer will almost always have healed in this time. If the ulcer has not completely healed when the stitches are removed then the vet may advise replacing the stitches and removing in another one or two weeks or the vet may advise a different kind of operation. The other kind of operation is called a conjunctival flap and it is not as simple to perform. A conjunctival flap involves moving a strip of the conjunctival membrane which covers the whites of the eyes over the ulcer in the cornea and stitching it to the cornea. I have found that it is rarely necessary to do this second operation as most cases heal with the simpler and cheaper operation of the third eyelid flap. If however the ulcer refuses to heal or if it is so deep that the risk of the eyeball bursting is very high then the conjunctival flap may be the only option.

Boxer dogs are the most susceptible breed with regards to developing corneal ulcers for no apparent reason. Researchers suggest that boxers are more at risk for developing corneal ulcers because they have a genetic flaw in the microscopic structure of the cornea. This means that some boxer dogs may develop ulcers more often than other dogs and the ulcers are more difficult to treat as they will sometimes refuse to heal without or sometimes even with surgery. Although slow healing corneal ulcers are more common in boxer dogs than other breeds they are not very common and only very few of them will cause major long-term problems.

6 Anterior uveitis

Anterior uveitis means that all the structures and membranes in the front part of the eyeball are inflamed. This means that the eye appears red because the dog has conjunctivitis, keratitis, and the inflammation also involves the structures inside the eyeball like the iris (the coloured part of the eye), the inside lining of the eyeball and the fluid in the eye. The cause of anterior uveitis is often not determined when dogs are initially examined and vets often assume that the causes of this condition are largely similar to the causes of conjunctivitis and keratitis as discussed earlier. Thus treatment consists of antibiotics and anti-inflammatories used in eyedrop form and often also in tablet form to ensure that the treatment reaches not just the surface of the eye but also the inside of the eyeball. The most serious concern that the vet may have when they diagnose anterior uveitis is that the inflammation inside the eye will obstruct the normal flow of fluid inside the eye and the eyeball may develop glaucoma. Glaucoma means that the eyeball is swollen and most often the pressure of the fluid inside the eyeball is much higher than normal. This high pressure causes severe pain and may permanently damage the inside of the eye and result in permanent blindness. Thus, if the vet diagnoses anterior uveitis they will want to check regularly the condition of the eye and the pressure in the eye because if glaucoma develops the best chance of saving the sight in that eye hinges on starting glaucoma treatment immediately. Treatment for glaucoma consists of specific types of eye drops and tablets and sometimes even advanced eye surgery.

14
MY DOG IS COUGHING

Dogs may develop a cough for the same reasons that human beings may develop a cough. The most common causes of coughing in dogs are problems with the respiratory system or heart problems. The respiratory system consists of several parts and is basically a system of tubes which carry air into and out of the body. The heart is basically a pump which pumps blood through another system of tubes (veins and arteries) around the body.

We should start by discussing the process of normal breathing. Air is drawn into the body via the nose or mouth. The air then moves through the back of the throat (the pharynx) into the voice box (larynx). The voice box (larynx) is literally a hollow box made of cartilage which contains the vocal cords. The air then moves down the windpipe (trachea) towards the lungs. The trachea is a tube (airway) for carrying air in and out of the body. The trachea splits into two smaller tubes (branches) as it passes over the top of the heart to form the left and right main stem bronchus. The right bronchus delivers air to the right lung and the left bronchus delivers air to the left lung. The right lung consists of four main parts called lung lobes and the left lung consists of three main parts also called the lung lobes. The right bronchus thus splits into four smaller tubes (branches) each supplying one of the right lung lobes and the left bronchus splits into three smaller tubes (branches) each supplying one of the left lung lobes. Once the branch of the bronchus enters each lung lobe it branches into many more branches each becoming slightly smaller as they continue to give off more branches. The smallest branches of this system of air tubes are called bronchioles. Each bronchiole ends in a small chamber called the alveolus. It is in the alveolus that oxygen moves out of the air into the blood supply and carbon dioxide moves out of the blood supply into the air in the alveolus. The plural for alveolus is alveoli. There are literally millions of alveoli in each lung lobe. Because air is constantly moving through all these air tubes (airways), the lining of the airways would tend to dry out. The lining of the airways thus contains special cells which secrete fluid and mucous to keep the airways moist. This mucous lining also helps to trap solid particles like dust, which are breathed in. The respiratory system can be divided into two components. The upper respiratory tract extends from the nose and mouth to the point where the trachea branches out to enter the lungs. The lower respiratory tract extends from the point where the trachea starts branching and includes the lungs.

Breathing consists of two stages – breathing in (inspiration) and breathing out (expiration). During inspiration air containing oxygen is breathed in through the system of air tubes into the alveoli where the oxygen moves into the blood supply. During expiration carbon dioxide moves out of the blood supply into the air in the alveoli and this air is then breathed out as waste gas.

The heart is simply a pump which pumps blood around the body. The heart, the blood and all

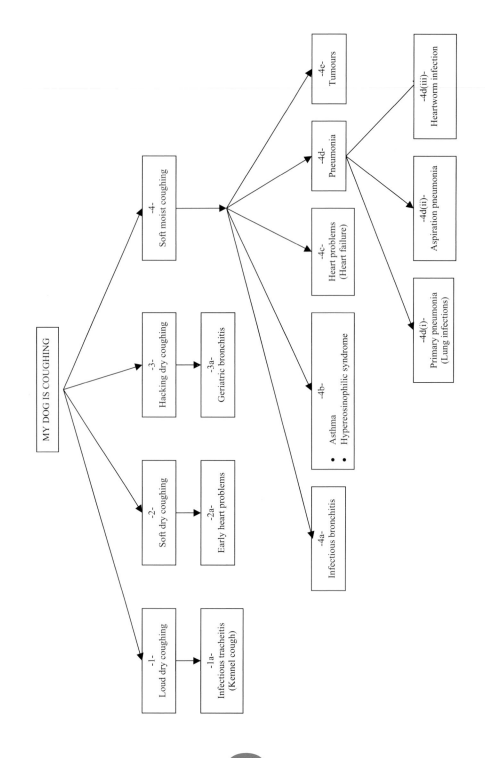

MY DOG IS COUGHING

-1-
Loud dry coughing
→ -1a-
Infectious tracheitis
(Kennel cough)

-2-
Soft dry coughing
→ -2a-
Early heart problems

-3-
Hacking dry coughing
→ -3a-
Geriatric bronchitis

-4-
Soft moist coughing

-4a-
Infectious bronchitis

-4b-
• Asthma
• Hypereosinophilic syndrome

-4c-
Heart problems
(Heart failure)

-4d-
Pneumonia

-4e-
Tumours

-4d(i)-
Primary pneumonia
(Lung infections)

-4d(ii)-
Aspiration pneumonia

-4d(iii)-
Heartworm infection

the veins and arteries and capillaries in the body form the cardiovascular system (circulatory system). One can think of the circulatory system as a system of tubes that carry liquid throughout the body. The liquid (blood) is pumped through this system of tubes (blood vessels) by a pump (the heart). The tubes which lead away from the pump (the heart) are called arteries and the tubes which lead back to the heart are called veins. The arteries are connected to the veins by very small tubes called capillaries. Oxygen, carbon dioxide, food and waste products move into and out of the cardio-vascular system through the capillaries. The heart consists of two sides – the left side and the right side. The left side pumps blood to and from the body and the right side pumps blood to and from the lungs. The right side thus pumps blood into the lungs where oxygen is absorbed from the air in the alveoli and carbon dioxide is released into the air in the alveoli. The blood is now full of oxygen and returns to the heart. The left side of the heart then pumps the blood to the rest of the body where the oxygen is absorbed by the cells of the body. The carbon dioxide released by the body's cells moves into the blood to be carried back to lungs to be breathed out as waste. The arteries, veins and capillaries thus lie in-between the alveoli and air tubes in the lungs.

The process of coughing is a self-defence mechanism which the respiratory system has developed. When the respiratory system feels that something is interfering with the movement of air in the system of air tubes it will produce a cough. A cough is simply a short, forceful way of shooting air out of the airways back into the atmosphere. The objective of a cough is thus to force out (cough out) anything in the airways that may interfere with the normal movement of air. Thus anything that affects the airways will cause a cough. When an individual coughs it means that the lung is aware that something is interfering with the flow of air in the airways. The lung will not know what is causing the interference with the flow of air so it does the only thing it can to try to correct the situation which is to try to cough up anything which may be stuck somewhere in the airways. Thus the lungs will produce a cough irrespective of the real cause of the problem because it is the only self-defence mechanism that they can perform.

A cough is a symptom that the lung is trying to clear out something that is interfering with the airways. There are many types of problems that may interfere with the airways.

The most obvious possible problem is that the individual has breathed in something solid like food, dust, pieces of grass etc. These objects interfere with the airways and the cough is the self-defence mechanism to get rid of the problem. In these cases the process of coughing is the obvious solution to the problem.

The second possible common cause of coughing is inflammation at any point in the respiratory system. Inflammation in the walls of the tubes of the airways will cause thickening of the walls of the airways and thus the airways become narrower. The lungs will realise that something is inter-fering with the movement of air in the airways. The lungs have no way of knowing what is causing the problem and thus they will produce a cough in case the cause of the problem is that something solid has been breathed in. The cough in this instance will obviously not solve the problem because there is nothing to cough out but a cough will always be produced because it is the only immediate defence mechanism the lungs have. If the inflammation in the airways does not resolve very quickly then the second defence mechanism of the lungs will be activated. This is the process of mucous production by the special cells lining the airways. These cells will increase their production of mucous to produce a thick protective layer on the inside of the airways. This thick layer of mucous is intended to trap solid objects like dust or pieces of food or grass so that they do not move into the smaller airways and get stuck there. Once the mucous has trapped the solid object, the continued coughing has the best chance of getting rid of the solid object. The mucous layer has a second purpose which is to protect the airways from infections trying to enter the body. Once again the objective of the mucous is to trap the infection and this stops it penetrating into the body's cells and also creates the situation where repeated coughing will cough out the mucous (phlegm) containing the parasites. As more and more mucous is produced, the mucous itself may start to obstruct the airway and thus the coughing will become more frequent and forceful as the lungs try to cough up the mucous (phlegm). Thus inflammation and increased mucous production in the airways will cause a cough. There are many causes of inflammation in the airways; the most common causes are infections, allergies (asthma), tumours and inhaled solid objects like dust, pieces of food or grass etc.

The third possible common cause of coughing is increased external pressure on the airways. This means that if something outside of the airways is pushing the walls of the airways inwards, the effect is that the airway is narrowed. The lungs once again have no way of knowing what is causing the problem and thus they will produce a cough in case the cause of the problem is that something solid has been breathed in. The cough in this instance will obviously not solve the problem because there is nothing to cough out but a cough will always be produced because it is the only immediate defence mechanism the lungs have. Two factors can cause pressure to be exerted on the airways i.e. tumours or fluid accumulations. If a tumour develops next to an airway it will press against the airway and this makes the airway narrower than normal and thus a cough will develop. If fluid accumulates next to an airway it will also press against the airway and thus cause a cough. Fluid may accumulate in-between the airways in cases of heart failure or high blood pressure. In these conditions the fluid may accumulate around the airways and/or inside the airways. If more fluid continues to accumulate or if the tumours continue growing in size then the cough will become more severe.

The symptom of coughing only tells us that there is a problem with the respiratory system or heart. I have explained that a cough may be caused by the three mechanisms described above. The clue to trying to determine which of these mechanisms has caused the cough is often the type of cough that is produced i.e. a dry cough or a moist cough. A dry cough which is very loud, has developed very suddenly and is produced frequently throughout the day tends to suggest that the cough has been caused by inflammation in the upper respiratory system caused either by an inhaled object (e.g. dust) or by a sudden infection (e.g. kennel cough). A dry cough which is not very loud and has developed over a period of a few weeks tends to suggest an upper respiratory problem caused by inflammation or external pressure. A soft, moist cough tends to suggest that the problem is situated in the lower respiratory system due to inflammation or fluid accumulation.

When a vet is presented with a coughing dog they will ask you a variety of questions to try to identify the type of cough. Some of the questions will relate directly to the cough and others will be directed to other symptoms that may be present at the same time. Your answers to the questions are very important and it is important not to try to guess the answer. It is better to answer a question with 'I don't know' rather than to guess, as the information that you give the vet will very often give them enough information to make the diagnosis without expensive tests. The questions will include some or all of the following.

- How old is the dog?
- How long have they had the cough?
- Are there other dogs in the household and if so, are they also coughing?
- Has the dog recently had contact with other dogs e.g. on walks, at training classes, at boarding kennels etc?
- Is the cough loud or soft?
- Is the cough a dry cough or a moist cough?
- Does the dog seem ill or unwell besides the fact that they are coughing i.e. are they alert and active and eating normally?
- Is the cough worse during the day or during the night or is it the same all the time?
- Does the dog cough only at certain times during the day e.g. during/after meals, only when they are excited, only while out for a walk etc?
- Is the dog losing or gaining weight?
- Does the dog become tired very quickly when they go out to walk and exercise?

Once the vet has asked you the above questions they will examine your dog with special attention being given to the respiratory and cardiovascular systems. They will examine the nose, throat and mouth and perform a test called the tracheal pinch test. This involves delicately squeezing the trachea (windpipe). A vet can make any dog cough by manipulating the trachea and this test is intended to see how easy it is to make the dog cough. If a cough is produced with very light pressure on the trachea then this is regarded as a positive tracheal pinch test and the most likely location of the problem is the trachea itself. The two most common conditions which cause increased sensitivity of the trachea are bacterial infections (kennel cough) in the trachea causing inflammation and 'tracheal collapse' caused by weak cartilage rings in the trachea. The vet will then listen to the heart and lung sounds and continue their examination of your dog as required.

Once the vet has collected all the information that they need their thoughts will go something like this. If the dog has a very loud dry cough and coughs throughout the day and night but seems active, happy, alert and is eating normally then the problem is most likely in the upper respiratory tract. If the act of coughing causes the dog to retch and gag and sometimes they appear to vomit white foam after coughing then there is most probably an infection in the upper respiratory tract. If the cough started after contact with other dogs (e.g. the dog has recently been in boarding kennels) then the cough is most likely due to an infection in the upper respiratory tract. If the cough started after going out for a walk or after the dog was exposed to dusty conditions then the cough may be due to something (e.g. dust or pieces of grass) lodged in the upper respiratory tract. If the dog has had a mild dry cough for more than two weeks then the cause of the problem may be the very early stages of a heart problem.

If the dog has a soft moist cough then the problem is most likely in the lower respiratory tract. If the dog seems completely normal (they are alert, happy and eating normally) despite the fact that they have a cough, then the cough is most likely due to mild inflammation in the lower respiratory tract or the early stages of a heart problem. Mild inflammation in the lower respiratory tract may be caused by solid objects (e.g. food) lodged in the lower respiratory tract or infections or allergic inflammation or the early stages of a tumour in the lower respiratory tract. If the dog has a soft moist cough and seems alert and happy but gets tired and out of breath very quickly when exercising then the problem may be a heart problem. If the dog seems very ill and is not eating and is lethargic with a moist cough then the problem may be severe infections (pneumonia) or severe heart problems affecting the lower respiratory tract.

As you can see, the type of cough does not always tell the vet exactly what the problem is but it will give a good idea of where to start looking for the problem. The most common diagnoses for a cough will be discussed individually.

1 Loud, dry coughs with occasional gagging/retching, which appear very suddenly

If a dog develops a loud, dry cough very suddenly i.e. within one or two days then the most likely explanation is that they have something lodged in the back of their throat or that they have an infection in the trachea. The vet will examine the back of the dog's throat to look for solid objects lodged there but it is very rare to find something lodged in the throat. The most common object that I find lodged in the throat is a grass seed which has punctured a tonsil. Once this object has been removed the cough will usually resolve within a few days.

The most common cause of a sudden onset, loud, dry cough is an infection in the trachea. The common symptoms are a very loud cough that occurs often throughout the day and night. The cough starts very suddenly and often the act of coughing causes the dog to retch and often they will 'vomit up' small amounts of a white foamy liquid. This act of gagging makes most people think that they have a bone stuck in their throat but this is almost never the case. The cough is often so loud that it has a 'honking' sound like a goose honking. The affected dogs are usually bright, alert, happy and eating normally despite the fact that they have this severe cough. When the vet touches their trachea it will usually start off another coughing fit. The affected dog has usually recently had contact with other dogs e.g. while out on a walk, in boarding kennels, at a dog show etc. If there are other dogs living in the same household they will often also start coughing within a few days.

1a Infections in the trachea are often called 'kennel cough'

This name comes from the fact that contagious infections which cause infection in the trachea with severe coughing are often spread from one dog to another while they are in kennels. This may happen because the bacteria which cause the infection are very easily passed from one dog to another and when many dogs are housed in a confined space it is very easy for the infection to spread. The same would apply to many people travelling together on an airplane for example. If one person had a cough, a cold or flu then this is the ideal situation for them to spread the infection. I do not like the name 'kennel cough' because it makes people think that the infection can be picked up only at dog kennels and this is not true. The infection can be passed from one dog to another in any situation e.g. at dog shows, while out for a walk, when friends and relatives visit etc. 'Kennel cough' is spread in the same way that colds and flu are spread between human beings.

The cough associated with 'kennel cough' is a very loud honking cough but it is rarely dangerous. 'Kennel cough' is not life threatening. The cough is caused by bacteria causing infection and inflammation in the trachea and the infection almost never moves into the lungs. The bacteria which cause the infection are very easy to eliminate using modern antibiotics. The most common bacteria which causes kennel cough is called Bordetella Bronchiseptica. If the cough does not resolve within seven to ten days of treatment then the vet may suggest taking a swab from the tonsils to run some tests. The swab is sent to a laboratory which will check for different types of bacterial and fungal infection and they will be able to determine the best treatment for treating that particular infection. Some vets feel that there is no need to treat these cases because they are 'self-limiting'. This means that, after several weeks, the infection should simply go away by itself in the majority of cases. This may well be the case but I tend to treat this condition because if I had a severe cough I would want to get rid of it as quickly as possible. I ask my clients to keep their dogs in their own houses and gardens for three weeks to avoid spreading the infection to other dogs in the community.

2 Soft, dry coughs which develop over the course of a few weeks

2a Early heart problems

If a dog has a soft, dry, 'tickly' cough which develops slowly over a period of a few weeks and is not necessarily coughing all day and night then one would consider the possibility of a heart problem. Many types of heart problems will cause the heart to stretch slightly. The bottom end of the trachea lies directly above the heart and thus if the heart stretches it will start to push against the trachea. This pressure on the trachea may cause a cough to develop (Fig. 17b). This happens because, as the heart enlarges (stretches), it pushes the wall of the trachea inwards, the effect is that the airway is narrowed. The lungs have no way of knowing what is causing the problem and thus they will produce a cough in case the cause of the problem is that something solid has been breathed in. The cough in this instance will obviously not solve the problem because there is nothing to cough out but a cough will always be produced because it is the only immediate defence mechanism the lungs have.

Besides the cough, the only other symptom that one may find in this very early stage of a heart problem is that the dog cannot manage as much exercise as they have managed before. People will often explain that the dog seems to run out of breath and energy more quickly than usual. This is called exercise intolerance. The dogs will continue to appear bright, alert and happy with a normal appetite despite the fact that they have the cough and mild exercise intolerance. The vet will often suggest taking an X-ray of the chest so that they can see the size of the heart and the position of the trachea above the heart. If the vet confirms that a stretched heart is causing the cough they will prescribe medication and possibly a change of diet to help the heart and alleviate the cough.

3 A hacking dry cough sometimes also coughing up phlegm in old dogs

3a Geriatric bronchitis

Old dogs may develop chronic bronchitis in the same way that old people do. Bronchitis means inflammation of the bronchioles (the very small airways in the lungs). Chronic means that the inflammation has developed over a long period of time. As we grow older all the tubes forming the airways in the respiratory system tend to become harder and less flexible. As the smaller airways

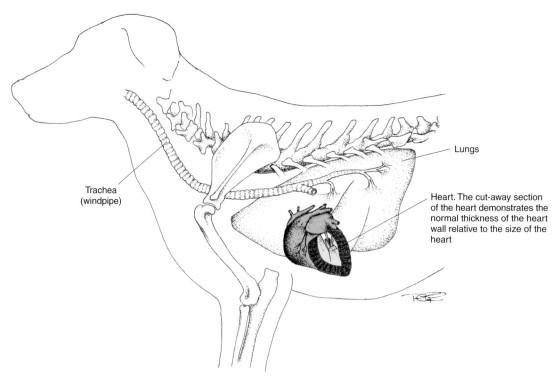

Trachea
(windpipe)

Lungs

Heart. The cut-away section
of the heart demonstrates the
normal thickness of the heart
wall relative to the size of the
heart

Fig 17a   A side view of the chest to show the normal size and position of the heart, lungs and trachea (windpipe).

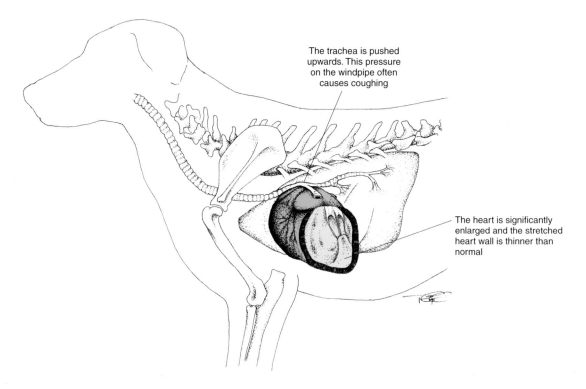

The trachea is pushed
upwards. This pressure
on the windpipe often
causes coughing

The heart is significantly
enlarged and the stretched
heart wall is thinner than
normal

Fig 17b   Heart failure causes the heart to dilate and enlarge. As the heart enlarges it pushes against
the lungs and it pushes the trachea (windpipe) upwards. This pressure on the trachea may cause coughing.

in the lungs grow older they become more rigid and less able to expand as we breathe. If you sit close to an old person and listen to their breathing you will often notice that they breathe more loudly than young people and often the breathing sounds slightly wheezy. Older people may also have an occasional dry cough. These symptoms develop because the smaller airways have lost their ability to expand to bring more air into the lungs. The lungs will compensate by taking more breaths every minute. Thus there is more air moving to and fro in the airways and the airways tend to dry out slightly more than in young people. As the airways dry out, they become slightly inflamed. This inflammation will cause a cough for the reasons described at the beginning of the chapter. This inflammation may also be caused by long term mild asthma. The final result is that the inflammation causes small amounts of 'scar tissue' to form in the airways and lungs and this further reduces the ability of the smaller airways to expand. This means that the lungs will again compensate by taking more breaths per minute and thus the airways will dry out even more. This is a vicious cycle and progressively becomes worse and worse. The treatment for these individuals is to use medications which will reduce the inflammation in the airways and stimulate the airways to dilate as much as possible. The treatments used for this condition are much the same as the treatments used for people who suffer from asthma because it is a very similar problem.

4 Soft, moist, chesty or rattly coughs developing over a period of a few days to a few weeks

A soft moist cough which occurs at any time during the day and night and which is associated with a 'chesty, rattling' sound tends to suggest a problem in the lower respiratory system. The 'chesty, rattling' sound is caused by fluid accumulating in the airways. This fluid may be mucous (phlegm) or a watery fluid that accumulates in the airways. The dog may sometimes seem to gag when they cough and may cough up small amounts of this fluid. The cough tends to develop over a period of a few days to a few weeks and gradually becomes worse. The affected dog will often not seem distressed but they are reluctant to exercise or go for walks. They usually have normal appetites. The possible causes in this situation include infections in the lower respiratory tract, 'allergic' bronchitis, early tumours in the lungs or heart problems.

The vet will carefully examine the dog and then they may suggest some tests. These tests may include X-rays, bronchoscopy and bronchial lavage and blood tests. The X-rays will allow the vet to see the size and shape of the heart and the condition of the lungs. Bronchoscopy is a procedure whereby the vet will pass a camera down the trachea (windpipe) and into the airways in the lungs. This procedure allows the vet to see what is going on inside the airways. Bronchial lavage is a procedure whereby the vet will flush a small amount of water through the airways in the lungs and then suck the fluid back into a syringe. This fluid is then sent to a laboratory which will perform several tests including testing for infections, tumours and allergic inflammation (asthma).

Once the vet has performed the required tests they may make one of the following diagnoses:

4a Infectious bronchitis

Infectious bronchitis simply means that there is an infection in the airways in the lower respiratory system. This infection is most commonly caused by bacteria but occasionally the infection is caused by viruses or rarely by fungal infections or lungworm. The tests the vet will have run will tell them what has caused the infection and this will determine the treatment they will use. The common treatments for infections in the lungs include antibiotics, anti-inflammatories, mucolytics (to loosen phlegm), expectorants (to dilate the airways) and deworming treatments (if the cause of the problem is lungworm).

4b Asthma or Hypereosinophilic syndrome ('Allergic' inflammation in the airways)

I use the word 'allergic' inflammation very loosely in this context. What I mean by this is that there is inflammation in the airways that is caused by on over-reaction of the immune system. This over-reaction of the immune system happens despite the fact that there is no sign of any other problem in the airways like infections or tumours. This is similar to hay fever which is characterised by severe inflammation in the nose which has not been caused by infections or tumours. This over-reaction of the immune system only happens in a small number of individuals. The over-reaction of the immune system may be a true allergic reaction to inhaled substances like pollens, cigarette smoke etc. in these cases the diagnosis is asthma which is the same condition as seen in human beings. Asthma is treated the same way that it is treated in human beings i.e. low doses of cortizone and bronchodilators (to dilate the airways to improve breathing). If we cannot find any explanation for the over-reaction of the immune system i.e. there is no sign of infections, tumours or asthma then we call the condition an autoimmune disorder. This means that the immune system is reacting to the body's own tissues for no apparent reason i.e. it is reacting to the respiratory cells as if they were pollen. This causes a severe accumulation of inflammatory cells in the airways which forms into a thick fluid in the airways. The dog will try to cough up this thick fluid and this causes the 'chesty, rattling cough'. This autoimmune lung inflammation is called hypereosinophilic syndrome and is treated using cortizone.

4c Heart failure

Heart conditions may cause congestive heart failure. The name congestive heart failure accurately describes the problem i.e. the fact that the heart is failing causes congestion in the lungs or other organs in the body. The first point to make is that a diagnosis of heart failure does not mean that the individual is necessarily going to die imminently. Heart failure simply means that the heart is failing to work as well as it should. True 'heart attacks' are very rare in dogs and most heart problems progress very slowly over a period of weeks to years.

The heart is simply a pump which pumps blood around the body. The heart, the blood and all the veins and arteries and capillaries in the body form the cardiovascular system (circulatory system). One can think of the circulatory system as a system of pipes which carry liquid throughout the body. The liquid (blood) is pumped through this system of pipes (blood vessels) by a pump (the heart). The pipes which lead away from the pump are called arteries and the pipes which lead back to the pump are called veins. The arteries are connected to the veins by very small pipes called capillaries. The heart consists of two sides viz. the left side and the right side. The left side pumps blood to and from the body and the right side pumps blood to and from the lungs. The right side thus pumps blood into the lungs where oxygen is absorbed and carbon dioxide is released. The blood is now full of oxygen and returns to the heart. The left side of the heart then pumps the blood to the rest of the body where the oxygen is absorbed by the cells of the body. The carbon dioxide released by the body's cells moves into the blood to be carried back to the lungs to be breathed out as waste. The arteries, veins and capillaries thus lie in-between the alveoli and air tubes in the lungs.

Heart failure simply means that the pump in the circulatory system is not working properly. This means that the liquid does not move through the pipes properly either. The result is that, as the pump fails, it pumps less fluid forward each time it pumps. Because the total amount of fluid in the pipes remains the same, this means that fluid returning to pump is not pumped through the pump as quickly as it should be because more fluid is arriving at the pump than is being pumped away from the pump. Compare this to a dam, which is used to pump water to irrigate fields. If heavy rains cause the dam to fill up faster than the dam pumps can pump the water into the fields, the dam will fill up and overflow. A similar process happens in the case of heart failure and fluid builds up in the pipes returning to the pump. As more fluid accumulates in these pipes (the veins), they start to overflow. This overflow from the veins means that clear fluid ('water') leaks out of the veins and accumulates in and around the organs in the body. If this 'water' accumulates in and around the airways of the lungs it will cause the individual to develop a cough which attempts to cough out the 'water'. This is why heart failure symptoms usually develop over a long period of time because the pump fails gradually over a long period of time and thus the overflow of water also takes a long period of time. If the pump stretches while it is failing we will hear a dry cough in the early stages of the problem (as discussed earlier) and as water overflows into the airways the cough will become a moist, rattling cough. The overflow of water is the result of congestion in the veins thus the condition is called congestive heart failure.

The vet will determine the cause and type of heart condition and will use treatment to correct the symptoms. It is important to stress that all treatments for heart conditions simply help the heart to function better and alleviate the symptoms caused by the failing heart. The treatment does not 'fix' the problem. The only way to 'fix' most heart conditions would be to replace the heart (pump) with a brand new pump. This is not realistic because replacing a heart is not as simple as replacing a pump in a piece of machinery. Thus the treatment the vet uses will be chosen depending on the exact problem with the pump.

Most cases of congestive heart failure are treated with a combination of medications. The most common medicine that appears in most combinations of treatment is a diuretic. Many people call diuretic tablets 'water tablets'. This is because diuretic tablets work by making the body produce more urine and thus pee more often. Thus, if the diuretic makes the kidneys produce more urine, the kidneys will have to take more 'water' from the blood to make this extra urine. Once more 'water' has been taken from the blood there is therefore less liquid for the heart to pump around the body and thus less liquid accumulates in the veins while waiting to be pumped by the heart. The final result is that the heart has less work to do and less congestion develops because less blood is accumulating in the veins and thus less water is leaking out of the veins. Once less water is leaking out of the veins less water accumulates in the airways and thus the cough either becomes less severe of goes away entirely. The other medications used in the treatment combinations will help the heart function in other ways. The combination of treatments used are intended to help the heart in as many ways as possible so that it can function as efficiently as possible. The process of heart failure is usually a slow and steady process and thus the types of medications used and the dosages used will have to be constantly adjusted by the vet as the weeks, months or years pass.

The symptoms of heart failure usually develop as follows: the initial symptoms are that the individual seems to get tired and out of breath more quickly when out for a walk or while taking exercise. This is called exercise intolerance and other than this, the dog seems quite normal i.e. happy, alert and eating normally. The next symptom to develop is an occasional dry cough. This cough develops as the heart stretches and pushes against the windpipe (trachea). This dry cough may be heard more frequently as the heart keeps stretching more and more. Once the heart function has been compromised more severely, then congestion will develop in the veins and 'water' starts accumulating in and around the organs of the body. If it is mainly the left side of the heart that is failing then most of the water will accumulate in and around the airways in the lungs and thus the cough will change to a soft moist cough as the dog tries to cough the water up. In the early stages of the congestion one may only notice the moist cough in the evenings when the dog is resting, but as the congestion becomes worse and more water accumulates, the cough will become more severe and the dog will cough during the day and the night. As more and more water accumulates in the lungs the dog's breathing will become more and more laboured and they are effectively drowning in their own fluids at this stage. The next inevitable stage in congestive heart failure is death. These are exactly the same stages we will see in human beings with congestive heart failure. The stages of congestive heart failure usually develop over a period of years. The vet will keep adjusting the treatment as new symptoms develop to ensure that the dog is comfortable and symptom free at all times and able to enjoy a good quality of life. In the very final stages of congestive heart failure the heart will be failing so severely that no amount of treatment will help the individual and it is at this point that you, or your vet, may decide that it maybe kinder to say goodbye to your pet. It is important to stress that most cases of congestive heart failure patients can be given good quality long lives by using modern heart medications.

If a dog with a moist, rattling or chesty cough seems very lethargic, depressed, weak or refuses to eat then one would consider the possibility of pneumonia or lung tumours. The word pneumonia simply means severe inflammation in one or both lungs without telling us what has caused the problem. The vet will usually also find that the affected individual has a fever and may be losing weight in addition to the symptom of coughing. The vet will usually suggest some tests to help them investigate and treat the problem. These tests may include X-rays, bronchoscopy and bronchial lavage. The X-rays will allow the vet to see the size and shape of the heart and the condition of the lungs. Bronchoscopy is a procedure whereby the vet will pass a camera down the trachea (windpipe) and into the airways in the lungs. This procedure allows the vet to see what is going on inside the airways. Bronchial lavage is a procedure whereby the vet will flush a small amount of water through the airways in the lungs and then suck the fluid back into a syringe. This fluid is then sent to a laboratory which will perform several tests including testing for infections, tumours and allergic inflammation (asthma).

4d Pneumonia
Once the vet has diagnosed pneumonia(inflammation in the lungs) they will try to determine what has caused the pneumonia, as this will determine the treatment to be applied. Most cases of pneumonia are caused by bacterial infection but may also be caused by viruses, fungal infections or solid

objects being inhaled into the lungs. In certain parts of the world, most notably in many states in the USA, inflammation in the lungs may be caused by heartworm infections. Once the vet has identified the cause of the pneumonia they will start the appropriate treatment.

4d(i) Primary pneumonia
Primary pneumonia is due to infections in the lungs in the absence of identifiable predisposing factors. Primary pneumonia is usually a viral or bacterial infection and is treated using some or all of the following: antibiotics, anti-inflammatories, mucolytics (to loosen phlegm), expectorants (to dilate the airways) and deworming treatments (if the cause of the problem is lungworm).

4d(ii) Aspiration pneumonia
If the pneumonia has been caused by solid objects being inhaled into the lungs then the above treatments are used but additionally the vet will determine what has been inhaled into the lungs. If an object like a piece of wood or grass has been inhaled, the vet will try to remove it using a special attachment on the bronchoscope (the camera that is used to look inside the lungs). If food has been inhaled into the lungs the vet may find that this has happened because the dog has a condition called megaoesophagus. This diagnosis means that the oesophagus (the swallowing tube leading to the stomach) has become 'paralysed'. There are a number of different causes of megaoesophagus but in many cases one cannot determine why the oesophagus has become 'paralysed'. What I mean by 'paralysed' is that the oesophagus is unable to move food from the mouth to the stomach. Food that is swallowed thus moves from the mouth into the oesophagus and then stays in the oesophagus. The oesophagus is normally a narrow muscular tube but when it stops working and food starts accumulating in it, it starts to stretch into a wide and flabby tube. The food that the dog eats then collects in this flabby tube and as the dog moves around during the day and night, small amounts of food will drop into the stomach when the oesophagus moves to and fro in the body. Unfortunately some food may also be rocked forward into the back of the throat and accidentally sucked down the windpipe when the dog breathes. If food does move into the windpipe the dog will usually immediately cough it out but sometimes they are unable to do so and the piece of food may be sucked deep into the small airways in the lungs. The food then becomes lodged in the small airways and the dog is unable to cough it out. This food in the lungs causes a severe reaction in the lungs and infection and pneumonia may develop, this is called aspiration pneumonia.

If aspiration pneumonia has developed because the dog has megaoesophagus, the treatment is much the same as in general cases of pneumonia i.e. antibiotics, anti-inflammatories, mucolytics (to loosen phlegm) and bronchodilators (to dilate the airways). The vet must also try to prevent more food from being aspirated into the lungs in the future. They will suggest that the dog should be fed several small meals during the day instead of one or two large meals. They will also suggest mixing water with the food to make a soupy texture and that each meal is fed from a high surface. This means that the food bowl should be placed high enough on a table so that the dog has to eat from the bowl while standing with their back legs on the floor and their front legs resting on the table. The idea behind all of these changes is to try to get the force of gravity to pull the soupy food down the oesophagus and into the stomach. Some dogs respond very well to this approach and we will have very few or even no recurrences of the aspiration pneumonia, but in other cases the dog will have repeated episodes of aspiration pneumonia which may prove fatal over time.

4d(iii) Canine heartworm disease

Dogs living in warm temperate climates in various parts of the world especially some states in the USA are at risk from heartworm disease. This condition does not occur in the United Kingdom as yet but as more people start to travel abroad with their dogs it may become a problem in the future. The Latin name of the heartworm is *Dirofilaria immitus*. The name of this condition clearly describes the nature of the problem i.e. the affected dog has worms living in the heart and the main artery leading from the heart to the lungs (the pulmonary artery). These worms are often the size of lengths of spaghetti when fully grown.

Dogs are at risk of becoming infected with the worms when they are bitten by an infected mosquito. The mosquito is called the vector i.e. it carries the infection from one dog to another. The mosquito becomes infected when it sucks blood from an infected dog. The infected dog will have worm eggs floating in the blood in the circulatory system. These eggs are produced by the adult worms living in the heart and released into the blood supply. The mosquito becomes infected when it sucks blood containing eggs from an infected dog. These eggs do not hatch inside the mosquito but when the mosquito moves on to bite another dog then the eggs can slip out of the mosquito and into the dog. The eggs then hatch into their immature stage called microfilariae in the dog's blood supply. These immature worms then develop into adult worms which live inside the heart and inside the main artery leading to the lungs. The effect of the worms living in the dog's blood vessels is that they damage the lining of the blood vessels. When some of the worms die they are carried by the flow of blood into the lungs where they cause an inflammatory reaction in much the same way as a thorn in your foot will cause an inflammatory action. The symptoms caused by heartworm infection thus depend on how many worms are living in the dog and what the worms are doing inside the heart and pulmonary artery.

The most common symptoms associated with heartworm infection are coughing and breathing difficulties. These symptoms develop as a result of the worms damaging the heart and lungs. The damage to the heart and lungs causes inflammation which in turn leads to fluid accumulating in the lungs. If you live in an area where heartworm is a problem the vet will often suggest doing some tests to investigate the possibility of heartworm infection if your dog develops these symptoms during the mosquito season. The tests may include blood tests, X-rays and ultra-sound scans of the heart. Once the vet has confirmed that heartworm is the cause of the symptoms they will decide how to treat the problem. The way the vet will treat the infection will depend on how many worms are present in the dog, how much damage the worms have caused, where the worms are situated in the heart and the stage in the life cycle of the worm. The vet will often suggest using anti-inflammatory drugs for a few days initially to alleviate the inflammation caused by the worms before treating with agents to kill the worms. In severe cases the vet may even advise against killing the worms at all. This is because if a large number of worms are killed at once, all their dead bodies will be swept into the lungs and cause severe reaction in the lungs which may prove fatal to the dog.

Your vet will advise you on the best way of treating your dog to try to avoid heartworm infections if you live in a high-risk area. This is a very serious and dangerous condition and one should make every effort to protect your dog from becoming infected.

4e Tumors in the respiratory system

These may produce almost any kind of cough but usually one will notice a moist, chesty, rattling cough in a dog who is losing weight and may start to lose their appetite and become lethargic and depressed. The presence and type of tumour in the respiratory tract is identified by the vet when they run the tests we discussed earlier in this chapter. Lung tumours are most commonly seen and found when the vet takes an X-ray of the dog's chest. To determine the type of tumour the vet will have to take a biopsy from the tumour and send it to a laboratory for analysis. The tumour may be a single mass in the lung or there may be multiple masses in the lungs. The tumour may be a primary tumour or a secondary tumour. A primary tumour means that the tumour has developed from lung tissue. A secondary tumour means that although the tumour is in the lung it has in fact spread to the lung from a different organ in the body.

Some types of tumour may respond very well to treatment but others may not respond at all. I feel that if there is only one tumour present and there is no sign of any spread to other points then one would consider surgery to remove the mass. The way to check for spread to other sites is by X-rays, ultrasound scanning and blood testing. If one can confirm that there has been no identifiable spread of the cancer then the option of surgery may proceed. The surgery involves entering the chest and removing the affected lung lobe or possibly the entire lung on that side of the body. Two important points to consider when removing the mass is that not just the mass should be removed but also a margin of normal healthy tissue in every direction to try to ensure that no cancer cells are left behind. The second issue is that the mass can only be removed if vital blood vessels and nerves supplying other tissues and organs in the area can be left intact. A very frustrating situation arises when the surgeon finds that although the mass can be removed in its entirety, it would involve sacrificing the blood supply to other vital areas. This is often due to the fact that the blood vessels or nerves of other organs are trapped in the tumour mass and cannot be freed from the mass. This means that one then cannot remove the mass because it would cause the death of the dog. In these cases the only remaining option is to try to eliminate the mass by radiation therapy and/or chemotherapy. Many surgeons would want to at least attempt to debulk the mass prior to proceeding with the radiation or chemotherapy. This would involve removing as much tumour tissue as possible without damaging any vital structures trapped in the mass. In many cases, even if the surgeon is able to remove the mass, one might want to follow up on the surgery with radiation and /or chemotherapy to ensure that no tumour cells, which may have spread on a microscopic level to other tissues, are able to grow into a new tumour. There are many different types and ways of using radiation and chemotherapy and the most appropriate protocol will often be decided after a specialist histopathologist has examined the tumour. For this reason some vets would want to perform surgery even in cases where there is more than one tumour mass present or where there is clear evidence of tumour spread to other parts of the body. The object of the surgery in these cases would be to obtain a biopsy of the tumour for analysis by a histopathologist so that the best radiation and/or chemotherapy strategy can be formulated.

Many of my clients may not want to go through all the above steps for any variety of reasons and ask if we could just ' cut to the chase' in terms of trying to help the dog either cope with or over-come the problem. This would often imply one of two strategies viz. treat the symptoms for as long as possible and when the treatment fails to alleviate the dog's suffering then humanely put him or her to sleep. The most effective way of trying to achieve this is with a category of medication called glucocorticoids. These treatments are the same as for treating asthma in human beings with the difference being one would employ larger doses in treating these dogs. This treatment is intended to reduce the inflammation caused by the tumour and to make the dog feel more comfortable. In addition to this I would often use bronchodilators (to dilate the airways) and possibly diuretics (if the tumour is causing fluid to accumulate in and around the lungs). This treatment is intended only to alleviate the dog's discomfort and give them as much good quality, pain free, happy life as possible. I accept that this is not a scientific approach to the problem but many people do not have the financial resources to do more than this or they may not want to subject the dog to any more than this. The overriding consideration must always be the welfare of the dog and if this un-scientific approach delivers results in terms of alleviating the symptoms then I have no moral problem with this approach.

15

MY DOG IS HAVING DIFFICULTY BREATHING

Laboured breathing in dogs is most commonly caused by one of four mechanisms. The four common mechanisms causing laboured breathing are: inflammation in the lungs, fluid accumulations in the lungs, anaemia or any condition casing distention/enlargement of the abdomen.

- Inflammation in the lungs may be caused by infections(pneumonia), tumours or 'chronic bronchitis'.
- Fluid accumulations may develop in the lungs due to heart failure or bruising/bleeding in the lungs.
- Anaemia means that there is insufficient haemoglobin in the blood to carry enough oxygen to meet the body's requirements. Anaemia thus causes laboured respiration because the lungs are made to work harder in trying to get more oxygen to the blood to be transported to the body's tissues.
- Enlargement or distention of any of the organs in the abdomen may cause the distended organ to push against the back edge of the lungs and thus the breathing may become laboured because it is more difficult for the lungs to expand and fill with air. This sensation would feel similar to a lady wearing a very tight corset. Accumulations of large amounts of fluids in the abdomen may have the same effect.

When a vet is presented with a dog with laboured breathing they will ask you a variety of questions to try to identify the cause. Some of the questions will relate directly to the breathing and others will be directed to other symptoms that may be present at the same time. Your answers to the questions are very important and it is vital that you do not guess the answer. It is better to say 'I don't know' rather than to guess, as the information that you give the vet will very often give them enough information to make the diagnosis without expensive tests. The questions will include some or all of the following.

- How old is the dog?
- How long have they had the symptoms?
- How quickly did the symptoms appear?
- Is the dog vomiting/retching or trying to vomit?

199

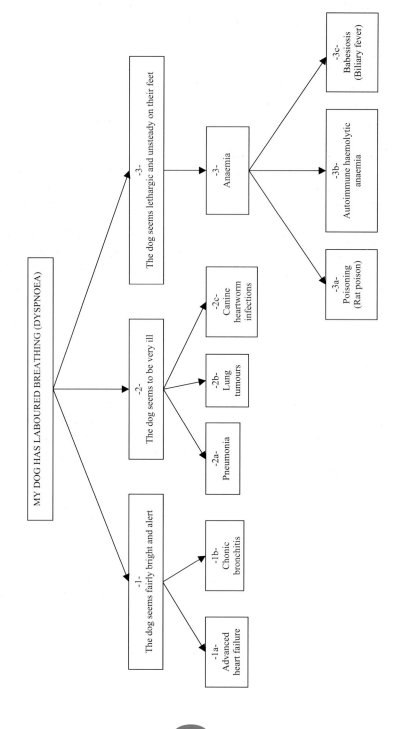

MY DOG HAS LABOURED BREATHING (DYSPNOEA)

-1-
The dog seems fairly bright and alert

-1a-
Advanced heart failure

-1b-
Chonic bronchitis

-2-
The dog seems to be very ill

-2a-
Pneumonia

-2b-
Lung tumours

-2c-
Canine heartworm infections

-3-
The dog seems lethargic and unsteady on their feet

-3-
Anaemia

-3a-
Poisoning (Rat poison)

-3b-
Autoimmune haemolytic anaemia

-3c-
Babesiosis (Biliary fever)

- Are there other dogs in the household and if so, are they showing the same or similar symptoms?
- Has the dog recently had contact with other dogs e.g. on walks, at training classes, at boarding kennels etc?
- Does the dog also have a dry cough or a moist cough?
- Does the dog seem ill or unwell besides the fact that their breathing is laboured or are they alert and active and eating normally?
- Is the dog losing or gaining weight?
- Does the dog become tired very quickly when they go out to walk and exercise?

Once the vet has asked you the above questions they will examine your dog with special attention being paid to the respiratory and cardiovascular systems. The vet will listen to the heart and lung sounds and evaluate the colour of the eyes and the gums. The vet will often recommend performing tests to investigate the problem and these tests will usually include X-rays, ultrasound scans and blood tests.

When the vet has collected all the information that they need their thoughts will go something like this: If the breathing became laboured very suddenly and the dog is trying to retch and vomit then the cause of the problem may be that the stomach is distended with gas. This condition is called gastric dilatation and may prove fatal very quickly – thus if you notice laboured breathing and repeated strenuous attempts at vomiting you should contact your vet immediately. This condition is discussed in more detail in chapter 2. Once the vet has discounted the possibility of gastric dilatation their thought processes will proceed as follows: In cases of pneumonia or anaemia the symptoms will usually appear and progress over a period of a few hours to a few days. In the case of heart failure, chronic bronchitis and lung tumours the symptoms may develop over a period of a few days to a few weeks. Pneumonia cases usually have a fever, tumour cases may sometimes have slightly increased temperatures and the other causes usually do not. Anaemia means that the dog has fewer red blood cells in their blood stream than they should have. Anaemia cases thus appear pale and this is most noticeable when one examines the colour of the gums and the conjunctival membrane in the eyes. If the dog has a cough in addition to the laboured breathing one would consider heart failure, pneumonia or lung tumours.

Dogs suffering from laboured breathing will usually fit into one of three categories viz. those who feel fairly bright and cheerful, those who feel very unwell and those who are anaemic. There may be significant overlaps between these categories but for the sake of this discussion I will consider each category individually.

1 Laboured breathing in a dog which seems fairly bright and cheerful with a fairly normal appetite but is unable to take much exercise and may also be coughing

1a Heart failure
Please refer to page 192 for the discussion on this condition.

1b Chronic bronchitis/pulmonary fibrosis.

The term chronic bronchitis, when used in the context of veterinary medicine, usually implies long-term, low grade inflammation in the lining of the airways in the lungs. This inflammation is similar to that associated with asthma in human beings in that it is usually not caused by an infection but rather by allergic or irritant mechanisms or is simply a result of old age. The effect of ageing or long-term inflammation in the lungs is that the 'tubes' lose their elasticity. This happens because inflammation over a long period of time will cause scar tissue to develop in the walls of the airways. This scar tissue is like scar tissue elsewhere in the body i.e. it is not as flexible(stretchy) as other tissues in the body. Old age causes a similar loss in elasticity of not only the airways, but also all other tissues in the body.

In an individual with normal healthy lungs, the tubes in the lungs are able to dilate when the lungs want to take in more air and they are able to take deeper breaths than normal. Thus, if the cells in the body require an increase in oxygen supply, the lungs will respond by dilating all the airways in the lungs and therefore more oxygen is taken into the body with each breath because we then breathe more deeply. This usually happens without us even realising that it is happening. In the case of an individual who has long term inflammation in the airways or simply old-age changes, the scar tissue in the walls of the airways will restrict their ability to dilate when the body requires an increased amount of oxygen. Thus if these individuals are unable to take deeper breaths to increase their oxygen intake, their only other option is to take more breaths. This process of taking more breaths may be noticed by the dog's owner as laboured respiration with rapid shallow breathing. This is, in fact, something that we are all familiar with. Consider occasions when you have been sitting next to an elderly person for a while and noticed that they seem to breathe more loudly than you do. This is because their airways have hardened with age and they need to breath faster than you do because they cannot breath as deeply as you do. This inability to dilate their airways also means that their breathing is noisier than yours because they are moving air more rapidly through narrower tubes. These elderly people often use asthma inhalers prescribed by their doctors to help improve their breathing. These inhalers work by reducing the inflammation in the lungs and by dilating the airways as much as possible. The reason that the anti-inflammatory inhalers help to improve the breathing is that the increased rate of breathing through the narrowed airways causes the lining of the airways to dry out faster than normal airways in a young healthy individual. This process of drying out causes inflammation which further aggravates the problem by causing more scar tissue to form in the long term thus further reducing the ability of the airway to dilate. In the short term this inflammation causes an increased amount of phlegm in the airways and this also impedes the flow of air in the airways and may also cause a cough.

Thus many dogs will suffer from chronic bronchitis either as a consequence of old age or as a dog version of asthma. The treatment in both instances is the same i.e. the vet will prescribe the same medication to dilate the airways and reduce inflammation as doctors do. The only difference is usually that dogs are unable to use inhalers effectively and thus we use the same treatments but we administer them in tablet form. The diagnosis of chronic bronchitis is usually made by evaluating X-rays, ultrasound scans and possibly bronchial washes. The response to treatment varies wildly from one individual to another i.e. some respond very well to treatment and others may hardly improve at all. The most commonly affected breed is the west highland white terrier. The treatment for this condition only serves to alleviate the symptoms and does not undo pre-existing scarring in the lungs and it only serves to slow down the rate of ongoing scarring. The result is that after weeks, months or years of treatment most dogs with this condition will deteriorate. In the early stages the vet will simply adjust the doses of the medication and will try different types. Most dogs with this condition will eventually deteriorate to a point where their respiration is so laboured that their quality of life is very poor and they may be in a permanent state of distress. In these instances the affected individual is effectively slowly suffocating and the final option may be to consider humanely putting them to sleep to avoid a traumatic and distressing end for a dear friend.

2 Laboured breathing in a dog which seems very lethargic or ill, may have a fever and may also be coughing

2a Pneumonia
Please refer to page 194 for the discussion on this condition.

2b Lung tumours
Please refer to page 197 for the discussion on this condition.

2c Canine heartworm disease
Please refer to page 196 for the discussion on this condition.

3 Anaemia as a cause of laboured breathing is associated with pale mucous membranes and a dog who suddenly seems very weak and wobbly on their legs

The word anaemia means that the dog has fewer red blood cells than they should have in their body. The red blood cells are responsible for carrying oxygen from the lungs to all the cells in the body. If there are too few red blood cells to carry oxygen, the affected individual will respond by breathing more rapidly and the breathing will be more laboured. This is an attempt by the body to supply more oxygen to the red blood cells. There are many causes of anaemia but the most common type of anaemia that causes laboured breathing is a sudden onset anaemia and the most common causes of this are accidental poisoning by rat poison and autoimmune haemolytic anaemia. In certain parts of the world (not currently in the United Kingdom) anaemia may be caused by a parasite called Babesiosis which destroys red blood cells. I will discuss each of these conditions individually.

3a Anaemia caused by rat poison
Most commercial rat poisons contain a chemical called warfarin. This chemical interferes with the blood's ability to clot and thus in cases of rat poisoning the individual will haemmorage (bleed) throughout their body. The warfarin interferes with the clotting ability of blood by inactivating vitamin k in the body. This bleeding may be seen as many bruises in the skin, gums and eyes. Each bruise may be as small as a pinhead or as large as a pancake. This bruising is caused by the warfarin

which causes blood to leak out of the blood vessels. If a large amount of blood leaks out of the blood vessels into other parts of the body the dog may have insufficient red blood cells left in the blood stream to carry oxygen around the body. If the blood leaks out of the blood vessels directly into the lungs then this will further worsen the dog's ability to breathe. Thus if the vet is presented with a dog with laboured breathing and the dog has many bruises on its body they will ask you if it is possible that the dog may have eaten rat poison. Once the diagnosis of poisoning has been made the treatment consists of injections of vitamin k followed by a course of vitamin k tablets.

3b Anaemia caused by immune-mediated haemolytic anaemia

This condition is called an autoimmune disorder and it means that the body's own immune system is attacking its own cells for no apparent reason. It seems that the immune system simply fails to recognise that red blood cells are normal cells and it then attacks them as if they were invading bacteria. As the attack on the cells continues, the cells become damaged and unable to work efficiently and eventually the cells being attacked will die. It is not understood why this process should happen for no apparent reason but unfortunately it does. This condition usually develops very suddenly and large numbers of red blood cells may be destroyed very quickly. Once large numbers of red blood cells have been destroyed there will be too few of them left to carry enough oxygen around the body. The affected dog will try to compensate by breathing more quickly and the breathing becomes more laboured. The gums will appear very pale and in severe cases the dog may collapse and be unable to stand. The vet will diagnose this condition by performing blood tests and treatment consists of high doses of cortisone to suppress the immune system. The vet will often start the treatment with injections and then start a course of cortisone tablets. The most commonly used tablets are prednisolone or prednisone. These tablets are usually given twice daily at a high dose for one or two weeks until repeated blood tests prove that the immune system is under control and no longer attacking the red blood cells. The body will make new red blood cells and the blood should return to normal. The vet will then slowly start to reduce the dose of the tablets over a period of several weeks. The vet will keep repeating the blood tests to confirm that the condition is under control. Many dogs will eventually be able to stop all treatment but others will have to stay on treatment for the rest of their lives to keep the immune system under control. Unfortunately a small number of dogs will not respond to treatment and will die despite our best efforts to save them.

3c Anaemia caused by canine babesiosis (biliary fever)

This condition only occurs in warm climates in parts of the world where certain types of ticks are encountered. The disease is caused by an organism called babesia canis. The organism is a blood parasite and lives inside the red blood cells in dogs. The disease is transmitted by ticks. When a tick bites and sucks blood from an infected dog it may ingest some of the babesia organisms. The babesia does not harm the tick but instead waits for the tick to bite another dog and it then slips out of the tick and into the dog. The babesia organism moves into the red blood cells in the dog and starts to multiply until there are so many of them in the red blood cell that it bursts and releases the organisms into the blood stream. Each of these new organisms then moves into a new blood cell and the process will keep repeating itself until all the red blood cells have been destroyed. Thus the infected dog will become progressively more and more anaemic and if the parasite is not stopped it will kill the dog.

The symptoms one will see with babesia infection will depend on how many parasites there are in the dog's blood and how rapidly they are multiplying. In the early stages of the infection the dogs will appear generally unwell i.e. they seem lethargic and lose their appetite. As the condition progresses and more red blood cells are destroyed, the dog becomes very lethargic and completely loses their appetite due to a high fever. The mucous membranes on the gums and in the eyes will become progressively paler until they may appear almost white. In severe cases the mucous membranes will appear very yellow and this indicates severe infection with massive destruction of red blood cells. This yellow appearance is called jaundice.

When your vet is presented with a dog with these symptoms in a region in the world where babesia is known to exist, they will suggest some simple tests. They will make a blood smear to check for the presence of parasites in the red blood cells and they will measure what proportion of the red blood cells have already been destroyed by the parasites. The way the vet will treat an infected dog depends on how severely infected they are and how far advanced the disease is. In early cases and mild infections a single injection is often sufficient to kill the parasites. In more advanced and potentially life threatening cases the dog will require intensive care including blood transfusions, intravenous fluids via drip lines and oxygen therapy in addition to treatments to kill the parasite. This is a very serious condition which may develop very rapidly and kills many dogs every year. One should make every effort to avoid the condition in the first place by using regular tick treatments as advised by the vet and being very vigilant for the symptoms especially in the warmer months of the year. My advice to people living in regions where babesia strikes is to have your dog checked by a vet if they seem even mildly ill because it is a condition which is cheap and easy to diagnose and if caught early it is easy to treat. Once the condition is advanced the treatment becomes far more dangerous to the dog and far more difficult and expensive to treat.

16

My Dog Has Smelly Breath (hallitosis)

People often find that their dog's breath has become very smelly and unpleasant as they grow older. The most common reason for this is the same as for human beings who suffer from halitosis (smelly breath). Bacteria which live in the mouth cause smelly breath. The more bacteria there are in the mouth, the smellier the breath will be.

The mouth is full of bacteria and some of these bacteria cause plaque. Plaque is the 'furry' feeling you feel on the surface of your teeth with your tongue when you have forgotten to brush your teeth. The bacteria attach themselves to the surface of your teeth and most noticeably in the groove between the tooth and the gum. This groove is called the gingival sulcus. Most of us do not realise that the very edge of the gum lying against the tooth is not attached to the tooth. This edge of the gum actually just lies against the tooth and thus there is a groove between the gum and the tooth. This groove is usually less than one millimetre deep. Most of us have used a toothpick at some point in our lives to remove a piece of food stuck in this groove (like popcorn). The piece of food is easily seen because the groove is very shallow and most of the piece of food sticks out of the groove.

This groove (the gingival sulcus) is the easiest place in the mouth for bacteria to live and grow. When we brush our teeth every day we remove most of the bacteria but as soon as you put your toothbrush down, the bacteria start growing again. Most people do not brush their dog's teeth everyday and thus the bacteria are not removed everyday. The body's immune system wages war against the bacteria in the mouth every minute of our lives. The immune system is very good at keeping the numbers of bacteria down even if we do not brush everyday and this is the only defence most animals have against plaque bacteria.

Some individuals simply have better teeth and gums than others do; this applies to human beings and dogs. This means that some individuals will naturally have healthier teeth and gums than others despite not brushing their teeth as regularly. This is because some individuals have more effective immune system patrols in their mouths and the conditions in their mouths are less favourable for the growth of bacteria. The conditions in your mouth are affected by the food you eat and the type of saliva (spit) that you produce.

We are all well aware that eating a lot of sugar is not good for our teeth and gums and much the same concept applies to dogs. Dogs are very unlikely to develop rotten teeth like we do despite what they each. This is because their teeth have a different design and they are naturally resistant to tooth decay. The food that a dog eats does however affect the health of the teeth and gums in other ways. Dogs who eat only soft foods and never chew bones or chewing toys will have more bacteria in their

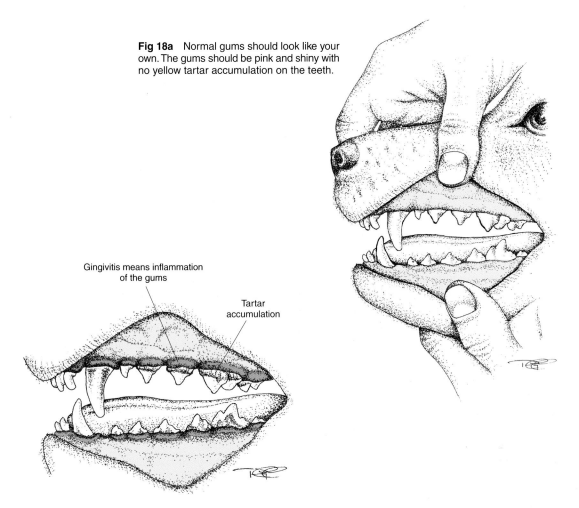

Fig 18a Normal gums should look like your own. The gums should be pink and shiny with no yellow tartar accumulation on the teeth.

Gingivitis means inflammation of the gums

Tartar accumulation

Fig 18b Mild gingivitis and mild tartar accumulation on the teeth.

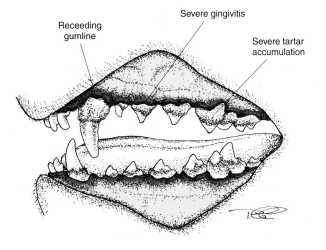

Receeding gumline

Severe gingivitis

Severe tartar accumulation

Fig 18c Advanced gingivitis and periodontal disease with large deposits of tartar. The gums are inflamed and are receeding.

mouth. This is simply because chewing dry foods, bones and toys does help to scrape bacteria off the teeth. The second reason is that chewing for a longer period of time changes the acidity level of the saliva which makes it more effective at killing plaque bacteria. Humans get the same benefit from chewing gum i.e. as we chew gum we constantly produce saliva and after producing saliva for about ten minutes the acidity level of the saliva changes. This change in the acidity level in the saliva makes it much more efficient at killing bacteria in our mouths. Thus dogs who spend more time chewing and salivating will have less bacteria in their mouths. Some individuals simply just have a better acidity level in their saliva all the time and thus they will have naturally healthy teeth and gums and are less likely to have smelly breath because as this saliva rinses the gingival sulcus it kills the bacteria hiding there.

We have determined therefore that smelly breath is caused by bacteria living in the mouth especially, the bacteria living in the gingival sulcus (the groove between the gum and the tooth). The more bacteria there are in the groove, the more the breath will smell. Bacteria which accumulate in this groove cause **gingivitis**. Gingiva is the medical word for the gums and the suffix 'itis' means inflamed, thus gingivitis simply means inflammation of the gums. Initially gingivitis is seen as a dark red or purple band of colour on the edge of the gum lying against the tooth and the most common cause of gingivitis is the accumulation of bacteria in the gingival sulcus (Fig. 18b). These bacteria cause plaque to form on the surface of the tooth and if this plaque is not removed it will turn into tartar. Once plaque has turned into tartar, it can only be removed by a dentist or a vet as it is very tightly stuck to the tooth. Tartar is a very hard substance similar to cement. The dentist or the vet removes this substance when you go for a 'dental scale and polish'. The process of removing tartar is called 'dental scaling'.

Tartar is often visible on one or more of your dog's teeth as a brown deposit on the surface of the tooth. Once a deposit of tartar has formed on a tooth the lump of tartar will continue to enlarge until it is removed. The enlarging mass of tartar pushes into the groove between the tooth and the gum and makes the groove deeper which then invites more bacteria to live and breed in the groove. As this process continues, the groove and bacteria move deeper and deeper inwards into the tooth socket in the bone of the jaw. Ultimately the tooth root may become loose and the tooth will fall out. This process of bacteria and infection moving deeper into the gum and ultimately into the tooth socket is called **periodontal disease** or **periodontitis** (Fig. 18c). Thus if we do not constantly remove tartar the teeth will be lost. The tartar thus also makes the breath smellier as it invites more bacteria to live in the mouth.

The most common cause of smelly breath is thus bacteria, plaque and tartar on the teeth. Some individuals are more prone to these problems than others but you can help your dog by ensuring that they eat and chew properly to reduce the number of bacteria in the mouth. You can further help them by brushing their teeth every day and if you do notice tartar developing in the mouth, ask the vet to remove it. Once the vet has removed the tartar you must continue brushing and encouraging your dog to chew coarse food, toys and bones to slow down the re-appearance of plaque bacteria. This is because, just like us, the minute you leave the dentist's chair after a scale and polish, the war against the bacteria starts again immediately. Dogs, just like us, will need to have their teeth professionally cleaned regularly. Just like human beings some dogs will need more frequent cleaning than others.

INDEX

Ear diseases 155–61
Ear mites 103
Eclampsia 13, 88
Ectropion 178
Elbow joint conditions 114–22
Entropion 176–8
Epilepsy 84–5
Eye diseases 173–82

Fistula(s), peri-anal 47
Flea allergy 91, 97–100, 104–6
Food allergy 92–3
Forearm problems 113–14
Foreign bodies, intestinal 21–3
Foreign bodies, nasal 165
Fractures 111, 112, 114, 120, 128, 129, 131, 143
Fungal infections, nasal 166
Fungal infections, skin 103

Garbage disease 20–1
Gastric dilatation-volvulus-torsion syndrome 23–4, 201
Gastro-enteritis 17–31
Gestation 3
Gingivitis 208
Glucose, in diabetes mellitus 50

Hallitosis 206–8
Hay fever 165–6
Heart failure 87–8, 192–4
Heartworm disease 196–7
Hepatic disease 86–7
Hepatic encephalopathy 86–7
Hip joint conditions 143–8
Hock disorders 129–30
Humerus conditions 114–22
Hydrocephalus 85
Hyperadrenocorticism, see Cushing's disease
Hyperparathyroidism 68
Hypoadrenocorticism, see Addison's disease
Hypocalcaemia, in eclampsia 88

Hypothyroidism 102, 106–7

Icterus, see Jaundice
Incontinence, see Urinary incontinence
Inflammatory bowel disease 27
Insulin therapy, see Diabetes mellitus
Intervertebral disc problems 151–2
Intestinal conditions 21
Intussusception 26–7
Irritable bowel syndrome 27–9
Itching ears 94–5
Itching skin 89–107

Jaundice 60, 205

Kennel cough 188–9
Keratoconjunctivitis sicca 178–9
Kidney conditions 56–60, 70

Labour, see Whelping
Large intestinal conditions, see Colitis
Legge-Calve-Perthes disease 144
Liver conditions 60
Lumbosacral joint disease 150
Lung conditions 199–205

Mange 103
Mastitis 15
Medial coronoid process, fractures of Megaoesophagus 195
Metaldehyde poisoning 86
Metoestrus 2
Mites 103–4

Nail disorders 110–11, 127–8
Nasal cavity disorders 167
Nose, disorders of 162–7
Nystagmus 85

Oestrus 2
Oestrus cycle 2–3